The Metaphysical
of Being-in-the-World

The Metaphysical Presuppositions of Being-in-the-World

A Confrontation between St. Thomas Aquinas and Martin Heidegger

Caitlin Smith Gilson

continuum

The Continuum International Publishing Group Inc
80 Maiden Lane, New York, NY 10038

The Continuum International Publishing Group Ltd
The Tower Building, 11 York Road, London SE1 7NX

www.continuumbooks.com

Library of Congress Cataloging-in-Publication Data
A catalog record for this book is available from the Library of Congress.

ISBN: 978-1-4411-9595-1 (paperback)

Typeset by Newgen Imaging Systems Pvt Ltd, Chennai, India
Printed in the United States of America

To my dearest Fred, far along the way of the Cross

To my little loves, Mary Alison and Lily Grace, who have just begun

And to my beloved grandmother, Mary, who found her way home

One has today so few companions upon the roads of metaphysics that one does not dare recall to them the word of Saint Augustine: "When you think these things, it is the word of God in your heart." But the modern man hardly thinks anymore of these things. He bathes in the divine without being aware of it.

Etienne Gilson, *Linguistics and Philosophy*

Contents

Contents   ix

Preface

Chesterton once reminded us that there exist basically three types of Western man.[1] First there is Roman Man, the citizen of that great cosmopolitan realm of reason and order, the man who makes straight roads and clear laws, and for whom good sense is good enough. Then there is, according to Chesterton, the Man in the Forest, who is harder to speak of. He walks behind us on every forest path and wakes within us when the wind wakes at night. He is the man of origins, the man in the forest. Heidegger is such a man and his thinking has the vastness, the depth and the seductiveness of a dark wood. And then there is Christian Man, who unites the numinous obscurities natural to origins with the simple clarities of public things, and who incarnates a mystery.

My book is an analysis of the irreconcilable confrontation between Heideggerian and classical notions of intentional being-in-the-world, with St. Thomas Aquinas as the supreme representative of the classical tradition. Consequently, some remarks on format and methodology are in order to enable the reader to orient himself. First, this analysis is not intended to be a historical glossing of notions of being-in-the-world, but rather a theoretical research into its essential nature, and is intended methodically to address the factors and essential confrontations that played their necessary roles in the metaphysical enunciation of Being at the historical origin of philosophy.

Being-in-the-world affirms that "*I am the other as other*" because "*the soul is in a way all things*," because "*the same is for thinking as for Being*." But the question remains as to the way in which the soul is all things and the way in which thinking and Being are the same without negating either the extra-mental reality or otherness of the world or man's radical dependency on becoming it for all his knowledge.

For St. Thomas Aquinas and for Heidegger intentional being-in-the-world roots the progressive revelation of Being to consciousness in an asking into the Being of truth (what we call truth and why) as well as into the truth of Being (how or why it is that something is true or is truly); it is at its core profoundly *aletheiological.* But how truth is a relation; how, one must ontologically ask, into the source and nature of that relation irreconcilably separates the thought of St. Thomas from Heidegger. In a word, how or why such a relation insists itself between man ("ex-sistence") and Being ("sub-sistence") is the central question: the question of truth's in-sistence.

The inquiry into this essential confrontation will be delimited by the need to grasp the genuine nature of truth as it is consistently identified in the act of intentional being-in-the-world. The analysis will be anchored by what I understand to be the four central components of classical being-in-the-world. The *aletheiological* orientation of classical being-in-the-world reveals itself through a fourfold intentional presuppositional structure; this structure is found in every genuine asking into the question of the meaning of Being.

This fourfold comprises (1) finitude; (2) the intentional presence (i.e., the knowing subject or privileged being, who participates in the meaning and the *formation* of Being; (3) causality; and (4) the *ananke stenai*, the necessary stop in the order of explanation that fully ratifies our knowledge of existence as genuine. The constitutive elements of the fourfold nature of the intentional presupposition are hermeneutically designated as mutual implications and are therefore the demonstrable components of man's nondemonstrable presuppositional being-in-the-world as a knower.

The irreconcilable difference between a metaphysical and a phenomenological understanding of intentionality rests in Heidegger's isolation and rejection of two critical constitutive elements, namely causality and the *ananke stenai.* For him, these are founded upon an illegitimate reductio of the meaning-phenomena into the merely present-at-hand and are then mistaken as the primordial mode of understanding Being-as-such.

To articulate the metaphysical-intentional enterprise, its *aletheiological* structure must be shown to be the genuine thinking of Being. It is not a ladder of reduced beings relegated to partial effects in terms of a higher Being, but the framework of the intentional and ineluctable ground—*the same is for thinking as for Being*—in which the knower becomes the known, again and again, in ever intensifying degrees of *likeness.* To demonstrate this point it is essential to return to the beginning through a direct examination, a close reading of the essential texts of three thinkers: Parmenides, Plato and Aristotle. The intent of this interpretive methodology is to remain close to the primary texts in an effort to show the essential interdependency of each of the elements of the fourfold.

As a historico-theoretical tracing of the fourfold, the first chapter is dedicated to an intensive historical tracing of the formation of the fourfold.

Poem of Parmenides, Plato's *Parmenides* and Aristotle's *De Anima* will help us to uncover the essential confrontations and conceptual difficulties that accompany these primordial askings into the meaning of Being. These texts are particularly important for each contributes essentially to announcing the primary components of classical intentionality at its very origin, even if only implicitly; indeed even where the unsaid is more important than what is said.

1. The *Poem of Parmenides* articulates man's intentional nature as the primary fact of existence. Intentionality is not itself knowledge precisely because it is the ground of all knowledge. Therefore it first announces itself in a manner that befits this distinction, i.e., in the hieratically compact Parmenidean pre-cognitive presupposition: the same is for thinking as for Being. This announcement gives birth to the chasmic divide between Heideggerian and metaphysical notions of the meaning of truth and cannot, therefore, be passed over.

2. Once that ontological proclamation is made, it is thereafter necessary to unpack epistemologically this compact intentional presupposition. Plato's dialogue *Parmenides* is the pivotal but overlooked dialogue for the delineation of the problematic of the intentional presupposition. The problematic of the dialogue is to take the totality of Parmenides' compactly announced epistemology—*the same is for thinking as for Being*—and expand it conceptually without reducing it to a founded doctrine that forsakes the world and its intelligibility. The dialogue fails repeatedly to accomplish this task, each argument entering frustrating infinite regressions, the antitheses of the *ananke stenai*. But by doing so, the dialogue has grasped the core of metaphysical intentionality, and the kind of truth that corresponds to it.

3. While Plato's *Parmenides* exposes the *ananke stenai* as the necessary precondition of truth *qua* knowledge, framing and completing the intentional experience of the ultimate Other as other, Aristotle's *De Anima* goes a long way in epistemologically laying bare its necessary structure. The *De Anima* is the concise account of the insights, failures and accomplishments of the earlier thinkers leading to the hallmark of classical intentionality: *the soul is in a way all things*.

The second chapter is an organic explanation of the fully realized *fourfold structure* in its supreme representative, St. Thomas Aquinas. The metaphysics that form the total structure of the fourfold will be laid bare; the elucidation of its onto-theo-logical structure will ultimately divide Heidegger from St. Thomas Aquinas.

Anchored in Heidegger's commentary on Kant's *Critique of Pure Reason*, the third chapter examines the irreconcilable difference between a causal and a phenomenological understanding of intentional being-in-the-world as resting on Heidegger's isolation and rejection of the latter two constitutive elements, causality and the *ananke stenai*. For Heidegger, these latter two elements inject an illicit otherworldliness (i.e., the entrance of the deity into philosophy) that effectively reduces *aletheia* to *veritas*, to a causality of correctness, rectitude and exactness that have come to dominate not only the perception but the very appearances of Being. This chapter will trace the fourfold as it enters its own recoil in modernity, altering decisively the meaning of each constituent. For example, in the classical vision, finitude is the vehicle of transcendence, while in modernity it becomes the stumbling block to knowledge. We will show how Heidegger attempts to utilize these *fourfold reversals* in a more primordially nonsystematic manner. But his effort to rid ontology of the deity and thereby to ground the phenomenological lived-world leaves him in a deontological impasse as the most unique idealist in the history of thought.

The final chapter is devoted to bringing into the clearing the *fourfold intensities*. The essential confrontation between Heidegger and St. Thomas is intended neither to merge the two in some facile reconciliation, nor to make of Heidegger a straw man with which to beat modernity in favor of a thirteenth-century theology. This confrontation will uncover the fourfold as it is embedded in the very core of Being, at the original source of the beginning *qua* end of the asking into the meaning of Being. Heidegger himself remarked in his own work on Nietzsche: "Confrontation is genuine criticism. It is the supreme way, the only way, to a true estimation of a thinker. In confrontation we undertake to reflect on his thinking and to trace it in its effective force . . . in order that through the confrontation we ourselves may become free for the supreme exertion of thinking."[2] The intensities will bring forth, as best possible, the *what-it-is* of the ground at which we necessarily come to a stop in the order of explanation and in the order of Being. At this point the "uncanny" or the un-familiar will emerge as the divine. The questions of the *aeviternal*-historical structure of man, of his *deiformitas*, of his freedom and of the *radical possibility of Christian Philosophy* as the context in which he asks into the meaning of Being will be seen as umbilically linked to the fourfold.

Acknowledgments

I am forever indebted to Professor Francisco Fernández Labastida for his generous spirit, intelligence and guidance.

I would also like to thank Professors Juan Andrés Mercado and Juan José Sanguineti for their insightful comments and thorough evaluations as well as Jeanmarie Pinto for her invaluable editorial assistance.

Chapter 1

The Fourfold Historical Origin of Metaphysics

But that is not what you were asked, Theaetetus. You were not asked to say what one may have knowledge of, or how many branches of knowledge there are. It was not with any idea of counting these up that the question was asked; we wanted to know what knowledge itself is or am I talking nonsense.

Plato, Theaetetus, *146e*

* * *

Tracing I: How the Deity Entered Philosophy

Parmenides' philosophy is a speculation on the Eon, *on Being. The symbol "Being" appears for the first time; and without exaggeration it can be said that with Parmenides the history of philosophy proper, as the exploration of the constitution of Being, begins . . . Parmenides has no predecessors, and his concept of Being has no prehistory. The historical process which results in the concept of Being does not itself move on the level of philosophical speculation; it rather is the process of the soul in which Being as absolute transcendence comes ultimately into experiential grasp.*[1]

The Return to the Origin

The mares that carry me, as far as desire might reach, were taking me as far as my heart desired, when they brought and placed me upon the much-speaking route of the goddess.

Poem of Parmenides, *1 1–2*

We are already confronted with the disposition of the specifically human self-transcendent intentional presence. Characteristically erotic, man is carried *as far as desire might reach* into the presence of the goddess. Eros is a natural metaphor for the intentional structure of consciousness in its other-directedness. It is the privation that betokens the human need for understanding, anticipating Aristotle's famous "all men by nature desire to know."[2] This erotic tension, while presupposing division, is released into union, just as the permanence of Being mediates generation and destruction at the origin of both processes, or as the way the now balances the difference between past and future by underlying time, and as the threshold of the Gates of Justice mediates the split between night and day by underlying both ways.[3] Several interpretive points must be noted regarding the nature of this self-transcendent human presence erotically striving toward that which underlies, mediates and unifies:

1. The route of the goddess is *much-speaking*. Language: this is perhaps an anticipation of the nature of Being to be the same as thinking: ". . . that the dictum of the thinker speaks by bringing into language the word of this goddess."[4] Man as oracle of Being, the possibility of which requires an affinity, and even more than that, between man and Being.
2. The goddess *is truth*. Truth is not a mere characteristic or accidental property of the goddess, like a man who is indifferently either tall or short. Truth is the essential ontological condition of the Being of the goddess. In other words, goddess as Truth and thus as goddess, i.e., as divine. As Heidegger remarks, not the goddess of truth but the goddess as truth.[5]
3. Man is *brought, placed upon* this much-speaking route of the thinking-*qua*-Being of the goddess who *is* Truth. Man as knower is already the known. By entering onto the route of the goddess has he not become what the goddess is and knows? Again, the goddess is Truth and when man becomes the known he becomes the true. "Thus, the inherent compatibility of Thought and Being is built into the way things are; i.e., thinking is essential to being human . . . we choose to participate Being by becoming one with the way things really are."[6]
4. Can we simply disregard the "personification" of truth as the goddess as a mere remnant of a mythological vision; or does the goddess reveal a fundamental relational presence, the being-with and being-toward-the-world among the activities of human knowing, and thus a sharp contrast to the ideational abstractness that has infiltrated the notion of truth as the supposed condition of universality? Heidegger was one of the first to notice that this device of "hypostatizing" universal concepts as divinities

is not merely in order to give more fullness and color to otherwise "abstract" thoughts.[7] The goddess is, as truth, the paradigmatic exemplar of the Other.[8]

If intentionality is this relational being-with and being-toward-the-world, what possible constituents of the true allow for a real other to be really other, i.e., existentially distinct from man? In a word, if relational being-with and being-toward-the-world demands that the real (not abstract) other appear in the face of the "I," then hasn't man been already presented with a definite stop in the order of his intentional being when he comes face to face with this existential otherness, face to face with the object of his *need* or desire to understand? Is this stop only an origin or one that also conditions the knowledge of existence only in the framework of an end, the need to come to a stop as *arché* and *telos* of man's existential presence?

These four problematics compactly announce the profoundly "*aletheiological*" orientation of being-in-the-world. It is "a 'thoughtful' experience of things, a 'meditative' thinking in which we let things emerge and rise up in their own presence"[9] in order to be brought to and placed upon the much-speaking route; it is the conversion of the knower to the known, by becoming the known. Parmenides' truth is essentially intentional and his intentionality is profoundly *aletheiological.* What does this mean within the context of our discussion?

Aletheia as the Critical Indicator of Man's End

Let us suppose that when the philosopher is placed on the much-speaking route, this placement signals a kind of stop which enables a start, an end to the action that had brought the narrator to the route, but which functions as the beginning of wisdom. The end is his entrance into the knowable. The intentional act reaches its culmination or *telos* in the it-Is: this is no empty presupposition, but the presupposition with which I, as a knower, must begin. Intentionality is directed to the what only in consequence of the recognition of the it-Is of presence.[10] But what is the proper condition and fulfillment of this direction?

Daughters of the Sun were hastening to escort me, after leaving the House of Night for the Light, having thrown back their veils from their heads. There stands the gateway of the paths of Night and Day . . . (fr. 1 10–18)

This passage is our first hermeneutic clue as to whether *aletheia* for Parmenides has as its *telos* a metaphysical or phenomenological end. The Daughters of the Sun who dwell in the House of Night move toward the light by throwing back the veils from their heads and escorting the philosopher out of the night and into the light. Is their ascent into the light an anticipation of Plato's allegory of the cave and of the metaphysical ladder of Being that man must ascend to be a knower, "the cathartic way that will lead man from the Night of the mortals (the submarine existence of Plato) to the Light of eternal truth?"[11] The paths of Night and Day suggest that Truth is found in the mutual interpenetration of the dark and light, the former the concealed and the latter the unconcealed. The Daughters of the Sun, the off-spring of Truth, do not reside in the light alone for they dwell in the dark and must remove their veils in order to return to the light. The veils, as Gadamer notes, are "a symbol of the light of truth into which they are now entering."[12] They throw back the veils but they are not cast off completely. The veils are still attached, merely pulled aside for the moment of clarity: the time of unconcealment. The fact that the veils are only partially removed indicates they are to be used again. Does this characterize metaphysical truth or a phenomenological sense of the mutual interpenetration of the concealed and unconcealed? In a word, doesn't this conversion of the dark into the light, that "alludes to a concealedness in every unconcealedness"[13] support a phenomenological sense of truth, wherein truth is the endless Event (*ereignis*) of bringing Being out of its concealedness only to let it retreat again? But then again, mustn't the prisoner return to the cave?

There is, though, something *between* Night and Day, the concealed and unconcealed, that is often overlooked but gives us another clue to the kind of end or *telos* this Truth-Goddess embodies:

> Appeasing her with gentle words, the maidens cunningly persuaded her to push back the bolted bar for them swiftly from the gates; and these, opening wide, made a yawning chasm in the door frame . . . (fr. 1 15–18)

There is a *yawning chasm* when the gates between night and day have been opened. Let us focus on the two words, *yawning (achanês)* and *chasm (anaptamenai)*. The latter perhaps signifies an absence, a nothingness between Night and Day. Does this mean that there is nothing-of-importance between Night and Day or does nothingness characterize what Parmenides understands to be a fundamental Other-at-work between the concealed and unconcealed? Doesn't this Other that cannot be characterized seem to indicate that there is something underlying and guaranteeing the order of explanation? The chasm describes this stop in the order of being that cannot be articulated or explained like Night and Day but is their ground or unity. If this is not the Heideggerian unity, i.e., the ontological differ-ence, an equiprimoridiality among beings, but one reflecting hierarchical degrees of being, then is it the onto-theo-logical difference, serving to ele-vate the duality between Night and Day, the unconcealed and concealed, into its fundamental and necessary unity? If this chasm more closely adheres to the metaphysical *ananke stenai*, then wouldn't its yawning/gaping per-haps best describe the strangeness or other-worldliness of this radical Other-at-work between Night and Day? The yawning of the gate creates a hollow sound that augurs the uncanny into which man has entered; he has reached his limit as a knower, the end in the order of explanation, the point at which man reaches the door to the divine. The gates yawn because of the rarity of such an experience to be recognized for what it is: the ground of Otherness for which all things are appropriated because the beginning is the end. "The message might be that Parmenides' shamanic voyage is one that only few, if any, mortals are allowed to share in this life. Perhaps the gates of justice are so immense that they cannot but produce such an extraor-dinary sound. The message might be that the Gates are not man-made, that the journey itself is supernatural."[14] "Parmenides' 'roadway' (*hodos*) is nowhere to be found on this earth; it is rather the way of salvation."[15] Parmenides further expresses the rarity of this intentional experience that lies far indeed from the beaten path of ordinary men:

Welcome! For it is no bad fate that has sent you forth to travel upon this route (for it lies far indeed from the beaten path of ordinary men), but right and justice. And it is right that you should learn all things, both the steadfast [immovable] heart of well-rounded truth and the opinions of mortals, in which there is no true trust. But nevertheless you shall learn these as well, how the things deemed to be ought to have been deemed to be fully, pervading all things completely. (fr. 1 26–32)

An Epistemological Digression/Discursus

In order to unpack the Parmenidean *arché/telos* expressed in the goddess' telling remark "it is all one to me where I am to begin; for I shall return there again," (fr. 5) we must first examine the meaning of *aletheia* in the poem. If man becomes the true or known in the form of the knower, what is this Truth? Heidegger famously recognizes the a-privative in the Greek *a-letheia* and translates truth as unconcealedness over and against the Latin *veritas*.

We are pursuing the four directives provided by the name *a-letheia* as translated "unconcealedness". In this way we hope to experience something of the primordial essence of Greek thought. First, un-concealedness refers to concealment. Concealment hence permeates the primordial essence of truth. Secondly, un-concealedness indicates that truth is wrenched from concealment and is in conflict with it. The primordial essence of truth is conflictual. What "conflict" means here remains a question. Thirdly, un-concealedness, in accordance with the just mentioned characterizations, refers to a realm of "oppositions" in which "truth" stands. Since it is on the basis of the "oppositional" essence of unconcealedness that its conflictual essence first becomes visible, we have to consider more closely the question of the "opposition" in which truth stands. Western thinking accounts untruth the sole opposite to truth. "Untruth" is identified with "falsity" which, understood as incorrectness, forms the evident and obstrusive counterpart to "correctness." The opposition holding sway at the beginning is known to us under the names *a-letheia kai pseudos, veritas et falsitas,* truth and falsity. We interpret the latter opposition as correctness and incorrectness; but truth as "correctness" is not of the same essence as truth in the sense of "unconcealedness". The opposition of correctness and incorrectness, validity and invalidity, may very well exhaust the oppositional essence of truth for later thinking and above all for modern thinking. But that decides nothing at all concerning the possible oppositions to "unconcealedness" thought by the Greeks. We must therefore ask how the primordial thinking of the Greeks sees the opposition to "unconcealedness".[16]

Verum, ver-, meant originally enclosing, covering. The latin verum belongs to the same realm of meaning as the Greek *a-letheia,* the uncovered—precisely by signifying the exact opposite of *a-letheia*: the closed off. The Roman verum, strictly speaking, should be taken as equivalent to the Greek pseudos, if the latter is indeed the counter-word to *a-letheia.* But the Roman verum not only does not coincide with *pseudos,* it is precisely the opposite of pseudos as understood in latin, i.e., *falsum.*[17]

Heidegger understands the latinization of "truth" not only to be fundamentally incompatible with the Greek *aletheia* but that its dominance on

[handwritten annotations: being-at-hand / aletheia / present-at-hand / veritas]

Western thought has resulted in a systematic restriction/dilution of being-at-hand to mere present-at-hand, ultimately undermining man's relatedness in and to the world. For Heidegger *aletheia* becomes *veritas* when *metron* becomes *meson* and *meson* becomes *mensura* and man becomes *mens*, and the entire apparatus of causality, correctness, rectitude and exactness come to dominate not only the perception but the very appearances of Being.[18] His potent etymological defense of this position is, if correct, a complete over-throwing of the deeply embedded notion that the comportment of the ontologic attitude is not only to arrive at the onto-theo-logic but to recognize it as the fulcrum and the confirmation of man's and Being's nature. And so before returning to the poem, we need to set the issue compactly but clearly:

1. Has truth as *verum* relegated truth as *aletheia* to a staid and static realm of factical and abstract assertion with no real bearing on actual existence, and is this perhaps the predecessor to the clear and distinct ideas of the idealist by way of the Platonic "correct vision" of the allegory?
2. Has metaphysics denied the essential role of the Parmenidean concealedness to bring forth the unconcealed (*a-letheia*) i.e., "*pseudos* involves a covering that simultaneously unveils,"[19] when it polemicized and destroyed the relationship between truth and pseudo, letting the former become mere correctness and the latter mere incorrectness?
3. And if indeed metaphysics has opposed truth to falsity in this way, has it thereby rendered all beings ordered by the supposed highest Being to have the Good, the Beautiful and the True only in the form of partici-pated effects and not as the primary and inseparable ontological characteristics that fully ratify and authenticate man's ontic commerce with and to the world? And don't these effects signal the systematic lessening of being-at-hand to mere presence-at-hand, converting the phenomenological lived-world into a founded causality?
4. In what way can *pseudos* (concealed) be the necessary conflictual con-trast to *a-letheia* (unconcealed), and still maintain its existential and irreducible distinction from it and not collapse into an idealistic sys-tem similar to either Hegel's or Schelling's? The very moral *entelechy* of human knowledge and its unity in Being depends on the legitimacy and nature of such a distinction.

For Heidegger, the goddess carries the concealed-unconcealed in a kind of reciprocity where there is no priority or hierarchy among truths and, as such, there can be no sense of truth in the form of *veritas* to stand against and in real distinction to the false. "The realm of the 'concealed-unconcealed' is, if we do not deceive ourselves, more immediately familiar and accessible than what is expressed in the banal titles *veritas* and 'truth'. Strictly speaking, the word 'truth' does not give us anything to think and still less anything to represent 'intuitively'."[20]

But can there be the intentional ground without the causal *ananke stenai* reached by the labor-intensive discrimination between true and false if the phenomenon is endless and endlessly shifting between the concealed and the unconcealed? Doesn't this approach a fundamental anti-theological groundlessness? If for Parmenides the goddess is not only unnamed, but because his understanding of Is does not even have a grammatical subject, aren't these factors hinting at a resolute unity of Night and Day in a higher theological Otherness?[21]

Let us suppose the goddess actually carried her two aspects *a-letheia kai pseudos*, the unconcealed and the concealed, equiprimordially. Wouldn't the unity of the two be a self-transcendence which could not lead to a greater Other beyond the phenomena or beyond the order of explanation and thereby not terminate in a genuinely mutual transcendence? The groundless appropriation of all things subsumes man into the other when he finds himself at an origin which is abysmal, which absorbs but does not contrast. Parenthetically, wouldn't then the distinction between good and evil be lost and its repercussions far reaching: the loss of the Christian God, the absence of the *ananke stenai* and causality and the problem of the moral constitution of man? But then Heidegger never claimed to have an ethical enterprise and the very loss of the Christian God and its self-same *ananke stenai* would rid philosophy for him of its alien elements.[22]

The charge that metaphysics forgets the nature of the concealed to bring forth the unconcealed and that it separates them into two opposed categories of mere correctness and incorrectness is not without merit. But are these charges fundamentally acceptable?[23]

Veritas as the "*Aletheia*" that Corresponds to Finitude

The concealed and unconcealed have not been displaced by metaphysics but elevated into their proper and unitary form. *Veritas* as enclosure maintains their unity and their distinction, but the need for truth as *veritas* has not yet been explicated. To identify the need for *veritas*, let us first examine in greater detail the kind of unity of which the goddess speaks.

For if it came-to-be, it is not, nor [is it] if at some time it is going to be. Thus, coming-to-be is extinguished, and perishing is not to be heard of. Nor is it divisible, since it all alike is; nor is it somewhat more here, which would keep it from holding together, nor is it somewhat less, but it is all full of what-is. Therefore it is all continuous; for what-is draws near to what-is. Moreover, changeless in the limits of great bonds it is unbeginning and unceasing, since coming-to-be and perishing have been exiled and true trust have thrust them out. (fr. 8 20–28)

From this fragment, Parmenides understood that the recognition of the unbeginning and unchanging Is/Being arises from within the limits of great bonds. How can we reconcile the hegemonic infinite nature of Being with the clear and definite symbols of finitude as perfection?[24] Several positions have arisen to defend this paradox against its possible contradiction, yet they fail to grasp its essential reasoning. On the one hand they argue for this reconciliation from the vantage point of Parmenides' many circle-metaphors or on the other hand from the idea that there is really no limit at all, but only an analogy designed to "account for balance, truth and infinite cosmic expanse in all directions."[25] The core of this paradox is the finite human presence in confrontation with its otherness. It is precisely his being a finite effect that enables and requires man to recognize that the terminus and origin of all his acts depend upon his existential involvement with the what-is.[26] We can understand what Heidegger means by calling man the shepherd of Being[27]: once man enters into the framework of the concealed and unconcealed, the structure of truth is realized. This realization is the conversion of the unconcealed into something other; the elevation of the concealed and unconcealed into the specifically human enclosure of *veritas*.[28] *The change: we "enclose" truth*

The elevation of the concealed and unconcealed into a kind of enclosure (*veritas*) does occur in the poem with the arrival of the specifically human self-transcendent intentional presence:

Remaining the same and in the same, it lies by itself and remains thus firmly in place; for strong Necessity holds it fast in the bonds of a limit, which encloses it. (fr. 8 29–31)

There are two fundamental and interrelated points in defense of the metaphysical resolution of *a-letheia* into *veritas*. The first lays the ground for the *ananke stenai*, revealing man not only to be a participant in the meaning of Being but also in its formation. From there, this participation reflects the fullness of the metaphysical intentional act to be not only an elevation of *a-letheia* into *veritas* but an elevation that signals a kind of need. In a word, the *aletheiological* character of the *Poem of Parmenides* in its goal or *telos* most acutely reflects the metaphysical need for an Other in divine terms to satisfy and secure man as a knower in the world.   *Ananke - necessity*

Strong Necessity conveys the finite intentional presence directed toward the what-is. If finitude is man's motive for and vehicle of self-transcendence, his way of and to Being is bound by a kind of necessity (*Ananke*) to adhere to the truth of that way. "Because man must be able to hold it fast, Being must not be unbound, but held by powerful *Ananke*"[29] and, by doing so, he has entered the ground of knowledge, the *ananke stenai*. The *ananke stenai* is man's *noetic* beginning and end and that which he has always and necessarily held fast; it is both the necessary precondition for his knowledge and the terminus (*stenai*) of his acts that gives him this knowledge. The intentional interplay between man and Other is the meeting ground of the *ananke* and the *stenai*. Call the former necessity, finite, mortal, and the latter Other, End, Divine: their union is found in the *ananke stenai*: the finite intentional presence meeting and recognizing as a necessity of thought the most radical Other. The *ananke stenai* "comes to be known," so to speak, by participation: man is the articulator of and as such assists in the formation of the meaning of Being. The Other is the meaning and is the ground for such a formation; because this Is cannot be predicated like its effects, it is not knowledge but the origin, condition and terminus of all knowledge. "This immortal being is determined as to its nature by the necessity of the Logos; and the same necessity determines its cognitive articulation."[30] Man becomes the what-is, not in its limitlessness but in the conceptual form of the knower who is marked by the finite bonds of a limit. As man holds fast in the bonds of limit to the what-is, i.e., the unconcealed, he encloses it. Because the known enters under the form of the knower, once unconcealedness as the known enters the knower it takes on the characteristic of the enclosedness or *veritas* of judgment. Why it takes on the form of *veritas* for Parmenides is not yet completely illuminated, except for that fact that there is a need for the unconcealed to be *veritas* when in the judgmental act of the knower.

The Formation of the "Same Is for Thinking as for Being"

This need that elevates *aletheia* into *veritas* and implies a kind of causal directed-ness, and where the unconcealed and concealed in man are not an endless

Event or conversion into each other but elevated into a teleological movement toward a definite Other in which all things including man co-inhere; this need presents an intentionality that is necessarily onto-theo-logically directed. The Truth that unites as "same" thinking-and-Being expresses the specifically metaphysical goal of self-transcendence.

In the poem the goddess assures the philosopher that she will reveal to him the "steadfast" heart of "well-rounded" Truth. As Voegelin points out "the attributes of Truth which appear in this assurance are the same (atremes, eukylos) that appear later as predicates of Being. The result of the speculation, thus, is not only a truth about being; it is the Truth of Being voiced through the 'knowing man' . . . the philosopher reproduces Being itself."[31] By becoming the Other, the philosopher gains access into the necessary prerequisite of Night and Day, the concealed and unconcealed, that which pervades all things completely. This notion of pervading all things completely describes pre-thematically the metaphysical hegemony of Being and the prerequisite of intentionality. Intentionality is not knowledge but the presuppositional ground of all knowledge, requiring but transcending all things, because Being is in all things. "The same is for thinking as for being" is the epistemological articulation of that presuppositional prerequisite and the philosopher learns of that which pervades all things completely by holding fast to what is.

> See how beings which are absent are, all the same, firmly present to mind; for [mind] will not cut off what-is from holding fast to what-is. (fr. 4)

He is able to know because he is able to hold on, and he is able to hold on because the same is for thinking as for Being. The mind will not separate from its *telos*—to *eon*—if it holds fast to it. Does this express a contemplative gaze that lets the truth of Being come to light in a phenomenological or in a metaphysical sense? For the former, the act of metaphysical judgment artificially reorders beings, not allowing Being to be. But for the latter, the contemplative gaze is characterized by a necessary abstraction that allows man to see firmly as present what-is even in its absence. To *eon*, as Gadamer says, "implies that it has nothing to do with the diversity of experiences, the listing of them, but rather that without the unity of being all of this no longer exists. This certainly means to *eon* cannot be separate from *tou eontas*; what Is possesses is cohesion (continuity) and unity. Obviously the universe [is meant] as universe in its unity, and this universe in its unity means at the same time the concept of being. To put it more precisely, it is not yet the concept but it is a full abstraction of the diversity of things. The singular is like an indicator of the beginning of the conceptual-speculative reflection."[32]

On this account it is not right for what-is to be incomplete; for it is not lacking; but if it were, it would lack everything. And the same is there for thinking and is that for the sake of which thought is; for not without what-is, to which it stands committed, will you find thinking; for nothing else is or will be besides what-is, since Fate has bound it to be whole and changeless. It is in reference to it that all names have been spoken. (fr. 8 23–40)

The fourfold intentional presupposition is aboundingly present in this passage.

1. Intentional presence in that man stands committed in his thinking and his being to the that of what-is.
2. Finitude in his emergence as the privileged being from the Fate that has bound Being to be whole and changeless.
3. Causality in that his finite intentional becoming is the necessary response and contrast to this origin *qua* end, and his causal tracking (naming) of Being.
4. *Ananke stenai* because man is capable of the above cited three only because the ground of what-is, is the necessary reference point, i.e., the *ananke stenai* in which all names have and can be spoken. These names are not "affixed by man . . . but by Necessity," outside time in the "supersensible where the tension between opposite forces in nature is arrested in contemplative oneness with nature."[33]

The Parmenidean Origin *qua* End as the *Ananke Stenai*

The foundation reached through the *ananke stenai* is that which gives all names but is itself beyond all names because it is the limit of explanation. In the poem the *ananke stenai* is personified in the unnamed goddess and it is in reference to the goddess *qua* stop that all is known. She represents the necessary stop in the order of explanation, the self-same stop in the order of Being that lets being be and the meaning of Being to be spoken. And we know this —"because the same is for thinking as for Being."

If everything is in reference to this stop/start-beginning/end, this referential standpoint signifies: (1) everything else to be "causal" effects of that end in some fundamental sense; (2) Parmenides, like Aristotle and St. Thomas, understood that there cannot be an infinite regress in the order of explanation and therefore in the order of Being; that there must be something that exists and is not dependent on its effects; thus, whose existence is separate from the existence of the world, that is, whose existence can be separated from the world.

The *ananke stenai* marks the irreconcilability between Heidegger's and St. Thomas' intentionality. Even if the goddess' understanding of Truth in its ground and application is pre-thematically metaphysical and as such the Greek/Parmenidean unconcealedness can be reconciled with the Latin *veritas*, we have not resolved whether metaphysics has relinquished and forgotten the trans-ontic non-entitative fullness of Being. Does metaphysical knowledge have none of the initial fullness, but only additions or semblances of a higher founded Being? Parmenides' hesitation to use the subject *Eon* with Is, or to speak in terms of an object when Being is no such thing echoes Heidegger's *Sein* and St. Thomas' *Esse* when they assert the primacy of existence over essence to safeguard the ontological, unifying, constitutive role for the act of being—actual existence—to play in our formation of knowledge. But whereas Heidegger sees only the loss of Being when it is distributed as causal effects from beginning to end, Parmenides in fact understands this to be the necessary precondition of knowledge. Unlike Heidegger, Parmenides saw compactly what St. Thomas sought to elaborate: that the privilege and possibility to assist in the formation of Being is the core of self-transcendence, and that this privilege is made possible by causal insight:

> The progress on the way towards the Light culminates in an experience of a supreme reality that can only be expressed in the exclamatory Is! . . . As far as predicates of a transcendental subject are concerned, the matter has been cleared up on principle by the Thomistic analogia entis.[34]

A discursus on the specifically Thomistic understanding of the nature of predication will later serve to make explicit what Parmenides understood ontologically only implicitly: beings, in their essence and existence, are effects ordered by a higher Being but these predicates are not additions to Being, rather they are each in themselves an essential visage of Being.

Intentionality and Its Onto-Theo-Logic Directedness in the *Poem of Parmenides*

The genius of Parmenides was to recognize that the unity of the limitless Being when in the form/identity of the knower/participant is this stop formed by man's limit or finitude. This relativity or relatedness of truth in knowledge is in point of fact that which insures the metaphysical independence of each term of the relation (*noesis-noema*), thus eschewing *ab origine* the possibility of any idealistic understanding of understanding. Being's onto-theo-logical difference provides both the backdrop for defining man as finite and for making possible this kind of participation. In itself, Parmenides' Being is "temporally without limits,"[35] but their "identity" signals a higher unity, whereby the onto enters the theological. "At this time the strongest religious motive for viewing the world philosophically still lies in the concept of unity. But Parmenides gives it new strength by endowing this unity with the properties of completeness, immobility, and limitation."[36]

At the origin/end of the order of Being, the onto-theo-logic has emerged. It reveals that man transcends the ontologic and enters into the theo-logic without ever leaving the world. The relationship between the immanent act of knowledge unfolding within the assimilatively self-transcendent act of becoming the known indicates man to be, by his very *noetic* structure, onto-theo-logically inclined. The interplay between the immanent and self-transcendent is the very formation of the causal *entelechy* that directs man via predications to the character of the foundation. The goddess' movement between the unconcealed and the concealed, *a-letheia* and *pseudos*, does not immanentize all things and divinize man, effectively obliterating the distinction between the two. She is the paradigmatic personification of metaphysical transcendence through levels of insight and predication. The immanent union of thinking and Being is upheld only in the self-transcendent participation with the Other wherein the concealed and unconcealed are elevated into their ultimate Truth.

When Heidegger asks, "How does the deity enter in philosophy"[37] he is questioning the validity of the onto-theo-logical unity characteristic of metaphysics, specifically of the ancient and medieval metaphysicians. The structure of metaphysics for Heidegger is oriented toward discerning the difference between Being and beings, while the question of Being as such remains inauthentically concealed and historically utterly forgotten. The experiential relationship of the subject and object and their corresponding appropriation in Being understood by intentionality is not the subject and object relationship of metaphysics, particularly not the transformationally theological metaphysics of someone like Aquinas. As Heidegger asserts, "both the contention that there are 'eternal truths' and the jumbling together of Dasein's phenomenally grounded ideality, with an idealized absolute subject, belong to those residues of Christian theology within philosophical problematics which have not as yet been radically extruded."[38]

For Heidegger, radically to free philosophy of its Christian residues is to return to the beginning and think about, as did Parmenides, Being itself. But, what is there to think of Being itself outside the onto-theo-logic, if the deity had not entered philosophy from the beginning as the beginning, with the *Poem of Parmenides?* "We need not ask whether his study of pure Being has a religious purpose, such as proving the existence of God in the traditional Christian manner; our question is rather whether his speculations about true Being strike him as having some significance that is in any sense religious, even though he does not call this Being God."[39]

Myth expands the realm of Doxa to include the incarnation of Truth. If the articulation of the Parmenidean range of problems would proceed in the same direction beyond Plato, we might anticipate an expansion of the Doxa to include the revelatory sphere itself; the Doxa as Revelation would be a truth beyond the Parmenidean truth of Being. This final step was taken, not within Hellenic philosophy, although its logic was immanent in its course, but only in the Hebrew-Christian revelation.[40]

The struggle between the Ways of Truth is the fundamental issue of Western intellectual history from the blending of Hellenism and Christianity to the present. And Parmenides is the thinker who has created the 'type' for this world-historic struggle through his unshakable establishment of the Way of Logos.[41]

In sum, we see in the goddess' explication of Being an intentional relationship of the knower to the known: it is both the primal and terminal act of being, framing the threshold of human existence as its *arché* and *telos* and constituting the two necessary interdependencies of immanence and self-transcendence. Intentionality is the radical maintenance of the specifically human self-transcendence through an immanent act, the act of knowledge itself. The four aspects of the intentional presupposition (the charter of metaphysics!) and the interplay between immanence and self-transcendence are essential to the poem and must needs be present to sustain man as a knower in the world: man is identical to the world and yet the world is existentially distinct, the beginning is the end but both stand apart in such a way that the immanent act of knowledge cannot be without self-transcendence. As a whole we can call the delicate and vital balance between the knower and the known the intentional presence. The breakdown of this conclusion is as follows:

1. "The lesson of the poem may just be that philosophy begins with transcendence, by passing through the gates of Justice, and not with the

    search for viable explanations of what is the case or what is true exclusively to this temporal world."[42]

2. That a beginning requires an end so much so that an origin is a *telos*, an intentional ground is an *ananke stenai*.

3. Because of its onto-theo-logical directedness, the beginning is the end; this does not signal the collapse of the real distinction between self-transcendence and immanence but upholds it in the face of irreducible Otherness, in the onto-theo-logical difference.

4. Knowledge is the first possibility and last effect of intentionality, and never leaves the intentional ground. From within this ground, man discovers the fourfold intentional presupposition that characterizes human becoming in the face of existential otherness: intentionality, finitude, causality, the *ananke stenai*, in a word, metaphysics.

5. We shall see that every substitute and surrogate for knowledge is founded on the loss of one of the aspects of the fourfold intentional presupposition that ultimately collapses the real distinction between, or denies the existence of, either immanence or self-transcendence.

6. And yet, this analysis has perhaps done nothing more than show Parmenides to be the first among many metaphysicians. How metaphysics alters or elevates being-in-the-world in terms of the theological must be further examined.

Parmenidean Origin versus Heideggerian *Ereignis*

The *aletheiological* origin of the Parmenidean what-is cannot be reconciled with *Ereignis*. The interplay between Night and Day, the concealed and unconcealed does not originate in time, not even in Heidegger's most primordial time. Heidegger's *Ereignis* cannot be a dialectical relationship between Being and time, it is not his "intention to resolve the mutual interplay between Being and time into some higher concept which unite the two in their higher truth."[43] But the Parmenidean origin is the resolution and unity of the relationship between the concealed and unconcealed; its beginning *qua* end is quantitatively closer to the metaphysical/intentional *ananke stenai*, than to Heidegger's in-time *Ereignis*.[44] Parmenides' "same is for thinking as for being" reflects the intentional presupposition specific to metaphysics; the known enters in the form of the knower only insofar as the knower belongs in, and in reference to, a higher Being. "The essence of the poem is that beings cannot claim the worldly essences that belong peculiarly and severally to them without there necessarily existing a transworldly, sourceless, and timeless Essence which gives of itself in the now."[45] Gadamer has noted that Heidegger sought to secure Parmenides' intentional pre-supposition (the same is for thinking as for Being) as an identification of the ontological difference over and against the metaphysical difference. "I can well understand why Heidegger wanted to hold onto that idea that Parmenides' main theme was identity (to auto). In Heidegger's eyes this would have gone beyond every metaphysical way of seeing and would thereby have anticipated a thesis that is later interpreted metaphysically in Western philosophy and has only come into its own in Heidegger's philosophy. Nevertheless, Heidegger himself realized that this was an error and that his thesis that Parmenides had to some extent anticipated his own philosophy could not be maintained."[46] But even if Parmenides cannot be subsumed by Heidegger we are still left with a major problem: is he just the first among many to have the metaphysically inclined disposition, i.e., the other-worldly temptress beckoning man to forsake the world of the existent and the particular in the search of a founded eternality? Does the metaphysical nature of causal predication inevitably invite man to pass over being-in-the-world in its epistemology? Or, contra Heidegger, does not the identification of Being and phenomenological appearing emasculate Being? Is it not deprived of an essential dimension: reality?[47] Our defense of classical intentionality and its metaphysical epistemology, it is to be hoped, will show that intentionality requires onto-theo-logic directedness not only in order not to end in an Idealism,[48] but much more positively to show that the denial of metaphysics is the denial of the mystery of Being, and thus of wonder, and thus of thought.

Again, Parmenides' intentional presupposition is

... not a vague supposition, for there is an uninterrupted tradition here. A confirmation can be found, for instance, in the sixteenth fragment, which consists of the only four undoubtedly authentic lines that are quoted by Aristotle (*Metaphysics* T5, 1009b 21). The text reads: *hos gar hekastot echei krasin meleon polukampton*—'as the relationship of the limbs of the organism develops itself'—*tos noos anthropoisi paristatai*—'so nous appears in human beings.' Put another way: thinking as consciousness of something, as intellectual perception, is related to the constitution of the organism; the one exists as soon as the other is present ... *To gar auto kai panti*—'it is always the same thing that thinks (namely) the composition of the organism in each and every person'; *to gar pleon esti noema*—'that which is perceived is always what predominates,' like the light that fills everything.[49]

Plato's dialogue *Parmenides* is next to follow in this uninterrupted tradition. It anticipates the Husserlian epistemology that Heidegger ambivalently rejects. The inseparability and immediacy of the perceived and the perceiving in Parmenides' presupposition is elaborated in the dialogue in such a way as to make the *Parmenides* the critical dialogue for the delineation of the problematic of the intentional presupposition. The problematic of the dialogue is to take the totality of Parmenides' compactly and hieratically announced epistemology—the same is for thinking as for Being—and expand it conceptually. All of the epistemological ways from the Platonic Forms to a pre-thematic anticipation of Husserl's phenomenology are a result of this explication. The goal of future thinkers will be to reconcile the Parmenidean presupposition with its appropriate conceptually predicative elaboration.

* * *

Tracing II: Plato's Parmenides

Those on one side drag all things down out of the heavens and the invisible realm, literally grabbing rocks and trees with their hands. They grasp all such things and maintain strenuously that that alone is which allows for some touching and embracing. For they mark off beinghood and body as the same; and if anyone from the other side says that something is that has no body, they despise him totally and don't want to listen to anything else. That's why those who dispute with them defend themselves very cautiously out of some invisible place on high, forcing true beinghood to be certain thought-things and disembodied forms. But the bodies of their opponents and what these men call truth, they bust up into small pieces in their arguments and call it, instead of beinghood, some sort of swept along becoming. And between these two, Theaetetus, a tremendous sort of battle over these things has forever been joined.

Sophist, 246a–c

Why the *Parmenides*?

Plato's *Parmenides* is, in every manner, from structure[50] to content, a perplexing series of contradictions that have left serious thinkers to assume it to be a game,[51] an esoteric exercise[52] or comic drama.[53] Parmenides himself in the dialogue calls his gymnastic a "worklike game."[54] It is a game, even a jeu d'esprit, but its "worklike" structure has a deadly serious goal.[55] This structure is a systematic unpacking of the intentional presuppositions: "the same is for thinking as for Being," and the necessity to come to a stop within the order of explanation. With particular emphasis on the meaning of the same and, as such, on the question of predication, this "game" is more like a wager: what happens to the knowledge of Being if the intentional ground is lost, and most importantly whether and which constituents of the four-fold intentional presupposition preserve that ground as intelligible?[56]

If Plato desired to lay forth his own epistemological doctrine in the *Parmenides*, mightn't he have done just that by means of a concise and ordered approach, as for instance in the *Phaedo* or in the famous "diagram of the line" in the *Republic*? But he did not. This dialogue must be examined less for its doctrinal content than for the aporetic invalidity of various meta-approaches, themselves critical indicators of something more fundamental than, but essentially related to, the knowledge of Being itself. In order to understand the dialogue, one must learn to think metaphysically.[57]

The most fundamental irreconcilability between a classical and a Heideggerian phenomenological intentionality is their contentiousness over whether, for the former, a causal *ananke stenai* or, for the latter, a phenomenological endlessness is the genuine prefigurement of *noetic* presence. For this reason, an analysis of Plato's *Parmenides* is of incalculable importance. The dialogue's seemingly unending series of hypotheses and contradictions not only provoke infinite regressions but also, by doing so, set forth the primary ontological questions implicit in this debate. The dialogue's rival contentions of the "One is-not"/"One is" lead the reader into an *aporia*, and into the sophist's thicket of nonbeing, of paradox and of contradiction. Within this *aporia*, that which always remains concealed, the intentional ground of knowledge, is exposed to be Necessary and metaphysically oriented. In a word, these infinite series of absurdities call to mind nothing other than the ontological need for a stop in the order of explanation—the *ananke stenai*. Therefore, it is the often overlooked but fundamental dialogue in support of a metaphysically directed intentionality, and indispensable to a historical tracing of the idea of intentionality.

On this account it is not right for what-is to be incomplete; for it is not lacking; but if it were, it would lack everything. And the same is there for thinking and is that for the sake of which thought is; for not without what-is, to which it stands committed, will you find thinking; for nothing else is or will be besides what-is, since Fate has bound it to be whole and changeless. It is in reference to it that all names have been spoken. (*Poem of Parmenides*, fr. 8 23–40)

Then if you say it once do you address whatever possesses the name, but if you said it many times you don't address this thing? Or whether once or many times you utter the same name, doesn't a great necessity force you always to mean the same thing? (*Parmenides*, 147d)

The *Parmenides* is of great importance because of its repeated attempts to unpack the meaning of the "same" between thinking and Being, anticipating both classical (the soul is in a way all things) and phenomenological (consciousness is always consciousness of) intentionality. The "same" is a question of predication and in the dialogue the question is specifically: How do the relative and the many relate to the universal, whether that be the Forms or the One, whether Being or something beyond and more original than Being?

Throughout the dialogue, this "same" is expressed in a multitude of ways: univocally, equiprimordially, idealistically and analogically. The first three expressions in varying degrees contribute ultimately to a phenomenological predication. Each turns away from the factical, pre-cognitive, presuppositional ground of intentionality and into a series of absurd hypotheses that remove the ground of Being, constituting an infinite regress. These types of predications accomplish this because either they do not start with the intentional presupposition (the nondemonstrable but descriptive fact of existence), but rather assume it to be one or another hypothesis in need of proof. Or, on the other hand, they begin with the descriptive facticity of intentionality but do not follow the presupposition to its necessary metaphysical conditions and in effect remain stranded in description, unable to turn toward the knowledge of the other as other.

This manifold analogical "same" of thinking and Being is grasped within the context of a twofold Necessity within the dialogue. In the *noetic* interplay between man and Other, or the different things and the One, Necessity is found to be their forceful adhesive. We maintain here that Necessity is known on the side of man as positive finitude and on the part of the Other as the *ananke stenai.* Both necessities are aspects of Necessity itself, constituting and appropriating man's *noetic* relationship with the world as onto-theologically directed. Finitude is the self-transcendent act moving naturally toward its end or *ananke stenai* unless derailed *contra naturam* by a failure to keep the fullness of the intentional presence. This framework alone allows man to turn toward thinking about Being through proper participation in and predication of Being.

The dialogue's attempts to conceptualize the hieratically compact "the same is for thinking as for Being" dead-end at the "notion" that the "One is-not." Just as the "same" between thinking and Being has several overlapping and even contradictory readings so does the idea that the "One is-not." These notions of the "One is-not" can be divided into two categories each with a number of implications:

1. The deprivation of beinghood: the primary conclusion for the "One is not." This deprivation or nonexistent One results from the loss of the factical quality of the intentional ground. The arguments enter into absurdity in their struggles to grasp the One by attempting the impossible, hypothesizing the unhypothetical, the ground of all knowledge, the "unhypothetical ground,"[58] and by doing so, systematically extrude Being from existence.

2. No-thing: of crucial importance, it signals that the One is not-a-thing like everything else within the order of Being. This notion of no-thing is the final conclusion to all the arguments, even those that postulate the One to be deprived of beinghood. The absurdity in arriving at that deprivation expresses the need for the *ananke stenai*.[59] The two arguments of particular importance for expanding this idea of no-"thing" will be the "instants" and the "heaps;" the former supports that need while the latter compactly expresses the repercussions of rejecting it, in favor of a kind of phenomenological endlessness.

Both the problem of the Platonic forms and a pre-thematized Heideggerian groundlessness (within the argument of "heaps") are ontological offshoots of this second conception of the One is-not (no-thing). While the former can be viewed as a predecessor to Idealism, they are as well a defense against it. The unrelatability of the forms with the different things expresses a kind of no-thingness that must ground or give consistency or universality to knowledge, but this self-same unrelatability or inability of predication leaves it susceptible to an Idealist rendering that subsumes those qualities into the "I." Heideggerian groundlessness, on the other hand, arises when no-thing is denied any relation to, or anticipation of, the *ananke stenai*, and is thus not the *telos* of predications onto-theo-logically directed. As such this phenomenological no-thing ends in a deprivation of beinghood.

As the dialogue attempts to unpack the intentional presupposition, it presents a series of confrontations between the I and Other, the oscillation between the One is or the One is-not, and the question of phenomenological or analogical predication. At its core, these confrontations are directed at (1) the question of Necessity, and (2) how, epistemologically, does that which is finite, limited, relative relate to or know the infinite, unlimited, universal.

This confrontation is expressed in the very linguistic/hermeneutic structure of the dialogue, in a confrontation between two kinds of necessity, "Strong Necessity" and a lesser logical necessity. "Strong Necessity" is a profound expression of the intentional presupposition and its aforementioned onto-theo-logic understanding of twofold Necessity (finitude and the *ananke stenai*) as the linchpin of thinking and Being. Strong Necessity stands apart briefly, before reentering the argument's *reductio ad absurdum*.

The latter by necessity is a derivation of the intentional presupposition. Without relationship to Strong Necessity, it is a polemic between the two constituents, thinking and Being. By necessity needs Strong Necessity to convert the logico-analytic enterprise into its proper ontology, as onto-logical. In the dialogue by necessity stands alone, signaling the argument's affirmation or negation to be necessary in a purely logical, deductive manner. In a word, "the domain [by necessity] under consideration is solely the rational domain attainable by 'for the same is for thinking and for being.' And, in this domain, there is no room for contingency."[60]

Our intent is to examine both necessities for their fundamental meaning. The goal and meaning of the dialogue express (1) the need for the intentional ground to be origin *qua* end, and (2) that without the *ananke stenai* an ontology of Being is ultimately a deontologized infinite regress. Our analysis of necessity, particularly the emphasis on Strong Necessity as the true meaning of the "same" between thinking and Being, will prefigure the cardinal issues between Heideggerian and Thomistic intentionality.

The First Infinite Regress

The dialogue just commenced, young Socrates has laid out his theory of the forms to Parmenides and Zeno. The serious problems of the forms are recognized: if the different things can by no means participate in the form because such partaking would dissolve the latter's unity, how then do we posit these forms that need to-be in order for the different things to-be without committing the forms to suffer becoming? A resolution is proposed:

I think that you think that each form is one because of this: whenever many things seem to you to be great, it seems probable to you, as you look over them all, that there is some one and the same idea. From this you conclude that the Great is one . . . (Plato, *Parmenides*, 132a)

However this attempted resolution of Socrates falls into an infinite regress:

But what about the Great itself and the different great things—if, in the same way, you look over them all with your soul, will there not appear, in turn, some great thing that makes all of them, by necessity, appear great. (132a)

But this necessity that makes all great things great does not in fact reflect the need for a stop in the order of the hypotheses, but on the contrary demands, as necessary, a continuation of its "logical" enterprise: "a different form of Greatness, then, will be revealed, in addition to what was Greatness itself and the things that partake of it. And above all of these, in turn, another, that makes all of them great. And so each of your forms will no longer be one, but will be boundless in multitude" (132a–b).

The argument has posited the forms' unity, favoring a stream of hypotheses that will ultimately commit the greatest violence to the form, rendering it to be utterly impotent epistemologically. Because the form has become boundless in multitude, the argument has entered its first of many infinite regresses.

A Brief Move toward, and Rejection of Idealism

When the unrelatability of the forms to the different things provokes an infinite regress, a fundamental problem arises. Isn't this boundless in multitude fundamentally contrary to the unitary nature of the form? And if this boundlessness must persist where then can the forms be posited as one and not suffer becoming?

Socrates' answer anticipates the move to a sort of nominalist/conceptualist/conventionalist idealism and even to the I-constitution of the world as the necessary prerequisite for the forms as clear and distinct ideas: "couldn't it be that each of these forms is a thought and properly comes to be nowhere but in souls? Then each in fact could be one and would not still suffer the things you just mentioned . . ." (132b). Parmenides responds, noting that since each thought is a thought of or about something, the inherent danger of reducing the form to a thought originating nowhere but in the soul is as an abstract existence solely of thoughts where "either each thing consists of thoughts and everything thinks or, although thoughts, they're thoughtless"(132c).

After Parmenides rejects that idealistic variant of the forms, Socrates concedes that the forms and the different things must participate in one another. He relates the two in a kind of analogy of likeness wherein the "forms stand in nature like paradigmata. The different things resemble them and are likenesses, and so the different things' participation in the forms turns out to be nothing else than to be made in their likeness!" (132d). At this point, the first Great necessity appears to give an onto-logical foundation to the "same" or likeness in Socrates' analogy:

> But doesn't a great necessity force the like, along with the thing like it, to partake of one and the same form? (132d–e)

In a way, this great necessity elevates the first by necessity's logical intelligibility into its onto-logical necessity, whereas the former only spoke of a great thing that makes all else appear great, the latter recognizes the different things must, in order to appear at all, themselves partake in that necessity or unity in order to be a genuine likeness.

The argument then runs aground in its hypothetical aspect and the problem of likeness drifts into a characteristic infinite regress. The differentiating factor or unhypothetical aspect within that first great necessity, one that would ground a genuine likeness, is overlooked. The hypotheses of likeness continue in a vicious and endless series of conclusions that undermine their initial advance: "Nothing then, can be like the form nor can the form be like anything else. Otherwise there will always appear a different form beyond the form; and if that is like anything, another still. And there will never be an end to the genesis of new forms as long as the form becomes like the thing that partakes of it" (132e–133a).

If it is true, then, that nothing can be like the form, nor can the form be like anything else, are we not left at an impasse as to what this form is, that appears not to-be? By continuing in the same logico-hypothetical manner, thought becomes involved in a conceptual undermining, wherein the initial posited form becomes nothing existent at all.

The One, deprived of its beinghood as the ground of appropriation for all things like it or in reference to it, dissolves: "for knowledge among us would be only of the truth among us, because none of the forms is known by us and therefore we do not partake of Knowledge itself" (134a–b). If the form is not among us, but must be posited as is, who then possesses the forms?

Perhaps a god would possess it, for he presumably possesses the most precise knowledge. But that assertion fails to rescue the One, for if indeed this god possesses Knowledge itself, he can't know the things among us, because the things among us cannot partake in the Forms (134d).

In a word, between thinking and Being the "same" has broken down; knowledge among us does not reflect the knowledge of Being itself. This breakdown is far reaching, for that god would be outside the possibility of thinking or speaking Being: "What an altogether wondrous speech, if it strips the gods of knowing!" (134e)

> The forms must by necessity have these problems and many more still, if there are these ideas of the beings and if one distinguishes each form on its own. The result is that whoever hears this hits a dead end and argues that these things are not; and if, at most, they should be, well, then, great necessity keeps them unknown from human nature. . . . Only a naturally gifted man could learn that there is a certain kind and beinghood, in itself, for each thing; and only a still more wondrous person will discover all these things and be able to teach someone else to judge them clearly and sufficiently for himself. (134e–135a)

The argument at this point has recognized the logical conundrum of the forms: if the form cannot be related to the many things, it cannot be spoken of; if it cannot be spoken of, does it exist? The very Great Necessity by which the forms are required is seemingly subverted by its own purely logical difficulties. In a word, the same between thinking and being has been annihilated. The result is a dead end, wherein the logical aspect of this argument hits a thoughtless, beingless impasse in which the man of this domain can't help but speak that these things are not.

But is this dead end in fact the locus at which the logical aspect necessarily merges into that which it needs in order to be logical, i.e., an ontological directedness? The forms or One that cannot be known signal a much more profound idea than mere deprivation of beinghood: What if this form or One or Being is really no-"thing" at all; what if it is the end in the order of explanation and is therefore something else altogether?

What does it mean when Parmenides states that great necessity keeps the forms unknown to human nature? Shall we say, quite pragmatically, that if it is unknowable, it might as well not exist? If only a god-like man could know or judge them for himself or teach them with clarity to others, how can it mean anything or apply to our everyday being-in-the world? And yet, on the other hand, this no-"thing," or perhaps Nonbeing, "puts its refuter too, into perplexity, and that as a result, whenever someone attempts to refute it, he's compelled to contradict himself about."[61]

It seems that this no-thing is inescapable in language; it cannot be circumvented or suppressed, but neither can it be managed in the same way that everything else that appears is spoken of or predicated. There is something fundamentally necessary that accompanies the notion of the forms and without it, knowledge is lost:

> If someone in turn, Socrates, after focusing on all these problems and others still, shall deny that there are forms of the beings and will not distinguish a certain form of each single thing, wherever he turns he'll understand nothing, since he does not allow that there is an ever-same idea for each of the beings. And so he will "entirely destroy the power of dialogue."(135b–c)

And dialogue itself is the manifestation of the dictum "the same is for thinking as for being" within our every day being-in-the-world. It is also, parenthetically, the ground of the moral and political order, custom, *nomos*, tradition, and of the pursuit of the realm of transcendence and the relationship between the open and closed societies in the domain of *paideia*.

Parmenides takes over the course of the dialogue at the point at which the One is-not is presented as a possible referent to a pre-predicative ground, prior to explanation and hypotheses. This proper method of his gymnastic is "not only to investigate the results of a hypothesis if each hypothesized thing is, but also hypothesize that this same thing is not" (135e–136a). Parmenides expresses his concern over commencing this deadly serious worklike game. He must be like the strong mares of his youth that had taken him to the goddess truth, but he is old, and knows fully both where this journey will lead and the strain and difficulty that must be accepted in order to understand:

> Then Parmenides said, "Necessary it is to obey. And yet I seem to be suffering something like that Ibyceian horse, which, as a prizewinner but old, is about to take part in a chariot race and, being experienced, trembles at what is about to happen. Ibycus says that he resembles the horse since, although he is so old and unwilling, Necessity forces him to fall in love. And so I seem quite fearful, since I remember what sort of and how great a multitude of speeches I must swim through at my age. Nevertheless, I must show you this favor, especially since, as Zeno says, we are by ourselves." (136e–137a)

As the gymnastic commences, the problem of necessity will take on a new weight; not only will it waver between the logical and the ontological, but also, with the recognition of this no-thing, the question of the onto-logical will in turn reveal onto-theo-logical implications.

The Argument and Its Movements Understood through the Fourfold Intentional Presupposition

The first argument begins with the hypothesis that the One-is, and is in a sense an elaboration of the earlier pre-gymnastic discussion of the problem of the forms. It demonstrates through all these examples, parts to the whole, motion and rest, same and other, like and unlike, equal and unequal, younger and older, being and nonbeing, that if the likeness between the One and the different things is derived solely from within the logical order of univocal explanation and predication there will inevitably be a fundamental unrelatability between the universal limitless One and the negatively finite limitation of the different things.

Every sub-argument instigates an infinite regression that ultimately annihilates one of the bipolarities of Being. Every argument concludes that if the One is, it is nothing. This argument, like the result of the analysis of the forms, is juggling with notions of the One is-not; either it is nonexistent or it is a foundational no-"thingness." The former ends in absurdity but the latter in the profound truth of the intentional ground.

Argument II contradicts argument I only insofar as each of its sub-arguments argues that if the One is, it is everything. But this argument's underlying issue is the same, the problem of grasping a positive and genuine conception of finitude. If the different things are defined by limit, how then can they be related to the One, which must be, in order to be the One, boundless and without limit? We saw a variation of this issue or paradox in the *Poem of Parmenides*. This argument's worklike game is directed toward confusing the notion of finitude, as something involved solely in a finite series of events rather than as a genuine dependency. These two notions are not opposed to one another, but the former reflects only the logical apparatus of finitude as limit, but on its own it cannot reflect a positive dependency that resides at the ontological (and perhaps onto-theo-logical) level. This confusion amounts to stating that the One is everything, but really amounts to nothing.

If the One and the different things interrelate solely on the logical level, the One is understood only in terms of mathematical primacy, as the first in a numerical series or as the unity of a set of parts that fit together but amount to a whole no greater than its parts. And if the whole or the One is no greater than the parts, even though it is everything together, it amounts ontologically to nothing at all. The explaining away of finite dependency occurs because the One is not fully seen outside its logical framework; the whole is never fully surmised to exist outside its parts as their foundation. The possibility of a positive finitude rests on finding a different way in which Being is attached or related to the thing (144c).

It is quite true that "if a thing is it must necessarily be something and not nothing." But how that finitude is attached to the thing will determine whether that statement avoids an infinite regress. The One is not genuinely attached if it's been partitioned or divided up and then spread among the order of things, for in that case the One is-not. It must be attached in a qualitatively different way:

> And yet a great necessity forces whatever has parts to be as many as its parts are. (144d)

The One's primacy must be metaphysical; it is not the parts that determine the whole to be One or Whole. Rather, the parts must have a genuine dependency, on some no-"thing" outside and independent of their composite whole that forces them both to be as many, and to possess individual unity.

The dialogue returns to its *reductio ad absurdum*:

> Therefore, not only is the being that is one many, but even the One itself, since it has been divided up by being, must, by necessity, be many. (144d)

The collapse of knowledge is twofold: Necessity loses its definitive quality, and finitude, its positive quality. Both are absorbed into the endlessness *qua* infinite regress of the phenomenon. "The One that is, then, is somehow both one and many, and a whole and pieces, and limited and limitless in multitude" (145a).

Without the twofold Necessity (*ananke stenai* and finitude) as that which expresses the relationship of the object to reason in its application to experience, or as the defining and distinguishing factor among things, or as distinguishing the I from the Other, how is the One distinguished from the different things or the different things as different from each other? Isn't the One forced into the position of distinguishing itself from the many:

> Insofar, then, as the One is Whole, its in something else. But insofar as it chances to be all those parts, it's in itself. And thus the One itself must, by necessity, be both in itself and in another. (145e)
>
> But whatever is always in the same thing must, by necessity, without a doubt, always be standing at rest. (146a)

In both of these "by necessity's," the One has been placed in a position to define or defend the ontological distinction that makes, for example, a plurality of subjects possible. Placing the One within the many breaks up the existential unity that makes the One to be One and indivisible. When placing the many within the One, in order to keep the One as One, the many cannot really be many. Therefore the notion of the many as complete ontological unities is reduced to partial effects, appearances, semblances of the real or One. "Surely everything is to everything else like this: either it is the same or other, or if not the same and not other, it would be a part of whatever it is thus related to or it would be as a whole is to a part" (146b).

Genuine Necessity is the differentiating component between the One and the many that allows the things to be as they are because, in a way, it names or announces the object-at-hand to be what it is, and not merely an appearance. This name necessarily communicates the Being of the thing. Naming is the spoken unity of thinking and Being. And to name something means that each time it is named the "same" thing is spoken of each time. It is the Necessity of Being that it be what it is:

> Then if you say it once do you address whatever possesses the name, but if you said it many times you don't address this thing? Or whether once or many times you utter the same name, doesn't a great necessity force you always to mean the same thing? (147d)

By naming the world "speculative thought achieves the leap to the metaphysical . . . for the world is Being."[62]

This insistence on "force" reflects how great necessity is the organizing principle that puts into being all things and therefore names them as they are. Just as great necessity forces whatever has parts to be as many as its parts are and, as such, the sum total of the parts can not be equivalent to the whole or One, so great necessity also forces the thing to mean and be the same thing no matter how many times it is named. Not only does this Necessity force the parts to be, but each part can never be anything else but its own part as this part or that part. When something is named it is named not as semblance or appearance or shadow but as the thing itself.

Because existence amounts to something more than the sum total of parts and because not everything is in its final place, there is then a reason beneath that limit, finitude or dependency. Rather than being seen as a stumbling block to the universals or on the other hand as obliterating the universal it becomes the crucial signate that names man's relatedness to something Other.

In argument II, there is a sub-argument specifically on the question of "touching." The argument confuses physical touching as the nature of the relationship between the One and the different things, but not to its detriment. This misapplied conception of their relationship actually exposes the motivating force behind this twofold Necessity as causality.

Metaphysical causality is the act of tracing the great chain of being until what is reached is something outside of and greater than the order of "things." Heidegger claims that this kind of self-transcendence misses the world of beings by reordering them in terms of a highest Being. If causality is not a passing over of the phenomenon of the world of being but rather the self-transcendent act of embedding oneself into its very origin or source, it must be shown that causality is the natural (not founded) act of being-with-others.

This sub-argument on "touching" begins with the assertion that if the One were in the different things, it would touch the different things, and in itself it would touch itself. But if it is to touch these different things, the question arises as to where it must be located so as to accomplish this touching of the different things while remaining as One. "And so, as though two, the One would do this and would come to be in two places at the same time. But as long as it is one, it won't be able to" (148e).

As the One, it cannot be like two and threes in the way it touches, for "the same necessity, then, that makes the One not to be two makes it not touch itself" (149a). The One, then, must touch the different things but not touch like everything else. If this touch is unlike everything else, how in the first place do the different things within the order of their kind of touch even recognize it? And if this utterly different touch of the One is at all necessary shouldn't it be known to man, shouldn't he be able to determine its presence and in its presence come to understand its necessity and thus his origin?

Causality is understood only in the world among the plurality of subjects that relate to or "touch" each other in every act of existence. Within every act of "touch," and understood only within its framework, is the causal relationship of the "touch" to the that which is "touched."

What is the *telos* of this being-in-the-world relationship? What does touch plus that which is touched "add" up to? What will each of the infinite additions lead to but an untouched touch, or more precisely, an uncaused cause: "And so, clearly, whenever one thing is added, one touch is also added and the result is that the touches are one less than the number of the multitude. For by an amount equal to that by which the first two exceeded the touches (by being more numerous than the touches), so every future number of things will also exceed all the touches. For in the future whenever one is added to the number of things, one touch will also be added to the touches" (149b–c).

What this means is that there is one more being than there are touches; something that just doesn't fit into the equal order of things and yet is needed to originate this order. Couldn't we call this an uncaused cause or untouched touch or unmeasured measurer, the unequal equalizer of all things, the ground in which all things find their affinity or accord or evenness? And hadn't the natural and causal state of being-in-the-world directed us to it by great necessity:

> Now, a great necessity makes whatever neither exceeds nor is exceeded be on equal terms, and it makes whatever is on equal terms equal. (150d)

The "Instants": The Move to the Ground of Being

Argument II reengages a series of absurdities on such matters as the nature of greatness and smallness, equal and unequal, younger and older. Each provokes an infinite regression along the same lines as the earlier ones. Then the argument takes a sudden and important shift in style and content. It is on the nature of "the instants" and its shift from the earlier sub-arguments might lead one to treat it as a new argument bringing the total number to nine, or to consider it an appendix to argument II, contending that it is not a separate argument because, unlike the other eight arguments, it does not begin with Parmenides' basic two hypotheses, that the One is or that the One is-not.

This argument is on its own. It does not begin with the two basic hypotheses because, perhaps, Plato intended it to reflect something qualitatively

different from the other arguments. It is, I believe, an argument that reaches
the conclusion of the earlier arguments, not by means of their logic but in
spite of it. For the most part, the earlier arguments' hypothetical gymnastic
ends in contradictory statements, whereas the goal of "the instants" is to
reach beyond this failing logical apparatus and to find the source of the
truth, stability and relatability of the One in an ontology that allows the
logical really to be logical.

While the earlier arguments debate the problem of participation within
the world and endless order of explanation, and by doing so systematically
deprive the One of beinghood, making impossible a genuine relationship
between the One and the many, "the instants" is the first argument thematically to look for the ground or the end in the order of Being as the source of
all things.

It gathers up the difficulties of the earlier arguments and asks the
most penetrating question: How can the One participate in all these
things mentioned, e.g., greatness and smallness, motion and rest, like
and unlike, without both taking and releasing beinghood, coming to be
and perishing (see 156a)? And while the earlier arguments had given, through
great necessity, a hint that knowledge and the order of explanation required,
in order to be meaningful, something like a causal *ananke stenai* to halt the
infinite regress (and thereby promote a positive finitude), it is only in "the
instants" that that claim is fully announced:

> The instant. For the 'instant' looks like it signifies this very thing:
> something from which there is a change in either of two directions. For
> while still standing at rest something cannot change from standing at
> rest; nor while still in motion can it change from motion. Instead this sort
> of momentary, out-of-place nature lurks between both motion and rest
> and is not in any time. Thus, into this and out of this, whatever's in
> motion changes to standing at rest and whatever stands at rests changes to
> being in motion. (156d–e)

The problem of the "instants" is not only an attempt to solve how the One
participates in the characteristic changes of the many, but just as much and
perhaps more, it attempts to find that which can differentiate and separate
these characteristic changes, giving each its own definable and irreducible
name. What accomplishes this cannot be within the endlessness of the in-
time realm of coming-to-be and perishing. For "certainly there is no time at
which something could at once neither be in motion or stand at rest"

(156c). Therefore there is posited to be "this out-of-place" thing that permits and promotes this change (156d). The notion of an "out-of-place" thing seems not only to express the conversion from the logical to the onto-logical but also to the onto-theo-logical.

When Aristotle asks Parmenides what sort of thing this out-of-place thing is, the answer is that it really is no-thing at all (156d–e). This no-"thing" emerges at the end of the order of explanation as a necessity of thought allowing beings to be with and distinct from each other. "The 'instant' is not a moment in time. It cannot be arrived at by subdividing the time continuum: whatever two moments of time are chosen, close to each other as they may be, the instant of change will always be 'between' them without forming part of the time continuum itself, since at any point in the time continuum the thing must be either in motion or at rest. In this sense, then, the instant is in no time."[63]

As such, no amount of time will "add up" to this instant for it is the beginning *qua* end, the framework of time, in an ontologically primal sense. Likened to the whole understood onto-logically as qualitatively greater than its parts, the instant is the unmeasured measurer, the unequal equalizer, and without its original instant-of-Being, time and the different things would cease to exist. "The instant is itself a disruption of time's continuity—a disruption, according to Parmenides' argument, that is required for change to take place at all."[64]

Although the argument has advanced considerably toward anticipating a metaphysical foundation as a final end, it fails to recognize that the central defining quality of the One must be the "instant"; that they are indeed two aspects of the same Being (156e–157a). Instead, the One, the many and the "instant" are seen as three separate entities wherein the out-of-time instant is construed in order for the other two in-time constituents to relate. In this way, the One is again reduced to the logical apparatus whereby the distinction between the One and the many is relegated to a mathematical ordering. And as such, the insurmountable problems of participation and predication reemerge, particularly the problem of articulating meaningfully the intentional presupposition.

Before analyzing thematically the aspects of the intentional presence, it should be noted that argument III revisits the problem of partaking or participating in the One.[65] This difficulty sets the stage for the meaning and importance of the intentional presence. The first sub-argument regarding the whole and its pieces revisits the problem of articulating the Whole as something more than the sum total of its pieces but it also makes the move toward a positive conception of predication when it remarks that each of the pieces must be a piece not of many but of a Whole:

> And yet the very whole must be, by necessity, one thing made up of many things—this whole of which the pieces will be pieces. For each of the pieces must be a piece not of many but of a Whole. (157c)
>
> And in fact, the same explanation also holds for each piece: it must, by necessity, partake of the One. For if each of them is a piece, then surely the "each" signifies that it's one, when delineated from the rest, in itself—if in fact it will be "each". (157e–158a)

Although this argument never really emancipates itself from the *reductio ad absurdum*, it nevertheless incorporates a decisive move toward a positive conception of predication. In particular, it grasps what is essential to the metaphysical intentional presence in terms of its referential relationship to Being. This relationship can be broken down in three ways:

1. the piece is utterly dependent on the Whole in order to be a piece; its name originates because it belongs in this whole—it is a piece not of many but of a whole;
2. and yet, that utter dependency must not invalidate the piece as a unity in itself;
3. while paradoxically, the complete unity of the piece occurs only within its unmitigated and essential reference to the Whole.

For the most part, the dialogue has been focused on the loss of Being in endlessness, but its effect on thought, the thinking that is the "same" as Being, has not been fully examined. In a word, every time the argument has entered an infinite regression, the One or Being has been systematically eliminated from existence and existentially nullified. If in fact this is the unfortunate result for Being, what then can come of thinking? Or more precisely, what happens to the intentional presence?

Intentional presence is the mode of being and the relational being-with and being-toward the world, the *noetic* bridge between man and world. Because of this the privileged being, man, announces or names or predicates that which is the "same" between thinking and Being. What are the preconditions for meaningful announcing and naming?

A genuine thinking of "same" analogically unites thinking and Being, and is understood under two aspects, finitude and the *ananke stenai*. As finite self-transcendence, man follows his onto-logical directedness, and enters into a nearness by means of the *ananke stenai*. The *ananke stenai* discloses the ultimate Other *qua* foundation, and man's knowledge is prefigured upon this union. This union constitutes the intentional presence or man's pre-cognitive "knowledge" of the "Same" because at this point language has finally caught up to Being.

The intentional presence exists only within the framework of this metaphysical foundation *qua* origin and end. Without it, language will never catch-up to Being and the things themselves will be only appearances without reference to any genuine likeness. When language does not catch-up to Being, or when the intentional presence is relegated only to the initial description of the world, then beings are reduced to a chain of "differences" not even able to be known as difference. Difference as difference can only be seen in the analogical and metaphysical understanding of the "same" between thinking and Being; the two constituents are distinct and mutual transcendences.

As the privileged being who acknowledges that the "same is for thinking as for Being," his moral/intellectual livelihood depends upon maintaining thinking and being as distinct but mutual transcendences related to each other and ordered by that which constitutes their difference as difference. When even the gods could not possess the knowledge of the different things, the intentional presence was lost, destroyed amid the reduction of one of the two entitative components (134e). And when Parmenides recognized not only the flaw in but the need for something like the forms, he recognized that the privileged being could not know or speak meaningfully without a metaphysical end as the source of knowledge. Without an ever-same idea for every being the power of speech will be destroyed, for this ever-same idea reflects the need for something (or rather a no-"thing") to maintain that difference as difference:

> If someone in turn, Socrates, after focusing on all these problems and others still, shall deny that there are forms of the beings and will not distinguish a certain form of each single thing, wherever he turns he'll understand nothing, since he does not allow that there is an ever-same idea for each of the beings. And so he will entirely destroy the power of dialogue. (135b–c)

And when Parmenides asserts that "surely there is nothing other besides them—something different than the One yet different than the different things, for everything is spoken of when one says, both the One and the different things" (argument IV, 159b–c), he grasps (before reentering the infinite regress) the *telos* of the intentional presence, that makes it to be, in a word, intentional. In one way, it is quite true that everything is spoken when one says both the One and the different things, except their difference as difference. And in that case there is then something different from the One and different from the different things. But not a difference merely in terms of this being or that being, but that the reality of their distinction presupposes their composition in something Other, and that this difference presupposes the actual reality of their unity as the "same." When this difference as difference is relegated in terms of this being or that, then the process of de-severing the One from the world will inevitably continue.

The intentional presence does not speak only about those things within the order of logical explanation; man's privilege is that he can announce the fundamental Other by concluding to it by a Necessity of thought within the order of explanation pointing to something beyond. If it is reached as a Necessity of thought, it must exist in the order of Being as fundamentally dependent upon and in a necessary relationship with Being. Why? Because the same is for thinking as for Being. Argument V reaches critical mass wherein this privilege is fully realized: man can speak of the One is-not, he can think of that difference as difference.

> Therefore he first means something known and then something other than the different things, whenever he says "one," whether he adds being or not-being to it. For whatever is said not to be is nonetheless known, and it is known to differ from the different things. In this way, then, we must say from the beginning, if one is not, what must be. First of all this must, so it looks, be the case concerning it: there is knowledge of it. Otherwise there'd be no way to know what is said whenever someone says, "if one is not." (160c–d)

This passage stresses the privilege of the intentional presence to understand all things in terms of difference as difference. The One is-not does not mean a mere deprivation in beinghood. If it was not known in any capacity, it could not be spoken of. How then would man think of the One or Being if it is different from all else? If it does not correspond ontologically to the order of explanation how do we think of it in terms of difference as difference? Man understands because he is ordered by a foundational Being. This is not a founded idea but the horizon of intentionality, realized in its privileged being. Man knows that the qualitative distinction between Being and beings belongs to Being: "For whenever someone says that the One is other than different things, he doesn't mean that otherness belongs to the different things, but rather to it" (160e).

By understanding this Otherness by means of difference as difference, man grasps something else altogether. What then is this thing or no-"thing" that is reached causally and intentionally by means of human finitude? Isn't this no-thing, this unmeasured measurer that gives measure to all else the *ananke stenai*, that stop required by the very nature of thought in the presence of Being?

Because each aspect of the fourfold intentional presupposition is inseparably interrelated, and are joined in a hegemonic unity within the *ananke stenai*, our examination of it will be something of a reiteration of the whole analysis. This section does not intend, though, merely to repeat but to bring into fullness the nature of the fourfold intentional presupposition.

If the One is-not reflects pre-thematically the *ananke stenai*, what then does this "is-not" imply:

> So it's not possible for the One to be, since it really is not, but in no way is it prohibited from partaking of many things; in fact, its necessary for it to do this, if indeed that One and not something different is not. However, if neither the One nor the 'that' will not be, then the speech is about something different and nothing can be uttered. But if the One and nothing else is hypothesized not to be, then it's necessary for it to have a share in the "that" and many different things. (160e–161a)

There is a categorical difference between the not-being of everything else compared to the One. And this difference as difference resides in some unitive and likening quality, some foundation, origin and *telos*.

And when, "nothing else but the One is hypothesized not to be, then it's necessary for it to have a share in the 'that' and many different things." This One therefore has a meta-physical nature. This One is-not has a share in everything else because it is the no-"thing" likening agent in which all other beings are ordered by the foundational Being. Thinking meets Being in the feature that differentiates them; in that which constitutes their difference as difference. That which constitutes that difference is reached at the end/ stop in the order of explanation but it is neither beyond being nor beyond knowledge. The *ananke stenai*, then, has an onto-theo-logic direction, implication and realization.

The One is-not, i.e., the *ananke stenai* is understood in a threefold manner:

1. it is the very core of that difference as difference grasped causally;
2. it maintains finitude as the proper vehicle of dependency to recognize the genuine "same" and otherness between thinking and Being;

3. and it gives the intentional presence the privilege to articulate that presupposition as a presupposition with which man as knower must begin. It is therefore not a hypothesis; it is the unhypothesized precondition of thought.

All else is in reference to and ordered by this no-thing. To speak truly of the things themselves is to understand them in their context, that there is an order or rather an orderer to their appearances that makes them not only apparitions but beings.

This no-"thing" does not change or move or transcend or perish, if indeed the "same" is for thinking as for Being. "The One cannot change from itself, whether it is or is not. For then this speech would not still be about the One—if in fact it changed from itself—but rather about something different" (162d). Therefore the different things must change only on the condition of the recognition or presupposition of the unhypothesized One:

> And yet indeed it is in motion, a great necessity forces it to change. For in whatever way it be moved, in this respect it no longer is as it was, but is otherwise. (162e–163a)

That which is reached by means of the *ananke stenai* has the ontological primacy wherein the sum total of the parts can never add up to the Whole; it is the converting or likening factor among all things that allows the soul to be, in a way, all things *because* the same is for thinking as for Being. And without concluding to this great necessity, the balance between thinking and Being cannot remain. This balance is likened to the way in which the beginning is the end, or in which the first principle is the final principle.[66] They are not the same in any sort of descriptive immediacy of being-in-the-world but rather find their "sameness" reflected only when their difference as difference enables man to arrive at the end and upon his arrival or necessary stop the end gives itself over as the beginning or the first all along, and thus enables knowledge to begin.

The "Heaps": In Anticipation of Phenomenology

In keeping with the dialogue's characteristic pattern of remaining within the thicket of NonBeing even when it places us in an *aporia*, the soul that was discovered to be in a way all things is soon given no way to be at all. In argument VI, the soul is lost. The is-not, the *telos* of all beings, is again conceived as nonexistent: "But whenever we say 'is not,' does it signify anything else than a deprivation of beinghood for whatever we say is not" (163c). This reverting from the argument's prior advances prepares us for the problem of the "heaps." The heaps are a solely appearance-based "stop" in the order of explanation; they endlessly become different phenomena upon closer inspection, denying any real stop in the order of Being. This phenomenon serves as a prime example of the far-reaching effects of the loss of the *ananke stenai* in the role of meaning and Being.

At the end of argument VI, there is a slight but important change in the notion of is-not from not only deprived but to having "no state at all" (164b). It opens the door to one of the most essential arguments, the "heaps" which anticipates the potential danger of phenomenological phenomena. This argument, in confrontation with the "instants," reflects prethematically the dispute between metaphysical and phenomenological intentionality. If this Being has now no state at all the question is:

> Will there be of the "that" or the "to that" or the "something" or the "this" or the "of this" or "of a different thing" or "to a different thing" or "once" or "hereafter" or "now" or knowledge or opinion or perception or definition or name or anything else of the things that are concerning the thing that is not. (164a–b)

The problem of the "heaps" anticipates the difficulty of acquiring any knowledge within the anti-*ananke stenai*, anti-onto-theologic endlessness of the phenomenon. The "heaps" are in utter opposition to the "instants." Even with all the ontological shortcomings of the "instants," it was the first thematic argument within the dialogue to attempt to ground existence in some momentary out-of-place and out-of-time no-"thing" that, in a sense was looking for the meta- of physics. On the other hand, the "heaps" not only deny this meta ground but are in themselves their own in-time "beginning." The elaboration of their nature hieratically but profoundly grasps that the same problem attached to an endless chain of hypotheses is present in the endlessness of the phenomenon, namely an infinite regress and the loss of the relationship between *noesis* and its *noematic* content.

The argument begins with the different things and how are they differentiated, if the One is in no state at all. It is surmised that "they're different than one another, then. For this is all that's left to them, or else they're different than nothing" (164c). But for the different things, to differentiate themselves is rendered only an appearance or seeming differentiation:

> Then they're all different from one another in multitude; for they could not be so one by one, since one is not. Instead each heap of them, so it

looks, is limitless in multitude. For even if someone shall grasp what
seems to be the smallest thing, just like a dream in sleep there appears
instantaneously a many in the place of what seemed to be one, and in the
place of the smallest thing there appears something very great in relation to
anything chopped off from it. (164c–d)

Positive finitude, necessity and limit are lost in this endless realm of seeming distinctions.

> And so will there be many heaps, each appearing to be one but not
> really so, if in fact there'll be no one? . . . And number will seem to
> belong to them, if in fact each seems to be one while they are many . . .
> And so some will appear to be odd and other even—but they won't be so in
> truth, if in fact there'll be no One. (164d–e)

But they won't be so in truth: the different things will be an endless chain
of appearing to be, odd and even, equal and unequal, great and small—
concealed and unconcealed for there is no One or truth, or end or *ananke
stenai* to ground these appearances in their reality. This is the no-way of the
Poem of Parmenides (fr. 6): "the one from which mortals knowing nothing
wander, two-headed; for helplessness in their breasts guides their distracted
mind; and they are carried deaf and blind alike, dazed, uncritical tribes, by
whom to be and not to be have been thought both the same and not the
same; and the path of all is backward-turning."

> And, to be sure, each heap will be thought to be equal to the many small
> things. For it would pass from greater to less, it appears, before seeming
> to enter into the middle—but this would be an appearance of equality.
> And so, while having a limit in relation to a different heap, does it have in
> relation to itself neither beginning nor limit nor middle? (165a)

If then there is no end to these heaps can there be a beginning? Can there
be anything Other at all? Can there be the same between thinking and
being? And if not, what about knowledge, and those who try to grasp the
"heaps"?

> Because whenever someone, by his understanding, takes hold of one of
> these things as belonging to such heaps, then a different beginning will
> always appear before the beginning, and another end will be left over
> after the end, and in the middle there'll be different middles more middle

than the middle—but smaller, since we can't grasp each one of them because the One is not. (165a–b)

The descriptive immediacy of the phenomenon brings a genuine appearance of otherness but without the necessary move toward its reference in Being itself, doesn't this description lose itself in endlessness and therefore lose its initial thrust toward intelligibility?

And so to anyone seeing such a thing from afar and faintly, won't it necessarily appear to be one? But to someone thinking about it up close and sharply, doesn't each one appear limitless in multitude, if in fact it's devoid of the One that is not? Just as to someone standing far from a drawing, everything there, appearing to be one, appears to have experienced the same situation . . . But when he comes closer they appear many and other and, by the appearance of the Other, of another sort and unlike themselves. (165c–d)

That which appears, the things themselves, are the initial entrance into truth in the form of the concealed-unconcealed, but it cannot be the final word. Just as the beginning is known to be the end only in the end, or the final principle is the first but only insofar as the final principle has been grasped, so the immediacy of being-in-the-world sustains its world in transcendence. This entrance into truth in the world is directed toward an end as en-closure, the very *veritas/ verum* Heidegger rejects. And without it there is, as seen in the final argument, no mode of Being and no truth at all.

Because the different things have no community—no way, no how—with any of the things that are not; nor do any of the things that are not relate to any of the different things. For the things that are not have no part . . . Then there would be no opinion about anything that is not among the different things, nor any appearance, and—no way, no how—whatever is not is not opined by the different things. (166a)

The dialogue has demonstrated the need to connect and secure knowledge to its origin *qua* end, the presuppositional intentional ground. It has shown this through its repeated failures to grasp the nature of the relationship between Being and thinking, I and other, universal and particular. At the core of each failure is the failure to come to a necessary stop which in turn promotes infinite regressions. If indeed the *ananke stenai* is the necessary precondition of knowledge, framing and completing the intentional experience of the ultimate other as Other, then one of the essential questions of intentionality must be the question of attachment. In a word, if the *ananke stenai* reveals that fundamental Other upon which man structures his knowledge, how then is man related or attached to this Other? Uncovering the nature of this attachment lies in a fully ratified and faithful epistemological expansion of the fourfold intentional presupposition. And while Plato's *Parmenides* has brought forth this need in its radicality, Aristotle's *De Anima* goes a long way in epistemologically laying bare its necessary structure.

* * *

Tracing III: Aristotle's *De Anima*

This tracing of intentionality arrives at its first organized epistemological explication in Aristotle's *De Anima*.[67] His examination into the breadth and nature of the soul raises the onto-epistemological question of attachment: what must be presupposed in order for the soul to be, in a way, and therefore to think, all things? In the order of investigation the question of what an agent does precedes the question of what enables it to do what it does.[68] And what it does of course involves the object of its activity. And thus the only starting point is, in a sense, the end of the activity, from which is tracked the nature of its operation, from which is further tracked the enabling ontological principle. What does this mean if not that we start from where we are and not from where we are not. And where are we? In the sensible world. While his predecessors arrived at the need for a first principle as the defining origin within Being to which existence and knowledge must relate, they had not been able to give a satisfactory account of that relationship of fittingness and attachment. The *De Anima* examines the attempts of both pre-Socratic thinkers and Plato, giving an account of their shared fatal flaw: their first principles could not withstand infinite regressions and consequent epistemological dead ends. By placing as "first" a property which operated within the material order, the pre-Socratic materialists had overlooked to their detriment the possibility that something qualitatively different must be the proper onto-logical first and as such the necessary origin and end in the orders of explanation and Being. Aristotle's overview of their ontological shortcomings uncovers the essential need for and working unity of each aspect of the intentional presuppositional fourfold. Therefore, it is necessary to begin this examination of Aristotle's

De Anima with his critique of his predecessors. In particular, the questions of the *ananke stenai* and finitude or attachment and the notion of "touch" as an analogy for the entire metaphysical-intentional apparatus of being-in-the-world serve to illuminate his understanding of how the soul is in a way all things.

Aristotle's Critique of Earlier First Principles

Aristotle's treatment of the various pre-Socratic theories can be divided into several themes, each pointing toward a fundamental interrelationships within the problem of knowledge: (1) confusing the nature of the First Principle as that which belongs within the elemental order of material explanation; (2) this confusion is occasioned by a further epistemological fumbling of the presupposition that "like is known by like," relegating that likeness to the material order; (3) the inevitable result of this problem is infinite regression and, as in Plato's *Parmenides*, each regression is a systematic annihilation of Being and therewith genuine knowledge; (4) as man enters this *aporia*, this thicket of nonbeing, Aristotle points toward the lack of and need for a genuine unifying or combining principle—a stop and end in the order of explanation—the proper complementarity to knowledge that makes it to be bounded or enclosed, i.e., that makes it to be knowledge. This notion of bounded calls to mind the question and nature of *veritas*. For Aristotle, truth is the form of knowledge in the way that the soul is the form of the body, the essence which gives the matter shape, limit, dependency and existence.

> The theory handed down from the Pythagoreans seems to entail the same view; for some of them have declared that the soul is identical with the particles of the air, and others what makes these particles move. These particles have found their place in the theory because they can be seen perpetually in motion even when the air is completely calm. Those who say that the soul is that which moves itself tend towards the same view. For they all assume that movement is the distinctive characteristic of the soul, and that everything else owes its movement to the soul, which they suppose to be self-moved, because they see nothing producing movement which does not itself move. (Aristotle, *De Anima*, 404a19–25)
>
> Empedocles, for instance, thought that the soul was composed of all the elements, and yet considered each of these to be a soul. (404b10–12)

In these passages, the primary mistake of the earlier thinkers was to consider the First Principle to be of the same substantial nature as the things that refer to it, namely material movement. With Empedocles the First Principle is rightly reflected within and by the soul, but unfortunately he does not separate the nature of the soul from the nature of that which it apprehends, thereby negating the reality of the soul *qua* soul, or as that which can exist for the sake of itself.

For Aristotle, that which can consider all things must be able to take on the form of the object, and as such must be potentially its object. Therefore the soul must be qualitatively different from that which it apprehends. If the soul were one or another material element within the order of explanation it could not become the other in thought, i.e., the apple cannot become the orange; at best it could only become another apple.

In a word, to the extent that a material thing can be said or conceived to "know" a thing, the only thing it could be conceived to "know" is of the same material nature, an apple to an apple and an orange to an orange; in no way could it know or become all things because knowledge is an inverse ratio to materiality. If the presupposition "like unto like" is confused as a comparison to the material order there is no genuine differentiation between the two likenesses. The conception of "same" would then reflect only a deprived state of being; they would be indistinct from each other, confined to their own posited identity. In the following passages this misapplied "like unto like" is exposed:

> In the same way, in the Timaeus, Plato constructs the soul out of the elements. For he maintains that "like" can only be known by "like," and that from these first beginnings grow the things which we perceive. (404b16–20)
>
>   Heracleitus also calls the first principle soul, as the emanation from which he constructs all other things; it is the most incorporeal and in ceaseless flux: he, like many others, supposed that a thing moving can only be known by something which moves, and that all that exists is in motion. (405a25–29)

This kind of "like unto like" presents the same difficulty evident throughout Plato's *Parmenides*; the whole is no greater than the sum total of its parts and thereby ultimately ceases to have any real and distinct existence at all:

> For they say that "like" is known by "like"; for since everything is known by the soul, they construct it of all the principles. (405b15–17)

Without an analogical and immaterial sense of "like unto like" wherein the likeness is based on a sameness of ratio or proportion between the respective terms or pairs, the presupposition will inevitably enter an epistemological absurdity, because ultimately whatever "likeness" posited is only to be unhinged in an endless and infinite series of existing things. That is to say, the order of explanation would go on to infinity "explaining" one thing that cannot account for itself by another thing which cannot account for itself, never reaching a stop and thus self-defeating as an explanation. If this likeness is not found in the respective ways in which the terms are related to each other in the two pairs, in a feature that differentiates the instances, then there is nothing different about the First Principle that really places it as ontologically first in the order of being as well as (and because) the stop in the order of thinking:

> Its supporters assume that like is recognized by like, as though they thus identified the soul with the things it knows. But these elements are not the only things existing; there are many—to be more exact, infinitely many—other things, composed of elements. (410a6–10)
>
> It is no use for the elements to exist in the soul, unless the ratios and the principle of composition also exist in it; for each element will recognize its like, but there will be nothing in the soul to recognize bone, for instance, or man, unless they too exist in it. (410a6–10)

In sum, reducing the metaphysical intentional presupposition "like unto like" to a base comparison of material factors, wherein the whole is no greater than its parts, provokes an infinite regress, wherein the mind can never grasp or exhaust the object it seeks to grasp:

> For if it is a magnitude, how can it think? With any one of its parts indifferently? The parts must be regarded either as magnitudes or points, if one can call a point a part. In the latter case, since the points are infinite in number, the mind obviously can never exhaust them; in the former, it will think the same thoughts very many or an infinite number of times. (407a11–16)

And if the mind can never exhaust these objects that are infinite in number, can it ever come to rest, can the mind know anything at all?

> Again, in each of these first principles there will be more ignorance than understanding; for each will know one thing but will know only one thing, but will be ignorant of many, in fact of everything else. On Empedocles'

view at least it follows that God must be most unintelligent; for He alone will be ignorant of one of these elements, namely strife, whereas mortal creatures will know them all; for each individual is composed of them all. (410b1–7)

The preceding passage mirrors quite strikingly the difficulty in Plato's *Parmenides* when the "same" between thinking and Being had broken down, when Socrates realized at a certain point in the gymnastic that the gods would be beyond any real possibility of thinking or speaking Being: "What an altogether wondrous speech, if it strips the gods of knowing!"[69] Similarly for Aristotle "like unto like" has collapsed epistemologically, for it lacked the feature that differentiates its likenesses. The result is quite clear: if the First Principle is not a real unifying or combining principle, and has no global role to play in the act of existence, then the knowledge of sensibles not only cannot reflect or relate to the being of knowledge itself but is actually opposed:

There would be a further difficulty in deciding what is the unifying principle, for the elements correspond to matter, and the force, whatever it is, which combines them is supreme; but it is impossible that anything should be superior to and control the soul or (a fortiori) the mind; for it is reasonable to suppose that the mind is by nature original and dominant, but they say that the elements are the first of all existing things. (410b11–16)

Aristotle's most remarkable insights concerning the difficulty surrounding the real nature of a First Principle are found in his criticism of Plato's identification of the movement of the soul with the spatial movements of the heavenly bodies. In effect Plato shares the same fatal flaw of the pre-Socratics: not grasping the idea that a genuine beginning negates the possibility of continuing *ad infinitum* within the order of explanation. "Clearly there is a beginning, and the causes of things are not infinite, either as a series or in a kind. For neither can one thing come from something else as from matter ad infinitum (for example, flesh from earth, earth from water, water from fire, and so on without end), nor can the source which begins motion (for example, a man is moved by air, air by the sun, the sun by Strife, and so on without limit) be such."[70] Again, a genuine beginning or first principle could not be valid if it allowed its referents to continue to infinity. This entails that a true and analogical understanding of "the soul is in a way all things," wherein "like unto like" and "the same is for thinking as for Being" require that thinking has its limit in the *ananke stenai*, thus uniting thought to Being:

> But, if it can only think when its whole circle is in contact, what does the contact of its parts mean? Again, how can it think that which has parts with that which has not, or that which has not with that which has? The mind must be identical with this circle; for the movement of the mind is thinking, and the movement of a circle is revolution. If then thinking is revolution, then the circle whose revolution is of this kind must be mind. But what can it be which mind always thinks?—as it must if the revolution is eternal. All practical thinking has limits (for it always has an object in view), and speculation is bounded like the verbal formulae which express it. (407a18–26)

Might we not anticipatorily compare the endless conversion of the Heideggerian concealed and unconcealed to the circle whose revolution reflects the mind's thinking? And without an enclosure *qua verum/veritas*— a first principle or beginning *qua* end reached by the *ananke stenai*, in which speculation is bounded like the verbal formulae which express it, then what happens to thinking about Being?: "Moreover, the final cause is an end, and as such it does not exist for the sake of something else but others exist for its sake. Thus, if there is to be such one which is last, the process will not be infinite; but if there is no such, there will be no final cause. But those who introduce an infinite series are unaware of the fact that they are eliminating the nature of the good, although no one would try to do anything if he did not intend to come to a limit. Nor would there be intellect in the world; for at any rate, he who has an intellect always acts for the sake of something, and this is a limit, for the end is a limit . . . for without it, knowledge would be impossible."[71] And thus, even ethics and the political realm would be rendered meaningless.

Aristotle has made it quite clear that a material first principle annihilates Being and knowledge because this kind of "first" denotes nothing more than a position on a grid, a numeric "first" of infinite points on a line, a first stripped of its privileged status. This kind of "beginning" does not possess the ability to end its succession of events and if considered to be "first" onto-logically will unfortunately introduce an infinite series eliminating the nature of the good. The *ananke stenai* is the antithesis of an infinite regress; it is the necessary stop at the end of the order of explanation that allows knowledge to be possible as knowledge of Being.

In the *De Anima* the soul and its tools, the sensible organs, share a participated likeness in the *ananke stenai.* This likeness or "sameness" discloses the
nature of the *ananke stenai.* But of course this "sameness" is understood
analogically; the soul is the "same," so to speak, because its total immaterial dependence on the *ananke stenai* is the framework of all knowledge.
A concise account of the qualitative nature of the *ananke stenai* will answer
how the soul is the form of the body as well as, in a way, all things.

When Aristotle's analysis of movement begins with the notion "that it is
not necessary that that which produces movement should itself move,"[72]
he has distanced himself immeasurably from the pre-Socratics. For he has
discovered that if all things exist in the context of something else, then
their cause-and-effect existence must necessarily be prefigured upon a
Cause that in no way was in turn an effect of a prior cause, i.e., this Cause
must exist in and for its own sake, in a word, movement must halt in order to
be movement:

> But that which has self-movement as part of its essence cannot be moved
> by anything else except incidentally: just as that which is good in itself is
> not good because of anything else, and that which is good for its own sake
> is not good for the sake of anything else. (406b13–15)

Aristotle appears to argue on behalf of this for-the-sake-of-itself-Cause,
this need for a stop in the realm of causes and movements through the
nature of the soul and its tools, the sense organs, as an analogy for
the *ananke stenai.* He notes that if all movement is a displacement of
that which is moved *qua* moved then the essential nature of the soul is
lost, subsumed by an endless series of movements:

> Moreover, if the soul moves itself, it is also itself moved, so that, if all
> movement is a displacement of that which is moved *qua* moved, then the
> soul must depart from its essential nature, if it does not move itself
> accidentally, but movement is part of its very essence . . . In general the
> living creature does not appear to be moved by the soul in this way, but by
> some act of the mind or will. (406b–26)

Isn't this endless series of movements *qua* movements like a series of
appearances wherein there is no real differentiation but only a seeming distinction between entities? Isn't this kind of continual upheaval of one
appearance by another similar to the difficulty in Plato's *Parmenides* when
"the heaps" anticipate the problem of phenomenological endlessness?

The problem of "the heaps" was that if the One is in no state at all, what then are the different things and how are they differentiated? The argument rejects a state of rest or meta ground in which being resides and is fully realized, and in a sense it affirms that movement *qua* movement can go on forever. It denies that "thinking seems more like a state of rest or halting than a movement" (407a32–33).

That the soul comes to a halt in thought reflects its participated likeness with the *ananke stenai*, the point to which all things necessarily refer in knowledge. This end evidenced in the soul's halting in knowledge allows man to name because it is the origin of all names which have and can be spoken, thus establishing what neither Plato nor the pre-Socratics could, the possibility of an unchangeable knowledge of changeable things! This halting of movement within the order of explanation is illustrated, for example, when soul and its tools are said necessarily to perceive themselves. They are able to accomplish this because without it nothing including themselves could be named:

> Since we can perceive that we see and hear, it must be either by sight itself, or by some other sense. But then the same sense must perceive both sight and colour, the object of sight. So that either two senses perceive the same object, or sight perceives itself. Again if there is a separate sense perceiving sight, either the process will go on *ad infinitum*, or a sense must perceive itself. (425b12–16)

Being-in-the-world is never outside the need to halt in order to accomplish the function of its respective faculty, from sensing to speculation. All things tend toward an end.

The *ananke stenai*, the non-entitative trans-ontic appropriating presence that causally defines entities, seems to be present both within and outside the soul as the combining or unifying principle or condition of all knowledge. "Within" the soul because the *ananke stenai* is evidenced by the soul as the form of the body. "Outside" of the soul because it is the reference point or *telos* of all the soul's knowledge including its self-knowledge. The paradox of this within-and-without relationship lies in the notion that the soul is analogously the "same" as the *ananke stenai*. This "same" captures, through a marriage of immanence and self-transcendence, the unbreakable, inseparable unity of the soul to its body and to its world in its participated likeness with the *ananke stenai*. Of course, death breaks and separates this unity of soul and body, and thus the question of immortality is the soul's natural problematic: does participation in the logos entail the immortality of the soul?

The *ananke stenai* is both within-and-without because it is not a thing, but rather as a no-thing, the combining or unifying causal principle that allows for the "same" between thinking and Being. The soul has an immanently existent sameness with the *ananke stenai* known self-transcendently. When an intellectual soul in act pursues an end, it pursues it in the immanence pertaining to its intellectual capacity. But the immediacy of the intellectual act is underscored paradoxically, but essentially, by the meaning of the soul as the form of the body. As the form of the body, the soul is, in a way, an exteriorized nature. In a word, the soul needs to be in the sensible world. Thereby the immanently speculative act is always accompanied by self-transcendence; this is not to its detriment but to its fulfillment, for self-transcendence is the onto-logical recognition that man's origin is found outside the "I," and thereby outside any idealist rendering. Through this marriage of immanence and self-transcendence, the soul is the "same" as the *ananke stenai*, but a sameness that is prefigured upon the soul's utter and total dependency on the latter, and without which the soul would lose its self-identity.

Aristotle identifies the unifying principle as something like an unmeasured measurer, that which is the onto-logical end *qua* beginning of the measuring process because it is the discernible agent of itself and its opposite: "only one of a pair of contraries is needed to discern both itself and its opposite. For instance, by that which is straight we discern both straight and crooked; for the carpenter's rule is a test of both, but the crooked tests neither itself nor the straight."[73] Thus the combining principle must give all the things which correspond or refer to it their unity. Unity is not the same as the total of units, i.e., a series of numeric parts equaling a numeric whole. Nor is it the phenomenological endlessness of the "heaps" wherein the difference between one phenomenon and the next is solely in terms of their position or order of appearance, no matter how descriptively rich.

> It would seem to make no difference whether we speak of units or minute particles; for if we suppose Democritus' spherical atoms to be converted into points and to retain nothing but their quantitative nature, there will still be in each of them something which moves and something which is moved, just as in a continuum. . . . There must, then, be something to give movement to the units. . . . But how can this possibly be a unit? Such a unit must differ inherently from the others. But what difference can a unit which is a point exhibit, except position? . . . And yet if two units can be in the same place, why not an infinite number? . . . For

there appear to be points infinitely many, indeed—in all of them. And again how is it possible to separate the points. (409a10–29)

Unity means that the whole or the combining principle is immeasurably greater (perhaps onto-theo-logic in nature) than the sum total of its parts; otherwise, without it, the descriptive tracing of parts would proceed *ad infinitum*.

> Some say that the soul has parts, and thinks with one part, and desires with another. In this case what is it which holds the soul together, if it naturally consists of parts? Certainly not the body: on the contrary the soul seems rather to hold the body together; at any rate when the soul is gone the body dissolves into air and decays. If then some other thing gives the soul unity, this would really be the soul. But we shall inquire again, whether this is a unity or has many parts. If it is a unity, why should not the soul be directly described as a unit? And if it has parts, the progress of the argument will again demand to know what is its combining principle, and thus we shall proceed *ad infinitum*. (411b5–15)

The combining principle evident in the soul's participated likeness with the *ananke stenai* must retain its identity when identifying and differentiating its referents, otherwise it would not be the soul, which is defined as, in a way, all things:

> Since what is tasted is wet, the organ which perceives it must be neither actually liquid nor incapable of liquefaction; for taste is affected by the object of taste, in so far as it is tasted. Hence there must be liquefaction of the organ of taste without loss of identity, but not liquid . . . what is capable of tasting is that which potentially has these qualities; and the tasteable is that which actualizes this potentiality. (422b1–145)

In a word, if "the senses perceive each other's proper objects incidentally, not in their own identity,"[74] then there must be an origin which does identify them in their identity. This origin is the combining or unifying principle that does not annihilate its constituents and thereby enables for identification.

Aristotle emerges from the Platonic *aporia* by relating the individual form to the particular sensible. The science of Being *qua* Being must extend also to the sensible universe and so to the causes peculiar to changeable things.[75] Man as the knowing referent announces the meaning of Being because his soul is in a way all things because in knowing I am the other as other because the same is for thinking and Being. Herein and only herein can be found the resolution to the epistemological-metaphysical problem of universals, upon the wreckage of which in the late medieval nominalist-realist debate all of modern thought was founded.

When following the causal clues to the world and his origin *qua* end, man is not as phenomenology contends passing over the world of beings. Rather, it is this action that corresponds epistemologically to his uniquely privileged soul: "it [the mind or reasoning faculty] seems to be a distinct kind of soul, and it alone admits of being separated, as the immortal from the perishable."[76] Participation in the logos entails, or rather means immortality, at least for the reasoning "part" of the soul. Here Aristotle reveals himself a genuine phenomenologist, for immortality is a fact to be described, like knowledge itself, and not a hypothesis to be proved. Further if man is the privileged being who announces Being, doesn't this privilege entail not only that he assists in articulating the meaning of Being but that he is a participant in the formation of the meaning of Being? This does not mean man constitutes the Being of the world, but that he does constitute his knowledge of the world, and that this active and appropriative constitution is precisely that which defines man as a participant (with a participated likeness) in the formation of the meaning of Being.

Thus the idea of causality is not a founded conceptual apparatus or artificial template but a reflection of man's nature. In a word, his privilege is his knowledge of causal being, and this causality exists on the level not merely of material explanation but in terms of the soul which "alone is immortal and everlasting."[77] And his nature which is causal and referential points not only toward the onto-logic but, as somehow immortal, to the onto-theo-logic.[78]

For Aristotle, all explanation of movement must come to a stop. The soul's participated likeness with the *ananke stenai,* particularly in the paradoxical interplay between immanence and self-transcendence, characterizes every act of human existence as rooted in its intentional structure. Therefore every act of this privileged being is directed toward an end *qua* beginning. The soul is a beginning for it is "the principle of animal life."[79] And it is the beginning *qua* end:

> The soul is the cause and first principle. Also the actuality of that which exists potentially is its essential formula. Clearly the soul is also the cause in a final sense. For just as mind acts with some purpose in view, so too does nature, and this purpose is its end. In living creatures the soul

supplies such a purpose, and this is in accordance with nature, for all natural bodies are instruments of the soul. (415b14–20)

Within this framework, the soul can be, in a way, all things because within it, the "same" is for thinking as for being. Knowledge is always coming to terms with existence when it affirms analogically the existence of what-is. The nature of the "same" between thinking and Being reflects the framework of intentionality when the end is understood as the beginning.

Intentionality is the starting point of being-in-the-world, as the ineluctable and necessary ground of all knowledge. The irreconcilable divide between Heideggerian and Thomistic intentionality will be at its core the debate over the nature of this ground. Is it causal and metaphysical wherein the beginning is the end as an origin *qua ananke stenai?* Or, is the "origin" quite the opposite, an in-time *Ereignis* grounding the appropriation of beings as they appear in a groundless and endless flux of the concealed and unconcealed? The answer lies in discovering whether it is a metaphysical or a phenomenological epistemology that "fits" and describes the intentional ground. Either the endlessness of the phenomena cannot account for knowledge because it never reaches the end and thereby never reaches Being, or metaphysical causality is a succession of artificially founded hermeneutic suppressions passing over the world of being-at-hand, reducing it to a mere and epistemologically manipulatable present-at-hand.

Our tracing of Aristotle's epistemology and its relationship to the intentional ground is not intended to resolve this debate, but only to lay bare his epistemological method as points toward a further analysis of the kind of "fittingness" proper to intentionality.

When Aristotle surmises that "if there is no one common method of finding the essential nature, our handling of the subject becomes still more difficult,"[80] he has asserted the relation between the intentional ground and its epistemological manifestation. Just as the intentional ground must be the appropriating base of all things, its epistemological method must mirror it, possessing a "common method of finding the essential nature" of the subject. Without this common method or starting point a milieu of epistemological difficulties ensue from infinite regressions to double truths and absurdities.

What then characterizes this starting point? There appears to be in Aristotle's epistemological methodology something framing or enclosing *qua veritas/verum* the intentional act of being-in-the-world. This enclosure is the epistemological abode of the end *qua* beginning evidenced by the starting point of knowledge as grasped within the underlying cause, i.e., the essential nature of the subject or the entity as announced. It seems that being-in-the-world not only requires but is this enclosure (*veritas*) in its two levels of beginning *qua* end, the onto-logical/metaphysical and the order of appearances. These two sets of origin *qua* end are fundamental interdependencies carving out the framework for which man is in the world as a knower wherein the "same" between thinking and Being has been cast against its proper enclosure, so as not to negate the absolute hegemony of Being. If the onto-logic origin *qua* end was posited to exist alone over and against the order of appearances then the problem of the Platonic forms and its idealistic deviants would undoubtedly emerge. On the other hand, the order of appearances divorced from any onto-logical combining or unifying principle would reduce the world of being to shadow semblances because Being, like the heaps, would have no state at all.

For Aristotle, all sensation is a being-affected. This does not mean that sensation is only purely passive. As we shall see, sense knowledge plays a fundamental and indeed revelatory part in the enunciation of man's being-in-the-world.[81] Being-in-the-world exists only insofar as man is affected and conditioned in knowledge by the framework or enclosure (*veritas*) of this twofold end *qua* beginning. Within this necessary enclosure man exists as the knowing subject affected by and affecting the entitative world. His self-knowledge is prefigured by these causal relational affections which are halted in the order of explanation or appearance so that man may announce the meanings of their being. This twofold end *qua* beginning, the order of appearances and the ontological order, are mirrored in the soul's paradoxical interplay of immanence and self-transcendence. As such, the soul's ontological grasping of the origin *qua* end is dependent upon the order of appearances but this order is realized because, the soul does not merely register these appearances by marking off their order as they become unconcealed and then re-concealed, but understands them. Man is in a way a participant in these appearances themselves as the epistemological enclosure (*veritas*) around them. Without this active participation, man could not speak of the things themselves. Genuinely to be the privileged being-in-the-world means not only to assist in articulating the meaning of Being but also be a participant in the formation of that meaning.[82] This active participation alone allows for thinking and Being to be the "same" while still maintaining the former as being-in-reference to the absolute hegemony of Being. His epistemological method culminates in the articulation of the most important definition of the intentional experience: "for in the case of things without matter that which thinks and that which is thought are the same; for speculative knowledge is the same as its object."[83] Aristotle announces this intentional truth, that the soul is in a way all things *qua* the same is for thinking as for Being, several times throughout the *De Anima*. An overview of the way in which the soul is the same as its object will lay the ground for articulating the core of classical intentionality.

The framework of beginning *qua* end allows for the real distinction and the real likeness between the soul and the world it apprehends. The likeness attained is based on locating the reality of the difference as difference i.e., "a thing is acted upon in one sense by like, in another by unlike; for while it is being acted upon it is unlike, but when the action is complete, it is like."[84] When the action is completed, man has reached his end, his *telos*, the difference as difference, the combining/unifying principle, the *ananke stenai* because, he has, in a way, enclosed (*veritas*) the object in knowledge. This enclosure is not a static likeness in the univocal sense of the pre-Socratics or an unrelatable and irreducible difference found among the sensibles in regard to the Platonic forms. The "same" that resides between the soul and its object is a dynamic and appropriative unity grounded in the difference as difference.[85]

This marriage of likeness and difference, immanence and self-transcendence is maintained within the soul's participated likeness in the *ananke stenai*. This participation reflects that the soul is in a way all things only insofar as it acts within the framework of thought needing to catch-up to Being, its *telos* or *ananke stenai*. Therefore the analogous nature of the "same" underscores the way in which the soul is all things. In a word, the soul in knowledge is ordered always in terms of dependency. This soul needs to enter its unity with its *telos* in order to be the "same" as the object it apprehends.[86]

This unity is achieved not because the soul passes over the world of beings in mere abstraction, rather, the soul needs to be an exteriorized existence in order to be the other in knowledge. Only in activity, in actuality, are the object and agent the "same." As Aristotle notes, "knowledge when actively operative is identical with its object."[87]

> If it [knowing] is analogous to perceiving, it must be either a process in which the soul is acted upon by what is thinkable, or something else of a similar kind. This part, then, must (although impassive) be receptive of the form of an object, i.e., must be potentially the same as its object, although not identical with it: as the sensitive to the sensible, so must mind be to what is thinkable. It is necessary then that mind, since it thinks all things, should be uncontaminated, as Anaxagoras says, in order that it may be in control, that is, that it may know. (429a12–19)

The potentiality to be the "same" is the necessary precondition of the privileged soul always in reference to its *telos*. In reaching its *telos*, the soul actualizes that precondition and becomes in a way all things, becoming the other in an immaterial act, enclosing the other in its knowledge. The soul does not reach this end by stepping outside the world. On the contrary, this end or sameness is reached only within the world. This end might be the door to the divine but it is not a reduction of the world; it is its fulfillment. This door is entered only through being a participant in the formation of the meaning of being and thereby acting in a manner that entrenches and exteriorizes the soul as being-in-the-world. The causal structure of the world is the door through which the soul becomes all things; it is a deepening of the intentional experience, that deadly serious game of trying to catch up in knowledge to Being. Where the soul is in a way all things *qua* the same is for thinking as for being, man discovers that the end was and is the beginning all along, in an eternality that unfolds in dependency, in being-in-the-world, reminding us of the goddess' cryptic remark: "And it is all one to me where I am to begin; for I shall return there again."[88]

It is essential not to overlook that the soul is in a way all things *qua* the same is for thinking as for Being primarily because the way in which the soul is the same as its object requires being-in-the-world as dependency or finitude. Aristotle uses the notion of "touch" as an analogy for the way in which the soul is an exteriorized nature extended out into the world of Being.[89] The exteriority of the soul conveys immanence as necessarily involved in self-transcendence, just as the I depends upon the other for its self-knowledge or the universal is realized in the particular. This last notion— the universal as realized in the particular—is of great importance for understanding the way in which the soul is all things. As earlier noted, the soul is the form of the body and form conveys limit or boundary. The soul gives the body its shape as this or that particular individual. The soul encloses around the body giving it its form and *entelechy*. Because it is fitted or attached not merely to any body but to a certain kind of existence, this particularity denotes dependency. For Aristotle, finitude as embodiment is not an impediment to reaching the first principles, the Universal or the *ananke stenai*, but is the necessary prefigurement of self-transcendence.[90]

Touch as Being-in-the-World

The distinguishing characteristics of the body, qua body, are tangible; by distinguishing characteristics I mean those which differentiate the elements. The tactile

organ which perceives them, i.e., that in which the sense of touch, as it is called,
primarily resides, is a part which has potentially the qualities of the object
touched. For perception is a form of being acted upon. Hence that which an
object makes actually like itself is potentially such already. This is why we have
no sensation of what is as hot, cold, hard, or soft as we are, but only of what is
more so, which implies that the sense is a sort of mean between the relevant sen-
sible extremes. That is how it can discern sensible objects. It is the mean that has
the power of discernment; for it becomes an extreme in relation to each of the
extremes in turn; and just as that which is to perceive white and black must be
actually neither, but potentially both (and similarly with the other senses) so in
the case of touch it must be neither hot nor cold.

(423b26–424a9)

Aristotle uses "touch" as an analogy for the soul as an exteriorized nature, as
that which is potentially all things because it is the mean or the combining/
unifying principle of its sensible constituents. Unlike the other senses, touch
does not have a medium between the sensible and the sense organ, and therefore the world is immediately apprehended.[91] In order for the other senses to
employ a medium or distancing factor, they must depend upon an underlying and immediate involvement in the world so that their knowledge is
genuinely entitative.[92] This immediacy of apprehension and the exteriorization of the soul as a kind of "touching" of the world are thereby an important
analogy for the legitimacy of classical and metaphysical intentionality. If
classical intentionality requires the "organ of organs" to be an exteriorized
nature, then it has understood being-in-the-world as the necessary and primary precondition of the intentional presence.

The world participates in the act of intentionality. Intentionality is
an inescapable component of existence just as "the first essential factor of
sensation that we all share, is a sense of touch."[93] If the soul is like "touch"
and "touch" exists only insofar as there is a world to grasp, then classical
intentionality has recognized that what makes both touch and the soul the
"most indispensable"[94] faculties are their inseparability from and immediacy
within the world.

As the privileged being who participates in the formation, meaning and
announcement of Being, man must be involved in the world, so much so
that the soul is, in a way, the "same" as the world. Compared to other animals, the human touch must be much more discriminating and that is why
of living creatures man is the most intelligent.[95] Therefore the combining/
unifying principle or mean that allows for the soul to be in a way all things is
not realized because the soul is postulated to be a "separate" existence apart

from the world. On the contrary, the privilege of the soul is the ability for the greatest involvement in the world. The soul, like touch, is potentially all things because it is the most available and most exteriorized to receive all things:

> It is also clear why plants do not feel, though they have one part of the soul, and are affected to some extent by objects touched, for they show both cold and heat; the reason is that they have no mean, i.e., no first principle such as to receive the form of sensible objects, but are affected by the matter at the same time as the form. (424a34–424b3)

The soul is the form of the body as the combining principle unifying the sensations, because it never leaves the world to define it as such:

> The other sense organs perceive by contact too, but through a medium; touch alone seems to perceive immediately. Thus no one of these elements could compose the animal body. Nor could earth. Touch is a kind of mean between all tangible qualities, and its organ is receptive not only of all the different qualities of the earth, but also of hot, cold, and all other tangible qualities. This is why we do not perceive with our bones and hair, and such parts of the body, because they are composed of earth . . . touch there can be no other sense, and the organ of touch is composed neither of earth nor of any other single element. (435a18–435b5)

The analogy of "touch," discloses finitude *qua* being-in-the-world as the vehicle of self-transcendence. This conception immeasurably distances the classical notion of intentionality from any Idealistic epistemology. But for finitude to be efficacious it must function within the enclosure, i.e., the beginning *qua* end wherein the unconcealment and concealment of appearances are elevated by man from their endlessness into their necessary form or end or enclosure.[96]

The elevation of the unconcealed into *veritas* discloses man as a participant not only in the articulation but in the formation of the meaning of Being. It is not possible ontologically to announce without this underlying formation of or adherence to or dependency upon Being. This formation occurs when thinking catches-up to Being, by means of the *ananke stenai*. At the point of reaching this end, knowledge is achieved but attached, with the radical understanding of our utter dependence on that end or formation or enclosure for our knowledge. To announce without formation would be to presuppose falsely an inordinate separation between the world and its privileged being (as for instance in the naive notions of "objectivity" contained in copy theories). Nor is it merely a separation in terms of the epistemological ability to abstract and become the object without matter, which rather would deny the need for the world in the most fundamental sense, in the act of knowledge itself. In a word, for Aristotle, finitude exists in the framework of the beginning *qua* end, because, for him, "all practical thinking has limits, and speculation is bounded like the verbal formulae which express it."[97] This is epistemological realism, and it has nothing to do with proving the existence of an external world or even the possibility of knowledge.

Pre-Socratics favored the unbounded, unending, indefiniteness of soul in any body, and thereby gained no real knowledge of the soul and the world of Being, plummeting into a *reductio ad absurdum*:

> These thinkers only try to explain what is the nature of the soul, without adding any details about the body which is to receive it; as though it were possible, as the Pythagorean stories suggest, for any soul to find its way into any body, which is absurd, for we can see that everybody has its own peculiar shape or form. Such a theory is like suggesting that carpentry can find its way into flutes; each craft must employ its own tools, and each soul its own body. (407b20–27)
>
>   It is not a body, it is associated with a body, and therefore resides in a body, and in a body of a particular kind; not at all as our predecessors supposed who fitted it to any body, without adding any limitations as to what body or what kind of body, although it is unknown for any chance thing to admit any other chance thing (. . .) for the actuality of each thing is naturally inherent in its potentiality that is in its own proper matter. (414a21–27)

Finitude reflects man's self-knowledge that holds man and world together, and without which man would cease to know and cease to be man. That which holds man and world together is the limit implicit in the order of explanation: the locus of the "same" is for thinking as for Being *qua* the soul is in a way all things. This power to preserve,[98] as found in the soul as the form of the body, means recognizing the prescribed limit of a thing as the crucial connective signate between the nature of its origin and the meaning of its end:

But in the addition to this, what is it that holds fire and earth together when they tend to move in contrary directions? For they will be torn apart, unless there is something to prevent this; but if there is anything of the sort this will be the soul, and the cause of growth and nourishment. To some the nature of fire seems by itself to be the cause of nutrition and growth; for it alone of all bodies and elements seems to be nourished and grow of itself. Hence one might suppose that it is the operating principle in both plants and animals. It is in a sense a contributory cause, but not absolutely the cause, which is much more properly the soul; for the growth of fire is without limit, so long as there is something to be burned, but of all things naturally composed there is a limit or proportion of size and growth; this is due to the soul, not to fire, and to the essential formula rather than to matter. (416a5–19)

Chapter 2

St. Thomas Aquinas and Classical Intentionality

In our tracing of the intentionality rooted in Aristotle and developed by St. Thomas, we shall endeavor to characterize and identify the necessity of intentionality as the pre-cognitive ground of all acts of knowledge precisely because it is the necessary precondition for articulating man's dependency upon the world as an essential and positive phenomenon. Finitude is for Aristotle and St. Thomas not a dense bulwark or impediment one must circumvent in order to find the world and establish knowledge, but the very vehicle of transcendence itself. The cogito, innate ideas, the a priori, existentialist engagement, the as-if, the absolute, the pragmatic principle of truth, what are these, but substitutes and surrogates for that for which there is no substitute: intentionality? These substitutes are united by the selfsame loss of the fourfold intentional presupposition, a loss which in turn inevitably summons the emergence of negative finitude as in-dependence. All are substitutes to enable man to navigate a world he cannot know.

For St. Thomas, the problem of intentionality is a complex issue when presented within a modern philosophical tradition where the intentional mode of being means a merely mental existence and where the intentional mode of existence is relegated only to a mode of naive or nominalist abstraction separated from sensible intuition, the immediate act of being-in-the-world.

For St. Thomas, the true being of the world is found in its progressive revelation to the consciousness of the human subject as phenomenon and as truth, a revelation that progresses only through the onto-theo-logic causal structure of a metaphysics of existence. This causal structure stands ultimately by and in reference to a fundamental Other which/who regulates our knowledge in each of the degrees of Being. Passing from one degree to the next (from one phenomenon to the next) requires an end, *qua ananke stenai*, in the order of the first phenomenon to enable man to gain *noetic* access into the next in ever deepening articulations and knowledge.

Let us also understand that for St. Thomas consciousness contains the world in the mode of intentionality and that the world contains consciousness in the mode of finitude or existentiality as mutual transcendences. In other words, the intentional presence can be defined by and as human activity in the real presence of actual existence;[1] it is the "nurse of becoming" that establishes the *noetic* relationship of the knower to the object known, as it is in itself. Therefore, for intentionality to be the intentional presence, intentionality must not reduce the object known to a mere representation of itself. For the soul is, to begin with, in a relation of potentiality to the world: and this potentiality is the pre-cognitive structural relationship of the human soul to its world under the immaterial mode of *esse intentionale*. This intentional becoming of the soul does not then duplicate the real world, even though it may represent it: it is not a pseudo-intentional leaping forth of the consciousness in a productive act; it is instead the ground of any such act, the relational being-with and being-toward that the soul is. The soul is, if you will, prefigured by the causal structure as a radical openness capable of encompassing the world of things and intelligibles, a reaching toward (*intentio*) that world.

The question of intentionality then is not whether but how Being reveals itself to the knower and, just as importantly, not whether but how the knower is able to respond to Being? For St. Thomas, as for Aristotle, because the soul is in a way all things, because it can become a thing other than itself, because it can become the other as other without confiscating the other's otherness, and without losing its own existential identity, the experience of thinking is not appropriated by a thinking thing through mere abstraction. Rather man and world are mutually appropriated by belonging in Being. In mutual response, together they define the experience of thought. The act of judgment for St. Thomas, then, is not a mere representation of the thing, but the intellectual act of man in the presence of Being.

Moreover, we must add that for St. Thomas language at its core must follow the order of explanation.[2] At the end of that order man finds a kind of knowledge of a Being beyond the world, but not in such a way that man is himself outside of the world or of actual Being. Quite the contrary, if judgment arises only at the end of an order of explanation that is prefigured by a prior necessary stop or *ananke stenai* in the order of Being, then in a way man reaches knowledge both of Being and indeed of himself only from reflecting upon this sheer irreducible and absolute Other (God) housed implicitly within the *ananke stenai*.[3] And the Other that man recognizes is radically other than himself and constitutes the onto-theo-logic unity of metaphysics. It is of great importance to note that in Thomistic intentionality, the four aspects of the intentional presupposition find their shared origination in an Other worth far more than the sum total of their individual aspects.

The soul is in a way all things: is this a massive naive presupposition or a fundamental inescapable descriptive fact? "*Et huius ratio est, quia actus cognitionis se extendit ad ea quae sunt extra cognoscentem, cognoscimus enim etiam ea quae extra nos sunt.*"[4] The act of cognition extends to things outside the knower in two ways: to sensible things through the senses and to intelligible things through the intellect. Therefore, nothing is essentially beyond the reach of the soul or consciousness. But we must proceed more slowly. In what sense is the soul all things; in what way?

The source of the Thomistic notion is of course Aristotle's *De Anima* Bk. III, ch. 7 (431b), where the Stagirite summarizes his findings with the most telling and influential remark, and then elaborates it in the following manner:

> Knowledge and perception are divided according to their objects, the potential according to the potential, the actual according to the actual; the perceiving and the knowing parts of the soul are potentially those things, the one the knowable, the other the perceivable. Those objects must be either things themselves or their forms. Not things themselves, for it is not the stone in the soul, but its form; so that the soul is as is the hand, for the hand is the organ of organs, and the intellect is the form of forms and sense perception the form of sensible objects.[5]

Let us note the following points:

1. Reality itself is, for Aristotle, to be understood in terms of actuality and potentiality: *dynamis* is the essential capacity or capability, a readiness to become (actual); *energeia* is the essential state-of-being-at-work, a functioning, or presence, or completion: the fulfillment of a capacity.[6] Reality or being, then, is no longer the being of the Eleatics,[7] that is to say it is no longer static, but is instead dynamic actuality.
2. Like the division in reality is the division in the soul whose faculties of knowledge and sense are also either potential or actual, directed toward either potential or actual sense and knowledge.
3. Within the soul itself, that is to say structurally, both knowledge and sense are in a relation of potentiality toward their respective objects. The soul is essential capacity-to-become its object. Knowledge is potentially what is knowable; sense is potentially what is sensible. In act, they are

actually their objects, not the objects themselves but their forms, for instance the form of the stone and not the stone itself bound, as it is, to its materiality.

4. Therefore the soul is like the hand, the tool of tools, the organ of organs, the instrument of instruments, that which makes praxis possible. The soul as the form of forms makes *theoria* possible. Or as St. Thomas says, "*et similiter anima data est homini loco omnium formarum, ut sit homo quodammodo totum ens, inquantum secundum animam est quodammodo omnia, prout eius anima est receptiva omnium formarum. Nam intellectus est quaedam potentia receptiva omnium formarum intelligibilium, et sensus est quaedam potentia receptiva omnium formarum sensibilium.*"[8] Through the use of the Aristotelian image of the hand as embodying sense in general, we could say that the hand has a thought and a language all its own: it is the key to the door of the world, as the soul is the key to Being; together they constitute our specific humanity.

When we said at the outset of this section that the consciousness contains the world in the four modes of the intentional presupposition, this is what is meant. Again, the soul is a radical openness capable of encompassing the world of things and intelligibles, a reaching toward (*intentio*) that world. But because being is said in many ways, we must be very careful at this stage of the discussion. It is the soul's ability to be all things cognitionally that makes present those beings under the finite mode of *esse intentionale* which stands distinct from *esse naturae*, that is to say to the being a thing possesses when it exists in its own nature, its finite delimited materiality. However, certain difficulties and obfuscations may emerge at this point concerning the distinctions between *esse intentionale, esse naturae* and immateriality: distinctions which can be clarified with the aid of St. Thomas and certain of his better commentators.

Let us recapitulate, in a sense, what we have ascertained to this point by turning to St. Thomas' Commentary on Aristotle's *De Anima*:

The term "universal" can be taken in two senses. It can refer to the nature itself, common to several things, in so far as this common nature is regarded in relation to those several things; or it can refer to the nature taken simply in itself . . . Now a nature—say, human nature,—which can be thought of universally, has two modes of existence: one, material, in the matter supplied by nature; the other, immaterial, in the intellect. As in the material mode of existence it cannot be represented in a universal notion, for in that mode it is individuated by its matter; this notion only applies to it therefore as abstracted from individuating matter. But it cannot, as so abstracted, have a real existence, as the Platonists thought; man in reality only exists . . . in this flesh and these bones. Therefore it is only in the intellect that human nature has any being, apart from the principles which individuate it.[9]

We have in hand the distinction between material mode of being and immaterial mode of being. They are strictly speaking manners of existence, ways of being-present, in themselves and to the spirit. It is here a question of representation. If intentionality is neither a copy theory, a static duplication of the real world or a pseudo-intentional leaping forth of the consciousness in a productive act but rather the relational being-with and being-toward that the soul is, then there must not be an irreconcilable dichotomy between the immaterial and material modes of existence but, on the contrary, a primordial unity rendering it possible for man to represent the other as other. Where is this primordial unity housed but in man's communion with Being? This communion already exists because man's finitude is, paradoxically, that which is immaterial in its origin but necessarily unfolds as fully invested in existence in an embodied state. Let us conclude with Maritain that

> Another kind of existence must . . . be admitted; an existence according to which the known will be in the knower and the knower will be the known, an entirely tendential and immaterial existence, whose office is not to posit a thing outside nothingness for itself and as a subject, but, on the contrary, for another thing and as a relation. It is an existence that does not seal up the thing within the bounds of its nature, but sets it free from them. In virtue of that existence, the thing exists in the soul with an existence other than its own existence, and the soul is, or becomes the thing with an existence other than its own [natural] existence.[10]

Housed within the intentional presupposition, the mode of finitude is part and parcel of an entirely tendential and immaterial existence, a being-for or toward, a relational mode of being which grounds the union of knower and known. In other words, because consciousness is tendential, it has both a positive and a negative reference: it is the Other (intentionally); it is not the Other (materially): it is immanent and transcendent, or rather transcending, because of its finitude. Finitude is that which first and foremost reflects our ontological association with the world, and secondarily that which makes possible our ontic commerce with the world: it is a being and a having: because we are the world (the soul is in a way all things) we can have a world (the soul is analogous to the hand): it is the common root, in one sense at least, of *theoria* and *praxis*, of word and deed, of being and doing.

Concerning the intentional mode of existence, we must beware of the possible misunderstanding we alluded to earlier. Does it mean that the world is had by the soul in merely "mental existence"? Is this what "intentional mode of being" means in our context? If such is the case, we could easily understand St. Thomas to be proposing a sort of copy theory, one in which intentionality would be an epistemological doctrine, a product of knowledge, a secondary attribute and not a primary precognitive characteristic of the act of knowing. The mental inexistence of the object would then be a representation of the object known "out there."[11] The object known, as an in-itself, would not in the final analysis be known at all, but only our representation of it. As such, we would be confronted with two worlds, the real and the ideal, and thus intentionality would have to assume the role of corresponding the two, of in fact accounting for their correspondence. And to this extent intentionality would become an epistemological and explanatory hypothesis. In such an analysis the union of knower and known becomes problematic, something to-be-achieved. This, however, does not seem to be what St. Thomas ever held or tried to say. For the soul is to begin with in a relation of potentiality to the world: and this potentiality is the pre-cognitive, structural relationship of the human soul to its world under the immaterial mode of *esse intentionale*. Again, this intentional becoming of the soul does not, then, duplicate the real world, even though again, it may represent it: it is instead the ground of any *noetic* act, the relational being-with and being-toward that the soul actively is. Still, this is not enough to counter the possible objections concerning a copy theory of mental inexistence. More is required, and this requirement is fulfilled with St. Thomas' doctrine of abstraction to which we shall now turn.

The Luminosity of Consciousness: Abstraction

There are, St. Thomas maintains, three grades of cognitive powers:[12]

1. The sensitive power or capacity which is the "act of a corporeal organ," and its proper object is the individual or particular, that is to say the form as existing in matter. Seeing, touching, smelling and the like: all these powers extend to the radical and corporeal particularities of

the object. Of the senses, sight is the most perfect because the least material, without natural immutation. In descending order of perfection sight is followed by hearing, smell, taste and touch.

2. That cognitive power which is neither the act of a corporeal organ nor in any way connected with corporeal matter is the angelic intellect,[13] whose proper object is form unrestricted by or through matter.

3. Midway in this hierarchy stands the human intellect. Not being the act of any sensorial organ, it is nevertheless and above all the knowing function or power of the soul. And because it holds the center position on the natural scale of cognitive powers, its proper object reflects that position and status.[14] "*Et ideo proprium eius est cognoscere formam in materia quidem corporali individualiter existentem, non tamen prout est in tali materia.*"[15] We have already seen what this means: the object of the soul's intellection may be an individual, but it exists in the soul intentionally and immaterially, without the natural limitations of the object's *esse naturae*, this as a whole comprises the specifically finite nature of man.

But we must now inquire into the specific "how" of the soul's finite intellection. Once the Platonic separate intelligibles have been removed, we must wonder just where the intellect gets its objects. How is the change from sense impression or object to intelligible object effected? We know that, for St. Thomas, the soul is *quodammodo omnia*. But what are, if you will, the mechanics of this structure? And most importantly, we must wonder if the abstraction that we will outline in this section turns out to be the same as the intentionality we previously discussed. [16]

Now there are two modes of abstraction:

1. *per modum compositionis et divisionis*: not unlike the Greek *synagoge* and *diairesis*, this mode of abstraction has as its goal the understanding "*aliquid non esse in alio, vel esse separatum ab eo.*"[17] This mode of abstraction may involve falsehood; that is to say, to separate things which in reality are not separate (as Plato did with the *eide*) leads to a false contemplation of that which has thus been separated: and so it becomes an abstraction.

2. *per modum simplicis et absolutae considerationis*: "*sicut cum intelligimus unum, nihil considerando de alio.*"[18] In this case, to abstract things which are, in reality, not really separate would not involve us in a falsehood. It is in this mode of abstraction a matter of separating the essential from the merely incidental individuating factors: "*Et hoc est abstrahere universale a particulari, vel speciem intelligibilem a phantasmatibus.*"[19] And the primary reason that such a mode of abstraction does not in itself convey a falsehood is that

"*alius sit modus intelligentis in intelligendo, quam modus rei in existendo, quia intellectum est in intelligente immaterialiter, per modum intellectus; non autem materialiter, per modum rei materialis.*"[20] And, as we have seen, the mode of the intellect is intentional and an immaterial finite existence, *esse intentionale*. Even at this point we have an implicit connection between intentionality, abstraction and knowledge as modes of the intentional presence. But prior to seeing how this connection works itself out, we must allow St. Thomas to explain more fully the doctrine of abstraction. And surely one of the crucial objections to this doctrine would be that it involves us in an "intellectualism."[21] If such an objection is well-founded it could be conclusive for the following reasons:

a. abstraction would be seen to violate the fundamental and manifest structure of the things we seek to understand: the intellect's attempt to know things by abstraction would lead instead to a knowledge of abstractions, and therefore

b. abstraction would indeed provide us with a new and different world from the one from which we ostensibly started; such a procedure would probably seek justification in

c. a copy theory of representations, crucial to which is the fact, whether admitted or denied, that the soul never does in fact extend to things beyond itself.

d. the philosophical upshot of this objection would most likely be either a Platonic variant on the one hand, or a nominalistic empiricism on the other.

Now St. Thomas of course is willing to accept neither of these alternatives. It is vital that he therefore show the objection to be at best confused. And this he attempts by noting the dual nature of matter, as it pertains to the question of finitude.

We have on the one hand individual or signate matter, strictly particularistic and peculiar to the object at hand. These material predicates are those aspects of an object which are not demanded by the nature of that object to exist.[22]

On the other hand, we have common matter which is the understood "basis of diversity amongst individuals within a species . . ."[23] Now common matter does indeed enter into the definition of material things, and to abstract from common matter would be to involve us in the difficulties previously sketched.[24]

Conjoin this with the principle that St. Thomas has previously stated, to wit: the mode of understanding is not the same as the mode of a thing in being, and we have likely, it seems, circumvented both the intellectualistic result of a false abstraction (one that would abstract from common matter) and the nominalistic empiricism that would result from rejecting a doctrine of abstraction that is false but assumed to be the only one. What St. Thomas is maintaining is that we can legitimately abstract (*per modum simplicis et absolutae considerationis*) the specific characteristics of the object in question without violating or denying the material character of that object.[25]

If the soul were purely passive, a receptacle for purely individual sense images, it could not be a knower, except by means of either the false abstraction already considered, in which case it would not know things, or by means of logical and epistemological construction, in which case it would not truly be a knower. But if we are to avoid the Scylla of hypostasizing Platonism and the Charybdis of empiricistic constructionism, and if we are to understand St. Thomas when he says that the soul knows and knows abstractively, then we must posit a certain action or activity on the part of the knower which enables abstractive knowing to be efficacious, which accounts for the transition from object of sense to object of intellect. And such is the distinction between active or agent intellect and possible intellect.[26]

Phantasms "have not the power of themselves to make an impression on the possible intellect": this is so because, as we have seen, the soul is immaterial and can only know immaterially and intentionally. A material sensory datum could not then impress itself upon the possible intellect, but only upon the corporeal organ corresponding to the phantasm. Let us be clear about the status of the possible intellect. We have already encountered it in our discussion of Aristotle's *De Anima.* The soul is in a way all things; it is in a relationship of potentiality to the forms of being; the faculty of knowledge is potentially its object. Now, "*omne quod exit de potentia in actum, potest dici pati, etiam cum perficitur,*"[27] that is to say it possesses the structural characteristic of the intentional possibility or potentiality even when it has been actualized. Because the proper object of the intellect is that which is intelligible, the intellect can be said to be in potentiality "*respectu intelligibilium.*"[28] Hence we must posit a passive or possible intellect.

Positing a possible intellect means to posit the intellect as possibility or as potentiality: the possible intellect is precisely a power, a mode of being of the intellect, a receptive openness.[29] As possibility, the possible intellect is prior to understanding.

But again, phantasms have not the power of themselves to make an impression on the possible intellect. For the soul actually to become all things, something must be posited by which it can do so, something by which the transition from sense object to intelligible object may be effected. For the understanding to be projected upon objects in their possibility, thus giving rise to intelligibility via the soul's abstraction, there must in the soul be an active power: only thus can those entities which the human subject has already encountered sensibly in the world, and which the soul somehow is, become objects of knowledge.

Through the power of the agent intellect, there results in the possible intellect a certain likeness produced by the attentional turning of the agent intellect toward the phantasms: where the possible intellect is receptivity, the agent intellect is productivity; it is in some sense a maker: a producer and maker of intelligibility. And it achieves this "*per abstractionem specierum a conditionibus materialibus,*"[30] by the dissociation of form from matter, and thus representing the phantasm to the intellect under the mode of intelligible species immaterially, intentionally, cognitionally, in the mode of the receiver. It is only a "certain likeness" for precisely that reason, and not the identical form that was in the phantasm, and from this emerges knowledge of that which is presented by the phantasms, but which had previously been only potentially intelligible.

> The soul *confers* intelligibility on the phantasms, and in this is an agent intellect; it *receives* determination from them, and in this is a possible intellect. . . . The sensible as such cannot penetrate the intelligible as such; and so it is our intellect which, aspiring to receive determination from the sensible, begins by rendering its action possible in raising it up to its own dignity.[31]

Because the sensible *qua* sensible cannot impress itself upon the intelligible *qua* intelligible, there must needs be such a power that can make the sensible "*redduntur habilia ut ab eis intentiones intelligibiles abstrahantur,*"[32] prior to the possible intellect's receipt of determination in a specific act of knowledge.[33]

Now the agent intellect performs its function of rendering sensible reality fit for abstraction—freeing, as Maritain observes,[34] the intelligibility contained potentially in sensible reality.[35] What then are we to make of the intelligible species? Are they the objects of knowledge? Is abstraction knowledge? Is the agent intellect equivalent to the *intellectus in actu?* Is abstraction equivalent to intentionality?

What are the intelligible species? From whence do we derive them and to what do they ultimately refer? They derive from the phantasms via the agent intellect's ability to confer intelligibility upon them. Ultimately, they refer to those phantasms (to material reality) *secundum esse intentionale*, that is, universally.[36] Intentional existence then is only the qualitative mode of being of that which has been abstracted and rendered intelligible. If intentionality is that capacity to become the other immaterially, abstraction is that whereby intentional becoming is accomplished. "Intentionality" refers only to the immaterial mode of existence and to the soul's capacity to assume, and put on the world (the other); it is relational. "Abstraction" accounts for the knowability of that material reality which has been objectified (made an object) in the intelligible species and by which the soul is objectified, becoming the other as other.[37]

For Platonism, what the soul comes to know are the separated ideas understood as abstractions. If, for the purposes of comparison, we say that for Plato the soul understood the intelligible species, then we can readily see that those species become the objects of Platonic episteme, and not the things which participate in the paradigm form. St. Thomas rejected such an understanding of knowledge. For Platonism man knows abstractions; for St. Thomas he knows the *things themselves* abstractly. St. Thomas' analysis of intelligible species should be seen as emerging from that same rejection.

Not only would the Platonic view (or a modern variant) involve the orientation of science toward things within the soul, but further it would result in the view of those who maintain that "*quod omne quod videtur est verum*"[38], that whatever seems true is true. Paradoxically this conclusion would lead back to the Protagorean principle that man is the measure of all things, a position that Plato specifically rejected.

In order then to safeguard the facts of human knowing, the integrity of the material reality under consideration, and the possibility of certitude and objectivity, the intelligible species must (1) not be seen as ontologically separate from its material ground and (2) be understood as "*habet ad intellectum ut quo intelligit intellectus.*" [39] Thus, the species of an object is not one being and the object another species. It is the very object under the mode of species.

In our discussion of the intentional mode of existence, we have twice asked if that meant having the world in merely mental existence, in which case the object known, as an in-itself (if that), would not in the final analysis be known at all, but only our representation of it. We can at this point see how very far St. Thomas is from a copy-theory, and just what the role of intelligible species is. While the intelligible species are in the intellect, they are not there as an object or referent of the intellect, but they are there as that through and by which the true object (the world) can be known. This is possible because the species are an intentional likeness of the thing by which man likens himself to the other as other. And if this is so, then we have not the problem of corresponding the species with the thing precisely because (1) the species is the resultant abstractive emergence of the thing's intelligibility via the agent intellect's illuminating power, and (2) "it is not the species of the object that is present in thought, but the object through its species."[40] It is not a question of corresponding the intelligible species with the thing, rather it is the intelligible species which makes possible any correspondence of thought and object; the species are not the termini of abstraction: the thing is the terminus, and once it is, of course, it is no longer mere thing, but object or at least ready-to-be-an-object, that is, a possible object of intellectual knowledge: "*Et sic species intellectiva secundario est id quod intelligitur. Sed id quod intelligitur primo, est res cuius species intelligibilis est similitudo.*"[41] In some sense at least, the intelligible species and, therefore, abstraction itself is prior to knowledge: it is pre-cognitive and potentially cognitive. It's man's being-in-the-world.

What does this mean? Because the species is the likeness of the thing understood, when that object is understood in act it is such that the species are the form of the intellect, the form that actualizes the intellect as potential. So that what is actually understood is the same as the intellect in act or the intellect as actualized.[42] In knowledge the soul is the other as other. But prior to the *intellectus* in *actu* is abstraction as that which provides the material for knowledge or understanding in act, and that material is the species, as a likeness (*similitudo*) of the thing. If the *intellectus* in *actu* then is the intellect as immediately ready to posit acts of knowing, we can say that abstraction is the pre-cognitive identification of man (the soul) and the world: it is the pre-cognitive identification *secundum esse intentionale* of man and his world which has been made ready for knowledge. If this is formularized as first I am the world and then I know it, it means that first I am the world via abstraction, the structure of which is intentional immateriality, and then I know it in act, operating on the intelligible species which have been provided by the agent intellect's abstractive action.

St. Thomas goes on to distinguish in the understanding that aspect which properly resides on the side of the thing from that which properly resides in the intellect:[43]

1. the thing which is understood (the side of the thing) and
2. the fact that it is understood (the side of the intellect).

Again, the purpose of this is to force the recognition that what is ultimately understood is not the intelligible species, even though understanding properly resides in the intellect. The world as understood is intelligibilized via abstraction and in that way retains its extra-mental integrity while becoming a possible object of the intellect. Or with Gilson we can say that "when a thing becomes intelligibilized in thought, it does not become anything more nor anything else than what it was. For an object with no consciousness of being, to be known is no event. It is as if nothing were happening to it."[44]

We have the clear distinction between abstraction and the *intellectus* in *actu*. Both *immutatio* and *formatio* are joined in the intellect: in the first place there is the effect produced in the possible intellect through the species by which it is informed—and this is *immutatio*; secondly, when the possible intellect is thus informed it formulates a definition or proposition (affirmative or negative) which is then signified in an enunciation— and this is *formatio*. Now it is quite clear that the former (*immutatio*) is but a description of St. Thomas' notion of abstraction, and that the latter is but a description of St. Thomas' notion of the *intellectus* in *actu*.[45] And it is equally clear that abstraction precedes actual understanding as expressed in language.

We have remarked in passing both that abstraction is pre-cognitive and that it is the source of the soul's existential assimilative identification with the world. If abstraction and intentionality are, for St. Thomas, the ground of man's being-in-the-world let us see what this means. Like abstraction, intentionality too is prior to any specific intentional act; it refers

1. to the fact that the soul is by nature directed toward an other and
2. to the immaterial mode of being of that other in consciousness, *esse intentionale*.

Intentionality is not an explanatory hypothesis or principle that can account for the possibility of transcending an inner sphere toward something which is grasped in an intentional act. The soul is already outside of itself intentionally and when it understands it understands intentionally. It is a descriptive fact, a phenomenologically descriptive fact, if you will. It is not an epistemological doctrine in any modern sense. This is an important point of contact between Heidegger and St. Thomas; it shows the depth at which they are united in implanting man in being-in-the-world but, as will be shown in Chapter 3, is, at the same time, the origin of their fundamental irreconcilability.

The Exteriority of Consciousness: Self-knowledge

Non ergo per essentiam suam, sed per actum suum se cognoscit intellectus noster.[46]

La conscience est purement et simplement conscience d'etre conscience de cet objet.[47]

The problem of self-knowledge and self-constitution hovers above and around almost the entire of modern philosophy: it is part and parcel of the problematic of transcendence—an understanding of the former is crucial to an understanding of the latter. But of course our purpose here is much more limited—it is to attempt an explication of what St. Thomas says on the problem and its relationship to what we have previously ascertained, and to what we will see in Husserl and, especially, Heidegger.

Setting out his definitive analysis of the problem in *De Veritate*, Question 10, Article 8, St. Thomas is insistent upon clarifying the terms of the question "Whether the soul knows itself through its own essence," for there are two ways of understanding that question:

> In the first, "through its essence" is taken to refer to the thing known, so that we understand that a thing is known through its essence when its essence is known, and that it is not known through its essence when not its essence but only certain of its accidents are known.[48]

But it is not in this sense that we are posing the question, and the reason seems to be this: we are not asking whether indeed we know the essence of the soul, but whether the soul comes to a knowledge of itself through (by means of) an unmediated apprehension (knowledge) of its essence, that is to say whether the soul comes to know its essence through its essence. Knowing "through its essence" in this first sense referred to by St. Thomas is, if anything, a conclusion and cannot therefore perform the function of posing the question that is being asked. Furthermore, "through its essence" in the first sense would, if employed, perhaps beg the question, for what we are asking is if and how the soul knows its essence and not what it means to know the essence. Therefore, we must look to the second sense of "through its essence" for aid in the endeavor:

> In the second way, it is taken to refer to that by which something is known, so that we thus understand that something is known through its essence because the essence itself is that by which it is known. It is in

this sense that we ask here if the soul understands itself through its essence.[49]

Does the soul, then, come to know itself by means of its own essence or by means of something else, something other?

And here a crucial distinction must be made, one by which we may distinguish the soul as presence from the soul as activity, as subject from object, as immediate, existential self-awareness from the knowledge of the nature of the soul in secondary reflection. Considered as self-experiencing subjectivity the soul is a core of incommunicability, a center both of ineffable flux and mysterious stillness: the crucible of self-hood, a world within the World. As such it is the fountain, at one level at least, of "mineness"; it is that which is most proper to my soul: it is presence, subjectivity, existential self-awareness, unseen and unseeable by the Other. It is, with St. Thomas, the knowledge by which the human soul understands itself only with reference to that which is essential to it, the knowledge of the soul as it exists in this individual. Thus it is through this knowledge that one understands whether the soul exists, as when man perceives that he has a soul.[50]

But even as such, another distinction must be made concerning this type of knowledge. The distinction is that between actual and habitual knowledge. Perceiving that he has a soul, that he lives or exists is dependent for man upon the prior experience or perception that he senses, understands and the like.[51] Now to perceive that he understands, man must first understand something. "For to understand something is prior to understanding that one understands. Therefore, through that which it understands or senses the soul arrives at actual perception of the fact that it exists."[52] First, then, is the apprehension of an Other after which there can be an apprehension of apprehension. So that even on this level of subjectivity and individuality the soul must gain a knowledge of itself indirectly, at least so far as actual cognition is concerned. Nevertheless, it is an actual cognition of an existential fact and not of generic or universal structure; we are still on the level of self-awareness. The knowledge of one's own existence is not then an irreducible and originary experiential datum of consciousness (the cogito) for St. Thomas, but is, if we may so call it, an intentional act in both senses of that term that we have employed: the broader sense indicating the other-directedness of the soul (as well as the immaterial mode of being assumed by the object of that directedness); the narrower sense indicating a specific intentional act culminating in a specific act of understanding or an actual cognition. The knowledge of personal existence follows upon the activities of personal existence.

There is however a legitimate analogical sense in which the soul does possess a direct actual cognition of its essential self, and this St. Thomas calls habitual knowledge:

> The soul has the power to enter upon actual cognition of itself from the very fact that its essence is present to it. This is like the case of one who, because he has the habit of some knowledge, can by reason of the presence of the habit perceive those things which fall under the habit. But no habit is required for the soul's perception of its existence and its advertence to the activity within it. The essence alone of the soul, which is present to the mind, is enough for this, for the acts in which it is actually perceived proceed from it.[53]

In such an instance the soul or mind is the principle "*cognitionem de mente habendam, sufficit ipsa mentis praesentia, quae est principium actus ex quo mens percipit seipsam,*"[54] and is in that sense present to itself. The soul knows itself because it is that which allows even the possibility of knowledge of anything at all and in that way is ever-present to itself.

But concerning knowledge of the generic and intelligible structures of the soul, neither the actual nor the habitual knowledge is sufficient, because although the soul cannot err in its apprehension of its own existence it may indeed, and often does, err in its understanding of the nature of the soul.[55] Now our apprehension of the nature of the soul is achieved through species which we abstract from the senses. Our soul possesses the last place among intellectual things, just as first matter does among the sensibles. For, as first matter is in potency with regards to all sensible forms, so too our possible intellect is in potency with regards to all intelligible forms. Thus it is pure potency within the order of intelligible things, as matter is within the order of sensible reality. Therefore, as matter is sensible only through some added form, so the possible intellect is intelligible only through a species which is brought into and accord with it.[56] The position of the intellect in the order of created being, the connaturality of soul and body, the doctrines of intentionality and abstraction: all these lead St. Thomas to maintain that knowledge of the soul's nature is gained indirectly, in the same manner that it gains knowledge of material reality.

1. *The position of the intellect in the order of created being.* Midway in the hierarchy between sensitive (corporeal) power and purely intellectual (angelic) power stands the human intellect. Not being, as we noted earlier, the act of any sensorial organ, it is nevertheless and above all the knowing

function of the soul. Its proper object reflects its status: it is proper and fitting to it to know a form existing in corporeal matter, but not as existing in this individual matter. For the angelic intellect, being fully actual, the act of understanding and that which is understood coincide in a unified cognition, and that is why the angelic intellect apprehends its own essence by means of itself. "Intellectus autem humanus se habet in genere rerum intelligibilium ut ens in potentia tantum," in which case there is not an actual cognition of its object, itself included, in which case while the cognition is actualized it is nevertheless indirect and achieved by means of the abstracted species: "*intelligat intellectus noster, secundum quod fit actu per species a sensibilibus abstractas per lumen intellectus agentis.*"[57] This mode of indirectness corresponds to finitude, properly reflecting the degrees of being for which man as finite engages in and to the world intentionally. Finitude is understood as the connaturality of soul and body.

2. *The connaturality of soul and body.* Because the human soul is a form joined to matter (as the form of that matter), though not thereby becoming material but embodied, incarnate, finite, it is potentially and not yet actually intelligible. We have seen that every form of this kind is known through abstraction of the species from individuated matter and from material conditions. Understanding, furthermore, is not accomplished by the soul alone, but through its conjunction with the body which would be unnecessary if the soul knew itself through its essence alone. Thus as we saw in the case of actual knowledge, the soul comes to a perception of its own existence through its acts and objects. And so far as actual knowledge of the intelligible structures of the soul is concerned, the situation is similar. And of course the key here is the soul's requisite turning to the phantasms, to sensible reality in order to gain knowledge. "From this," Gilson tells us, "result the numerous operations which such knowledge demands as well as the order in which they are presented. Our soul only comes to knowledge of itself because it first apprehends other things. . . . It knows first its object, then its operation, and finally its own nature. Now it perceives merely that it is an intellectual soul, since it apprehends the operation of its intellect. Then it is raised to universal knowledge of what is the nature of the human soul by a methodical reflection on the conditions required by such an operation."[58] The nature of the soul, then, comes to be known secondarily after the fact of knowing an other. The soul moves from itself to the other and then back to an understanding of itself. And the very movement toward the other which enables the soul's intentional presence to return to itself in secondary methodical reflection is the movement that we have called intentionality. This intentionality lays the ground for the longer way,[59] the way of finitude;

man does not come to know himself by means of his own essence but by means of something else, something intermediate. This intermediate exists in turning toward the world. The act of turning reflects the onto-theo-logic causal structure of metaphysics, because in turning man recognizes an end in the order of the phenomenon that acts as an entry into other phenomena and then, into Otherness as such, the locus of the *ananke stenai*. In other words, man is open to the infinite because he is finite.

3. *Intentionality and abstraction.* Concerning the knowledge of the soul's nature, St. Thomas Aquinas follows Aristotle in holding that the intellect understands itself just as it understands other things, quoting the Philosopher to the effect that intellect is understood through an intention in it, just as other intelligible things, and this intention is the intelligible species abstracted by the power of the agent intellect. Now this does not mean that the abstracted species is a likeness of the soul, that is to say, the species are not abstracted from the soul which is after all not a sensible reality. Rather, from a study of the nature of the species abstracted from sensible things we discover the nature of the soul in which such a species is received, just as matter is known from form. In other words, "*non ergo per essentiam suam, sed per actum suum se cognoscit intellectus noster.*"[60] The soul illumines the world and the world illumines the soul. The pre-cognitive abstractive and intentional unity of man and world is thus a unity of reciprocity as far as the soul is concerned.[61] The intellect becomes its object both in a transcending movement away from itself and toward its object and through a receptivity wherein it brings the object into itself, in an immanent cognitional activity. That double movement of receptive and projective activity thus lays the groundwork for the soul's knowledge of its own intelligible structure.

The Meaning of Self-transcendence

If we understand the notion of self-transcendence to embrace the reciprocal relationship between man and the world, we can see some of the things that it signifies.

It signifies first of all, objectivity: the conferring of intelligibility that was discussed earlier is an affair of objectification; it is that which transforms a mere thing into an intelligible object and it objectifies the soul in the world, by which it becomes the world in knowledge. And this is why, within the intentional identification of the soul and its object neither the specific otherness of the object nor the identity of the soul is eradicated or confiscated by the other term of the process. When, through abstraction, the intelligibility is liberated from the confines of individual matter what is this if not the freeing of the thing for objective knowledge? And so, if self-transcendence signifies objectivity, then objectivity implies intersubjectivity, that is to say a community of knowers.[62]

Now while actual cognition cannot be understood apart from the movement of self-transcendence, we must keep in mind that self-transcendence is primarily and for the most part pre-cognitive and existential (in the contemporary usage of that word): it is the world that man deals with, and the object appears against the background of the world. The object as known, as conceptualized in a proposition or judgment results from the prior intelligibilizing of the world through abstraction in the movement of intentional self-transcendence that characterizes the soul. Man is able to deal with the world because of that movement of transcendence which reaches the world in a dual manner:

1. by binding the soul to the world (the soul is in a way all things) in such a way that man is always alongside and along-with the world and
2. by separating, presupposing a distance, between man and the intelligible object which as an intellectual ob-ject can be investigated objectively and known independently of the soul. The question of the nature of the soul is logically independent of the question of the nature of an intellectual object.

Transcendence then constitutes man as both source and passion or as both activity and receptivity. It is both a projecting of intelligibility as the basis for a world and the submission to that objectivity as a conforming to the world. It is both a going out to the world and a bringing of the world into the soul. It is the co-inherence of the being of man and the being of the world.

While we do not yet deem it necessary to engage in a detailed comparison of St. Thomas and Heidegger, certain points of intersection should be made if only because it is Heidegger who has brought the notion of being-in-the-world to the forefront of much of contemporary philosophy.

Heidegger has made the following remark concerning the relationship between the human subject (Dasein) and the world:

As an *existentiale*, "Being alongside" the world never means anything like the Being-present-at-hand-together of Things that occur. There is no such thing as the "side-by-side-ness" of an entity called "Dasein" with another entity called "world". Of course when two things are present-at-hand together alongside one another, we are accustomed to express this occasionally by something like "The table stands 'by' ['bei'] the door" or "the chair 'touches' ['beruhrt'] the wall". Taken strictly, "touching" is never what we are talking about in such cases, not because accurate re-examination will always eventually establish that there is a space between the chair and the wall, but because in principle the chair can never touch the wall, even if the space between them should be equal to zero. If the chair could touch the wall, this would presuppose that the wall is the sort of thing "for" which a chair would be encounterable. An entity present-at-hand within the world can be touched by another entity only if by its very nature the latter entity has Being-in as its own kind of Being, only if, with its Being-there [Da-sein], something like the world is already revealed to it, so that from out of that world another entity can manifest itself in touching, and thus become accessible in its Being-present-at-hand. When two entities are present-at-hand within the world, and furthermore are worldless in themselves, they can never "touch" each other, nor can either of them "be" "alongside" the other.[63]

The almost complete correspondence between the view presented in such a passage and some of St. Thomas' ideas discussed should be unmistakable:

1. Unlike the material beings by which it is surrounded, the human subject (the embodied soul) stands out: so that through his soul a man is, in a way, all being or everything . . . able to assimilate or become all the forms of being.[64] The radical openness of the soul is that which separates it from the beings that surround it and thus posits a different kind of existence as well. Man is not "in" the world, nor is knowledge of the world "in" man in the same manner in which furniture is "in" a room. Material things can be said to be "in" something as that which contains them but man contains those things in which he is.[65] By means of the union of soul and body and by means of man's consequent cognitive presence in and to the world, he is found to be above and beyond the ontological calling of material beings although not beyond their call. Because the soul is on the confinium of spiritual and corporeal creatures . . . the powers of both meet in the soul ("*Et ideo penes huiusmodi differentias potentiae animae non distinguuntur*").[66] As embodied, man is on the horizon of Being; more, let us say that as incarnate man is the horizon of Being, and thus is open to infinite things, not "*determinari a natura vel determinatae existimationes naturales, vel etiam determinata auxilia.*"[67]

2. Because the soul's mode of existence is distinct from the beings that surround it, it requires different modes of being to reflect its *ontico-noetic*

relational being-with and toward the world. This fundamental difference in man is precisely that by virtue of which he is able to know the world, to have the world, to be the world.[68] The modern problematic from Descartes on acknowledges the difference in man but infers from it a fundamental disproportion making knowledge itself problematic, requiring substitute principles by which man can somehow negotiate and navigate the world he cannot know. This, again, is the difference between a positive and a negative finitude. St. Thomas' positive notion implies no cognitive disproportion, disengagement or isolation from the world. It is the very difference we have articulated that precludes or forecloses in advance and *ab origine* such disproportion, disengagement or isolation. The difference is the proportionality inherent in the very meaning of i*ntellectus* as an innermost knowledge, for *intelligere* is the same as *intus legere* (to read inwardly) for "*cognitio autem intellectiva penetrat usque ad essentiam rei.*"[69] This intellectual power flows from its immateriality, but the immateriality is not the intellect; rather it is the precondition of proportionality, of man's need and ability to know the world.[70]

3. The soul's understanding is actualized in knowledge, it does not first leap forth from some sealed center of subjectivity, but its "primary kind of Being," the very structure of the knowing subject as such is such that it is always outside alongside entities which it encounters and which belong to a world already discovered. Even when the intellect is actualized in knowing and determines the character of the object through a concept, even then it has not leaped forth from an inner sphere: the human subject is still in-the-world as knower, and the world is in the soul, under the soul's conditions, as known.

We must keep in mind the following tentative point of divergence in Thomistic and Heideggerian thought. For although St. Thomas and Heidegger claim being-in-the-world as the form, the vehicle and instrument of knowledge, their respective notions of intellect and of being-in-the-world amount to two vastly different polar accounts of the role and nature of transcendence. More precisely, in what way is man always outside, alongside entities which he encounters and which belong to a world already discovered? For St. Thomas the world is already discovered in the sense that the intelligible species have already been abstracted by the agent intellect and can now act as the material for any specific act of knowledge, any specific intentional act. Again for St. Thomas, the world is already discovered because the entities alongside which the human subject dwells and acts have been intelligibilized so that the soul can know them thematically, while the dwelling-acting stage is un- or pre-thematic, pre-cognitive in its mode of understanding. For both, the world has already been discovered; the soul is already in-the-world and alongside its objects: the soul is in a way all things. But is this soul for St. Thomas the same as Dasein?

To answer this question will involve the entire structure of the fourfold intentional presupposition, for it is that which sets St. Thomas apart from Heidegger, as it sets metaphysics apart from phenomenology or "fundamental ontology," because the dividing line between them is the problem of God or the role of the deity in philosophy.

Chapter 3

The Fourfold Reversals: The Displacement of Being-in-the-World

Now, in everyday life, the problem of putting a thing in its proper place is a comparatively simple one. It seldom amounts to more than putting it away always in the same place and remembering where it is. Not so in philosophy, where there is but one conceivable proper place for any given thing. Unless you find it, that thing is lost, not in the usual sense that it is not to be found where you expected it to be, but in the much more radical sense that it is no longer to be found anywhere. Out of its proper place, the thing simply cannot exist at all. For indeed, the place of each thing is determined there by its own essence, and unless you know first what the thing is you shall never be able to define its relations to what it is not.[1]

The goal of the earlier chapters was to lay bare the origins of intentional being-in-the-world by revisiting the essential components of the ground of metaphysics. The fourfold ontological structure, i.e., finitude, intentional presence, causality and *ananke stenai* provided the framework within which meaning reveals its faithful adherence to Being in order to become and maintain itself as meaningful. Each element, while conceptually distinct, was briefly shown to be, in actuality, one reality as the only way in which a genuine accord between thinking and being-in-and-to-the-world exists. The origin of this metaphysical framework purports the way as onto-theo-logical from its very beginning to its very end. The deity, the "*theo*," is not an adjectival attribute merely "picked up" along the *logos*-way of ontology; such would signal the possibility of discarding it and still retaining ontology as such. Instead, it is the central adverbial signate of man's finite need to be in accord with Being; itself it embodies the structure of truth as language ever desiring to catch-up to Being, to know what the experience of a life meant, to speak for a moment existentially. But laying bare the almost aphoristic fourfold in the ancients is not nearly enough to prove its irreducible centrality to and within being-in-the-world. Therefore, what must be sought is the essential confrontation over the ground of Being, shaking metaphysics as such to its core as either the primordial truth of Dasein or its greatest injustice.

Will the fourfold prove to be an empty edifice housing nothing more than conceptual distortions that say nothing of the originary appearances of Being? This is precisely the question-at-hand. The problem is, as Heidegger rightly sees it, the entrance of the deity into philosophy. Heidegger rejects causality and the *ananke stenai* because, for him, they represent the shift from ontology as such, i.e., Being *qua* Being, to beings artificially stripped of their finite *Ereignis* when ordered in terms of a highest Being *qua* God, onto-theology.[2] The repercussions of such a rejection are tremendous. A genuine examination of this rejection must not overlook either Heidegger's acceptance of the Husserlian notion of the phenomenon or his remarkable analysis of Kant's *Critique of Pure Reason*.[3]

Brief Discursus on Heidegger's Husserlian Influence

Heidegger's thought is clearly an attempt to restore the essence of man, *qua* meta-physical, to its original calling as the opening (clearing or place) for the manifestation of Being as Presence. As sheerly given presence, in its sheerly given totality, the essence of man would be at odds with the deity.[4] It is perhaps not yet clear to philosophers that this very attempt by both Heidegger and Husserl to re-situate man solely in the phenomenological appearance of Being is made within and on the basis of the same world created by modern thought in its inception; it was inherited by Husserl in his structural and original, transcendental, examination and given its most radical interpretation in Heideggerian thought.

Husserl inherited the uniquely and specifically modern world of the sheerly given totality of what-is, and reappropriated it (clarified, grounded and made our own) by way (*methodos*) of the *epoché*, through a pure, transcendental subjectivity, as a possibility.[5] For in order to comprehend and envelop the world, Husserl must willfully break contact with the world through employment of the reduction in order to establish contact with the constitutive framework of the world. The *epoché* was at heart an immanentized transcendence, and its pure possibility dislodged man from any genuine causal adherence to or relational dependency on the fourfold for his knowledge.

The essence of phenomenology as one of the truly great and perhaps final moments of modern thought is to be found within Husserl and, most uniquely, in Heidegger. In following, tracking or at least mapping their sometimes convergent, sometimes divergent paths through thought we can perhaps determine what it is that makes of phenomenology a movement of-and-within-thought, a genuine philosophy, and an authentic response to the world. In other words, let us see what constitutes its possibility. And far more importantly we shall see what phenomenology under the guidance of its masters does to-and-with-the-world. About phenomenology we must ask: How does it stand with Being?

The Phenomenological Ego: The Man Who Would Be King

Initially, Husserl considered the foundation of knowledge to reside in the original phenomena to which our concepts and ideas refer. But as his thought matured and quickened, and as the regions of phenomenology as a subject matter deepened, Husserl came to see human rationality not merely as an accidental and de facto ability of calculation and judgment but rather as an all-embracing, essentially necessary form belonging to all of what is now to be seen and known as transcendental subjectivity.[6]

> An obscure dissatisfaction with the previous way of grounding in all science leads to the setting of new problems and to theories which exhibit a certain self-evidence of success in solving them in spite of many difficulties that are unnoticed or . . . drowned out. This first self-evidence can still conceal within itself more than enough obscurities which lie deeper, especially in the form of the unquestioned, supposedly quite obvious presuppostions. . . . We can understand accordingly, that the history of transcendental philosophy first had to be a history of renewed attempts just to bring transcendental philosophy to its starting point. And above all, to a clear and proper self-understanding of what it actually could and must undertake.[7]

Now this clearly required a methodological conversion within the very historical movement of thought, one empowered by the Copernican "turn" from the unsophisticated and question-begging banalities of the naive-objective sciences and their unexamined world.[8] It was Descartes who planted the primal seed of transcendental philosophy,[9] in his Meditations as an attempt at an absolutely objectivistic grounding of philosophy through the apodictic ego.[10] But the meaning and import of the Cartesian cogito remained unclarified and ambiguous, becoming ultimately entangled within the nonsense of

a transcendental realism. Even Kant was unable to achieve the radical liberation from tradition required to penetrate to "the absolute subjectivity which
constitutes everything that is, in its meaning and validity, nor to the method
of attaining it in its apodicticity."[11] And even the new sciences born of the
Copernican Revolution lacked a proper self-comprehension and remained
instead solely within the status of *techne* (thus worldly), the ground of which
was essentially unknown. "The great transcendental philosophies did not
satisfy the scientific need for such self-evidence, and for this reason their ways
of thinking were abandoned."[12]

How then has phenomenology arrived at this transcendental starting
point of self-under-standing which was destined to remain beyond the
reach of Descartes and Kant and the later Idealists? What is it that constitutes for phenomenology its ground which enables and compels its radical
liberation from tradition? By tracing the nature of this phenomenological
starting point, and by uncovering its unique way of being the horizon of
Being, we will be brought face-to-face with the totality of Heideggerian fundamental ontology.

To begin with, Descartes and Kant fell short of the goal because they were,
according to Husserl, unclear about the very essence of their own reflective
moves. Modern thought prior to phenomenology merely posits the
world, its factical reality and its intelligibility, i.e., its scientific objectivity.
Never does it get beneath or beyond its own positional presupposition to the
very possibility of world-and-intelligibility itself. To the extent that the source
of such possibility precisely as possibility is not attained, the systems and
sciences involved must be contaminated by contingency and pseudo self-
evidence. It is left to the *logos* of transcendental subjectivity within itself to lay
claim to the "sole function of determining for itself what is possibly real purely
on the basis of what self-evidently appears to it."[13] Phenomenology grasps this
possibility, seizes it in, through, and by means of the *epoché* and reduction:

> The independent *epoché* with regard to the nature of the world as it
> appears and is real to me—that is, "real" to the previous and natural point
> of view—discloses the greatest and most magnificent of all facts: I and my
> life remain—in my sense of reality—untouched by whichever way we
> decide the issue of whether the world is or is not. . . . The phenomenologi-
> cal epoché . . . eliminates as worldly facts from my field of judgment both
> the reality of the objective world in general and the sciences of the world.
> Consequently, for me there exists no "I" and there are no psychic actions,
> that is, psychic phenomena in the psychological sense. To myself I do not
> exist as a human being, (nor) do my cogitationes exist as components of

my psycho-physical world. But through all this I have discovered my true self. I have discovered that I alone am the pure ego, with pure existence and pure capacities (for example the obvious capacity to abstain from judging). Through this ego alone does the being of the world, and for that matter, any being whatsoever, make sense to me and has possible validity. The world—whose conceivable non-being does not extinguish my pure being but rather presupposes it—is termed transcendent, whereas my pure being or pure ego is termed transcendental. Through the phenomenological epoché the natural human ego, specifically my own, is reduced to transcendental ego. This is the meaning of the phenomenological reduction.[14]

Now the *epoché*, as described by Husserl, is a very complicated, even delicate, notion. It is in one sense "a new way of looking at things" and this a (the) philosophic attitude or posture, "one that contrasts at every point with the natural attitude of experience and thought."[15] In another sense, the *epoché* is part and parcel of a method which appropriates the world through the *eidos* of primordial self-evidence-and-givenness in immediate, absolute, intuition.[16] Again, it is a total abstention from all previous philosophical theories and presuppositions.[17] Most crucially, the *epoché* is "the elaboration of a transcendental philosophy implying a genuine *metaphysical* decision concerning the ontological status" of the phenomena attained through its means.[18] Thus the *epoché* and reduction not only enable but even determine phenomenology to be an attitude or posture, and a method, and a science.[19] Because "transcendence" is put in question critically,[20] once the *epoché* has been employed we are left with the phenomenological residuum: the perception-*qua*-phenomenon, i.e., self-evident, purely and freely (absolutely) given presence under the form of intentional cognitive correlate. This is the residuum: the rest is de trop, and has been, as such, suspended, bracketed, ignored, refused. But now, what precisely has phenomenology suspended and refused admittance to? Most broadly, as we note in the passage above, the world in its existentiality, in its contingent and therefore dubitable worldly facticity. Of course, existentiality here refers only to the presential assumption (acceptance) "out there" of particular thing-substances (within-the-world), or to the totality of such thing-substances (the world), and this is exactly why it is suspended. Thus, with the general thesis of the world in its possible existence displaced, there must also be parenthesized the individual data of the world and the actual intentional referents *qua* actual, and this again because an existential referent *qua* existential is thoroughly irrelevant to the objectivity of the essential phenomenon which is, in this case, the phenomenological essence: the pure capacities of the ego. Remaining, *qua* phenomenon, is pure immanent activity:

> Consciousness in itself has a being of its own which in its absolute uniqueness of nature remains unaffected by the phenomenological disconnexion. It therefore remains over as a "phenomenological residuum," as a region of Being which is in principle unique, and can become in fact the field of a new science—the science of phenomenology.[21]

Not only does consciousness remain as a unique region of Being, but as absolute Being, unconditioned by any other being and thus the foundational source of absolute (free and underived) givenness,[22] it is a "self-contained system of Being . . . into which nothing can penetrate, and from which nothing can escape."[23] So understood, intentional referentiality becomes, and must remain, only a being-for-ego[24] (as it has continued to be for later, "non-idealistic" phenomenology), a being-for-ego in fact established, founded, and maintained, in a word, constituted, by the consciousness. The contingent world is now rooted. Thought is now a method because Being is now a system. An odd sort of finitude remains: as an ego I am dependent upon the very world I constitute! Intentionality is no longer the descriptive fact of existence; it is now an epistemological doctrine.

The Reduction: What Is It and Why Is It?

Are we able to say that the reduction is a procedure which can be employed independently of a more or less consciously explicit ultimate aim? What, in other words, is the original and abiding necessity for the reduction and the *epoché?* Wherein dwells the origin of its phenomenological requirement?

As early as 1907 Husserl was aware of the metaphysical impetus behind phenomenology. Because the natural attitude cannot authenticate and therefore justify itself by a critical, apodictic, a priori cognitional correspondence to an only allegedly existent, determining, objective world of nonnecessary things, such a naive posture is impotent in the face of the basic epistemological (critical) problems. What thought needs, with utmost and ownmost necessity, is a critical analysis of cognition.[25] And while it is true that phenomenology at this stage of its development is not engaged in an explicit idealistic endeavor, we must nevertheless be clear about its own self-conception, which is also its raison d'etre. True, Husserl has not developed the comprehensive doctrine of constitution which will enable-compel phenomenology to emerge as, and culminate in, an absolute transcendental idealism. But he does see phenomenology as the basis for a universal critique of cognition, in the service of a science of beings in an absolute sense:[26]

> This science, which we shall call metaphysics, grows out of a "critique" of the natural sciences which is based upon the insight into the essence of knowledge and into the distinctive basic forms of knowledge-objectivities (objects of knowledge) in the sense of the different fundamental correlations between knowledge and its objectivity won by the universal critique of knowledge.[27]

Indeed, we are aware of the necessity for critique within the more general awareness that natural cognition does not achieve an adequate comprehension of Being:

> Only epistemological reflection can produce the distinction between natural science and philosophy, and only through this reflection is it clear that the natural sciences of being are not the ultimate sciences of being. We require a science of being in an absolute sense.[28]

If a reflective epistemological critique stands in immediate service to a metaphysics of Being absolutely conceived, then phenomenology will stand in immediate service to that epistemological critique. Phenomenology is to establish the very need for and region of the absolute science of Being through its unveiling of the inadequacy of the natural attitude which, for Husserl, is both an epistemological and metaphysical doctrine. But in order to accomplish this, phenomenology must hold itself "purely to the task of clarifying the essence of knowledge and of being an object of cognition belonging to knowledge,"[29] i.e., remaining first in the service of critique, thus ignoring the metaphysical goals/conclusions of the critique, and this means abstaining from all questions concerning beings in an absolute sense.[30] That is to say, refusing all judgment concerning their ontological status as such, even to the extent of accepting their claims to existence at all. And herein rests the need for the *epoché*. It accomplishes the reduction of the world to sheerly given presential phenomenon-for-Ego, and does so in order to satisfy the conditions of (1) an independent and eidetic description of knowledge and of its objects and (2) a total and apodictic presupposition-less self-evidence. Taken in conjunction and phenomenology is able to provide the matter and method for an absolute science of being (metaphysics) which, for once and for all, is able to ground the very possibility of world.

While Heidegger has clearly rejected the second condition, clearly he has embraced the first.

In any event, it is quite clear, in the *Paris Lectures*, how phenomenology, so understood, is to deal with the world:

> We can no longer accept the reality of the world as a fact to be taken for granted. It is an hypothesis that needs verification. Does there remain a ground of being? . . . Is not "world" the name for the totality of all that is? Might it not turn out that the world is not the truly ultimate basis for judgment, but instead that its existence presupposes a prior ground of being? Here, specifically following Descartes, we make the great shift which, when properly carried out, leads to transcendental subjectivity. This is the shift to the ego cogito, as the apodictically certain and last basis for judgment upon which all radical philosophy must be grounded. . . . We can no longer say that the world is real—a belief that is natural enough to our ordinary experience—instead it merely makes a claim to reality . . . the entire concrete world ceases to have reality for me and becomes instead mere appearance. However . . . phenomena in themselves cannot be disregarded as mere "nothing." On the contrary, it is precisely the phenomena themselves which, without exception, render possible for me the very existence of both the reality and appearance. . . . I no longer judge regarding the distinction between reality and appearance. I must similarly abstain from any other of my opinions, judgments and valuations about the world, since these likewise assume the reality of the world. But for these, as for other phenomena, epistemological abstention does not mean their disappearance, at least not as pure phenomena. This ubiquitous detachment from any point of view regarding the objective world we term the phenomenological epoché. . . . Everything in the world, all spatio-temporal being, exists for me because I experience it, because I perceive it, remember it in any way, judge it, value, desire it, etc.[31]

And thus the world, unsurprisingly but dramatically enough, is interrupted, interrogated, arrested, suspended and reduced to the status of phenomenon, whose nature is to be purely presence-to-and-for-Ego. The *epoché* allows us to step behind the world and encounter the ultimate basis for judgment, the world-grounding cogito.

Given phenomenology's self-conception as the epistemological prolegomena to the absolute science of beings, thus requiring, as we saw, the *epoché* and reduction, we must see that intentionality can function only subsequent to the dual act of suspension and reduction-to-presence. Because Husserl sees epistemological critique as reflexive grounding and *noematic* founding he goes on to see cognition as purely infra-subjective, as a modification of and within subjectivity (so much so, in fact, that transcendence must ultimately be subsumed under immanence). And thus, what Husserlian intentionality does, as a function of the directly and immediately self-attained cogito, is to transform the world into constituted presence-for-cogito and, of itself, nothing more.[32] Functional intentionality in *actu*, that is to say in remembering, thinking, perceiving, judging, willing and the like, discloses the world as *noematic* correlate, as constituted inexistence.

To the thing itself, yes. "To the thing itself!" might cry a convinced phenomenologist. But the thing itself is the Self itself and nothing more. The world is an emission of consciousness, and as such fulfills certain necessary a priori conditions to which individuality and instantiation and actuality are perfectly irrelevant, thoroughly de trop.[33]

> We have a methodological insight which, next to the . . . reduction, is the most important in phenomenology: the ego, to use traditional language, possesses an enormous inborn a priori. . . . The actual facts of experience are irrational, but their form—the enormous formal system of constituted objects and the correlative formal system of their intentional a priori constitution—consists of an inexhaustibly infinite a priori. Phenomenology explores this a priori which is nothing other than the essence (Wesenform) of the ego *qua* ego, and which is disclosed, and can only be disclosed, by means of my own self-examination.[34]

Now again this Pure Transcendental Ego is no factual, historical, actual subjectivity. It is, so to speak, abstracted from history just as the world is abstracted, precisely, from existence, and for the same reasons. The Ego is an a-cosmic consciousness above this world because it is above any world. And this is the very core of Husserl's rejection of the Cartesian cogito. For it is exactly the unclarified groundless substantiality of the world (and the soul) that must be suspended in order to achieve apodictic grounding.[35] Phenomenology's task is to correct the theoretical imbalance between substantiality and self-evidence which Descartes left in the wake of his inadequate conception of subjectivity. This imbalance is the *negative disproportion* that must be overcome by immanentizing the transcendent world.

If modern thought, now revealed as Pure Phenomenology, reflects upon itself as the essence of thought and thus brings itself to perfect clarity in that reflection, it becomes ineluctably manifest that the reality of the world (the world as reality) and the existence of the world (the world as existence) quite simply do not and cannot emerge. And here precisely is the momentous advance beyond Descartes that constitutes phenomenology's inherent inevitability, given the world as conceived by modern Cartesian thought. For Descartes still requires a world as the matter upon and over which mathematical science could exercise its control as *techne*: thus the embarrassing problem of the causal bridge between cognition and *res extensa*. Phenomenology steps back and reappropriates that world through the *epoché*, dismissing the last vestiges of any in-itselfness beyond knowledge and beyond consciousness. What was a stumbling block for Cartesian Man is sheer folly to Phenomenological Man. Such remnants of existence are both stumbling blocks and folly. The reappropriation of the world is the self-appropriation of the Ego, "the return to the things themselves . . . a return of the cogito to itself, a return to the a priori of subjectivity."[36] There can thus be no phenomenology of causality. Heidegger will, as he must, follow Husserl here.

But there is still more. So autonomous, so aboriginal, so absolute (free) is the Ego that its concern with the origin of the world is, as noted above, both a-cosmic and a-historical. This is to say that it works through the history of the origin of the world (e.g., the Crisis) only to reveal the essential egological structures required for the emergence of any possible world at all in general. Phenomenology does not ask: What is the essence of this world? Rather, it asks: How is any world possible, what is the essence of World? The first question can not even be asked until the second question is answered. It is only on the way to its own self-constitution that the Ego tarries long enough to concern itself with the essence of what actually appears.

Phenomenology ostensibly began as a methodological apparatus—a tool— which could aid in the penetration of the fact of self-transcendence, which is the very mystery of knowledge. It was a way of examining the facts of our being-within-being, understood as the world.

Phenomenology has manifestly involved itself in a dual set of spiraling reductions. Internally considered, and from the reference of the object of thought, Husserl has reduced (1) transcendence to immanence, thus insuring the apodictic commensuration (fulfilled intention) of cogito and objectivity, (2) the world to the *Lebenswelt* as the primordial and ultimate source of meaning which, as reduced phenomenon, guarantees the impossibility of an existential metaphysics, (3) existence to the phenomenon (the methodological bottom line) thus limiting *noetic* analysis to the phenomenal objectivity inherent in a being-for-ego, and thereby freeing Reason for absolute penetration via constitution. Is Heidegger not a true disciple in his differently expressed adherence to these reductions?

Externally considered, from the point of reference of the phenomenological endeavor itself historically understood, Husserl has reduced intentionality from essential fact characterizing knowledge to a function of the cogito as the nonfactual, i.e., transcendental, *Eidos* characterizing thought: he has reduced man to the Form of his species (reason); reason to a mode of rationalism; philosophy to a science in quest of certainty. Has not the reduction precluded with perfect necessity any culmination other than some variant of rationalist idealism? Can the world, once reduced from existence to phenomenon (*Lebenswelt*) ever be or become more or other than the immanent, constituted, intentional *noema* required by the ideal of apodictic evidence? What has happened to its status as transcendent Other? Can it ever escape the sentence implicitly imposed, *ab origine*, of being sheer and constituted givenness-for-ego? Of being, in a word, both the prison and the prisoner of the cogito? Can human reason confront reality and demand from it apodictic evidence without remaking (reducing) the world to its own image? And indeed, what is that image? Is it not the reduction which makes of intentionality a function of its very antithesis, the cogito, thus forcing it into an unnatural role? Can we say that the reduction is at all epistemologically or onto-meta-physically neutral, rather than already a highly nuanced metaphysical de-cision, historically conditioned and placed? Are philosophy and science equivalents? Do knowledge and science follow the same rules, have the same structure, speak the same language?

Must reason be rationalist in order to safeguard human knowledge? Does the denial of Rationalism entail the affirmation of existential irrationality? Do we give up the claim to all knowledge when we give up the claim to absolute knowledge? Must reality have its source in human reason in order to be intelligible? Must a reality whose source is not in human reason be absurd? Or *noumenal*?[37]

Conclusion of the Discursus

Heidegger inherits this modern sheerly given totality and reappropriates it in a different manner through another *methodos*, but also phenomenologically. For in the new and fundamental ontology of Heidegger man dispenses with the pure and ontologically groundless transcendental subjectivity and thus takes the world as an existential matter of essentially metaphysical concern to actual *Existenz* in Dasein. In the forthcoming analysis of Heidegger's treatise on *Kant and the Problem of Metaphysics*, we will see how he utilizes the sheerly given totality to obtain a far more original result.

In sum, on the irrevocable basis of his radical methodological option, namely the absolutizing of the cogito beyond factical existent to an Essence,[38] and its resultant elevation to constitutive creator of the possibility of the world as possibility: on this basis Husserl is required to question (doubt) the truth of appearances or presences, i.e., the natural and naive attitude, and so to question in absolute detachment from the (essential) question of existence. But Heidegger's critique is not aimed at the truth of appearances as such in order to ground them in the primordial apodicticity of the transcendental Ego's mirrored self-reflection (the essence of which is precisely therefore constitution). Rather, his impulse is to attain the nonappearing essence of the appearing totality of what-is,[39] or, the Worldhood (Being) of the World, the presencing and essencing of Being, evoked necessarily from Nothing, as phenomenological phenomenon. Heidegger has brought the sheerly given into its phenomenological totality in Nothingness, because only there can Being engage its endless possibilities in a fundamentally ontological manner. Now as such phenomenon the non-apparent essence of being-in-totality is covertly prior-to-and-constituitive-of any possible conceptual or metaphysical reason, *intellectus et ratio*, and is therefore unattainable by or through such a rationality. The transition from Husserl to Heidegger takes us from Absolute Ontology to Fundamental Ontology, both understood and expressed phenomenologically. It is this transition that makes Heidegger the supreme and most formidable confrontation to the fourfold nature of metaphysics.[40]

Heidegger's Commentary on the Critique of Pure Reason:
Abyssus Abyssum Invocat

Within Heidegger's treatise on Kant's *Critique of Pure Reason* the origins of his problematic of Being as a problem are uncovered. While we return to it in a later section, some comments are in order at this introductory stage.

Heidegger finds in the first edition of Kant's *Critique of Pure Reason* an opening into the origin of *metaphysica generalis*, i.e., the meaning of Being *qua* Being, that must precede in primacy the sciences of *metaphysica specialis.* If the latter is to be proven a legitimate announcement of the various aspects of Being, it was for Kant necessary to rediscover the forgotten foundation of metaphysics, in fact to reground that foundation which alone can give man the parameters or measurements or limits or boundaries that essentially pertain to the nature of the foundation. If the foundation as "root Being" can be brought to the light of reason, then from its dimensions man can draw its relative ontological structure and begin to answer the question of the directional nature *qua* limits of ontology.[41]

Where must man begin his descent into the foundational ground of Being but in the world? If consciousness is always "consciousness of" because I am always, in knowing, the other as other, then the foundation is somehow wrapped up in the existential "mineness" as situated in and thereby dependent on the world for my knowledge. Both for Heidegger and St. Thomas finitude is the central component of man's intentional presence. If in advance one expects to find an original foundation autonomously absolute, independent of relational being-in-the-world and outside the grasp of finitude, then the regression to the origin of metaphysics will fail from the start.

Thus for the task at hand finitude will be our point of departure. But this starting point cannot be left behind along the way, for without it the way would obscure and then disappear all together. The question of the origin is at the same time a question of finitude. Because it carries the possibility of announcing Being in its most primordial sense, it is Originary. And as the point of contact, as well as the most profound division between Heidegger and St. Thomas, an analysis of the finite intentional presence at the origin of metaphysics will elicit the nature of *theo* in its real relatedness to the *ontos* and to the *logos*.

The kind of finitude that will serve as point of departure will be one intrinsically united to the other three aspects of the fourfold, so much so that uncovering the genuine foundation of metaphysics will depend upon the presence of this unity which is not a mere synthesis. Finitude enjoys the privilege of fundamental intentional correlate primarily because, beneath all aspects, it is man's intimate essence, i.e., it is the necessary prerequisite that allows him to extend his being via causality as an intentional presence to the *ananke stenai* in knowledge. Finitude can be considered either to be the stumbling block to knowledge or the very vehicle of transcendence. This is the difference between a negative and a positive finitude.

A positive finitude asserts man's dependence upon Being for all his knowledge, but presupposes thereby the ability to know Being. A negative finitude sees man's finite condition as an impediment to knowledge, a separation from Being or, in a word, in-dependence, with all the dangerous epistemological, moral, metaphysical and religious implications of that independence. This seemingly modest position, almost a skepticism, installs man at the center and primacy of the world, and triggers the search for some surrogate mechanism for intentionality by which I can navigate a world I cannot know. Thus: the a priori, the cogito, innate ideas, the "as if," the pragmatic theory of truth, existentialist engagement: what are these but substitutes for that for which there are no substitutes?

Nevertheless, Heidegger sees in Kant's Idealism a strange phenomenon, a reversal of sorts—a negative finitude that is both productive and yet the basis of transcendence. Whereas Kant would later deem this unacceptable to the construction of a metaphysic of pure knowledge and amend his thoughts in the second edition of the *Critique,* Heidegger sees in Kant's early thought and in his subsequent recoil an essential truth about the origin of meta-physics and of Being as such.[42] For Heidegger this so-called negative finitude is need in its basic originality; for him it is a more positive finitude precisely because its transcendence-as-need disallows the possibility of an onto-theo-logic orientation for Dasein. This notion of reversal of the funda-mental categories of metaphysics is fundamental to our understanding of the origin of Being.

Heidegger has indeed pinpointed a precise moment in the history of Western thought that cannot be overlooked. Kant's reversal transfers the properties once housed in a positive finitude, formation and transcend-ence to a negative finitude, a thereness that cannot procure a *logos*-way from man to world to God. This finitude is a phenomenologically grounded transcendence that does not depend upon causality and the consequent *ananke stenai* and thereby doesn't reach anything fundamen-tally beyond where it began in the Dasein of man. But whereas Heidegger sees in this a momentous advance, I believe this reversal is a serious offense against the meaning of finitude. Its effects are evident in modern and postmodern thought, but perhaps most profoundly in Heidegger. If indeed by Idealism is meant only the system constructs of Schelling, Fichte and Hegel, then Heidegger is by no means an Idealist, and to view him as such would neglect a body of work that has moved the finitude of transcendence outside the conceptual constraints of a systematic deontology. But as absurd as the following proposition may seem, it must, if we are to get to the source of things, be asked: Is there a preformation or horizon of Idealism even before the system, and has Heidegger perhaps grounded his anti-causal and anti-theological ontology in its roots?

Where Kant recoiled in the second edition of the *Critique*, Heidegger proceeds. Where has it taken him? If indeed metaphysical finitude is one aspect of a fourfold metaphysical unity, then this reversal into noncausal finitude must affect each of the other constituents. The presence of this finitude does not coexist with but annihilates the former finitude's onto-theo-logical necessities. While the fourfold guided our earlier analysis of classical intentional being-in-the-world, its undermining, the fourfold reversal, must be clarified in order to understand the decisive changes that gave rise to Heidegger's ontology. A preliminary outline of the fourfold corresponding reversals are:

1. *Finitude—In the fourfold*: finitude faces and is appropriated by the foundation as No-thing. This No-thing has its theological *telos* in the *ananke stenai.*

In the fourfold reversal: Nothingness confronts and overwhelms finitude. This nothingness is the absence of any theological *telos*; it is the abyss that never reaches a stop either in the order of explanation or in the order of Being. *Abyssus abyssum invocat.*

2. *Causality—In the fourfold*: Language plays "catch-up" to Being in the *noetic* act.

In the fourfold reversal: Thinking constitutes Being. The structure of "catch-up" dissolves and with it the existential independence of Being. In fact, causality as a viable notion is *dependent* upon this "transcendence" which imposes upon the phenomena a causal template. If causality survives at all it is dependent upon this finitude and transcendence which impose upon phenomena an a priori or pragmatically hypothetical causal template.

3. *Intentional Presence—In the fourfold*: the act of to-be gives essence its existence. This structure alone announces the finite need as positive and active as a necessary dependency that enables knowledge, not a deficiency that must be overcome.

In the fourfold reversal: the loss of the primacy of existence over essence to an essentialized deontology will be key to understanding the formation of Idealism and an antimetaphysical phenomenology that ultimately cannot maintain a positive finitude.

4. *Ananke stenai—In the fourfold*: the origin is an Uncaused cause.
In the fourfold reversal: a self-caused cause. This subtle shift from "un" to "self" is the capstone of all the reversals extruding and alienating the deity from ontology. This reversal is linked most acutely to the intentional presence reversal, to the primacy of essence over existence. All these rever-

sals in their most original inauthentic mode provide the ground in which a phenomenologically reduced lived-world can thrive.

Nothing or "No-thing"?

Classically understood, finitude is the recognition of our utter, unfailing, enabling dependency on the world for all our knowledge. Dependency is still at the heart of modern finitude but not as a genuine positivity.

Finitude must now be overcome in order to know. Dependency is now alienation.[43] It is a disabling condition. This is most readily apparent in the absolutist systems where, in order to reconcile finitude and the infinite, man truly becomes the center of all things effectively extending finitude to encompass the world, thereby maintaining but at the same time rendering the distinction between the infinite and the finite meaningless. Because man becomes the sole meaning-giver in the world, he becomes its originator. In the end, this finitude negates man's dependency on anything for his knowledge and the genuine primacy of God is lost as the ontological center of otherness.

But this is only the result of the reversal. What exactly is the point of origin of the finite reversal in terms of finitude itself? If the question of finitude resides in the nature of dependency and limitation then these signal adherence to something Other. But if Heidegger has resolved his ontology in the origins of Idealism prior to a system, we cannot merely say that his primordial Idealism neglects otherness and leave it at that. In the origins of his Idealism there must still be adherence but not to an Absolute and not to something that can lead anywhere and most certainly not to God. Perhaps we could say that he seeks to retain adherence but rejects its fundamental meaning as an adherence to, i.e., as a causal co-inherent reciprocity: the connection between the adherent to its adherence in terms of their union pointing toward another greater Other.

For Heidegger, at the horizon of Dasein's disclosive possibility is adherence to otherness *qua* nothingness. This "Nothing," understood more primordially than the Kantian *noumenon*, is the abyss. But this Nothing is not the causal No-thing of metaphysics. This Nothing is precisely that which persistently eludes the correlative inferences that make the meta No-thing a reference to and adherence to God. The former is man in the facelessness of nothingness, rather than man in the face of No-thing as Other. The latter No-thing is the clearing for the theological capacity of ontology, the

Heideggerian Nothing is a denial of *telos*; it is the font of the phenomenological thereness that situates man in the world of appearances. Ultimately,
can it really give meaning to man if this Nothing by virtue of its bottomless-
ness collapses the distinction between appearances and the thing (as end)
in-itself? Heidegger's intent was to ground man in the groundless thereness
of the appearance-aspect of the world, but because he reduced the dependency to an abyss of Nothingness rather than to a No-thing *qua* Other, this
conception ultimately leads to the absence of otherness and of ground. In
a word, Heidegger's Nothing is "other" than man but it is not the Other
that allows for genuine accountability, especially including moral accountability in the world, and therein resides his preformational Idealism.[44] This
Nothing's impenetrability leaves open for man the possibility and vulnera-
bility of assuming the stance of sole meaning-giver. Not perhaps in the
Kantian manner of approaching nature not as a pupil but as an appointed
judge who compels answers to questions of his own formulation (*Critique of
Pure Reason*, Bxiii). Heidegger rather seems to pick up the Kantian freedom,
which must be deontological precisely in order to be free.

What does this reversal of finitude entail for the other three elements
of the fourfold? We can concretize their reversals in the systems of modern
thought, and also find in them their pre-systematic primordiality.

Causality begins in Being, i.e., language through causal knowledge
must "catch-up" to Being. In the Kantian reversal causality is grounded in
the ego of "I think" that accompanies all experience. Thought needn't catch
up to Being, at least phenomenal Being, at all. It is here that the pupil-judge-
witness applies. This reversal of causality grounded in the ego doesn't even
maintain the notion of catching-up. Being must "catch-up" to thought insofar as thought conditions and forms Being. The signification of the Same is
for thinking as for Being is at issue here. It is one thing to say thinking must
adhere to Being, in which case there is an existential distinction between
thought and Being. This is not merely to say that I cannot separate meaning
from Being, for this holds true for St. Thomas as well as for Heidegger. For
both, I am a conscious intentional being, and when I ask the question of
Being, it is the same as asking the question of the meaning of Being.
But there is a fundamental difference between starting in the being of the
world and starting with the ego. It is an entirely different thing to say that
Being is reducible to or adheres to thought. The inseparability here between
thought and being in the meaning-structure of intentional existence
signifies that there is no real existential difference between the two, they are
one and the same. But that inseparability is the crucial signate of finitude, of
our dependency on Being for our knowledge. This unites St. Thomas Aquinas

to both Parmenides and Plato. Man cannot be separated from Being, because if he were he would not only not know, he would not meaningfully be man at all.[45]

Antimetaphysical Ontology and the Loss of the Intentional Presence

For Heidegger Kant's finitude, situated in the transcendental imagination, was an essential truth about the nature of being-in-the-world, rendering a decisive conclusion to the laying of the foundation of metaphysics in its limit, scope or directionality. The transcendental imagination, the source-origin of pure knowledge as "the intrinsic possibility of the essential unity of metaphysics,"[46] is the most primordial kind of time, and finitude, the temporal structure which temporalizes its meaning, is intrinsically bound to man. Through this structure of transcendental imagination and its primordial relationship to finitude, Heidegger conceived of a metaphysical transcendence that leads not to the classical deified origin *qua* end, but an "ontology accomplished as the disclosure of transcendence i.e., the subjectivity of the subject."[47] For him, the origins of *metaphysica generalis* and its limits are found in Dasein *qua* time: "is it not necessary to conclude that the ego is so temporal that it is time itself and that only as such in its very essence is it possible at all?"[48] Heidegger sees the original horizon of metaphysics as phenomenologically situated and temporally structured.

What is at stake is the need to clarify the mode of inauthenticity that has formed Heidegger's antimetaphysical ontology. Whereas Heidegger traces metaphysics as inevitably leading to Idealism, I contend that without a genuine metaphysics otherness cannot be maintained, and the result is Idealism and its most original formulation is Heideggerian thought. He is not the first idealist, but he is the thinker who has taken this mode of inauthenticity to its roots (not to its architectonic heights) utilizing it far beyond the system and its products.

For what reason would Heidegger embrace a primordial Idealism? What has been opened for questioning so far in our treatment of finitude and causality is the nature of existence that arises from their reversals. If Heidegger's goal is to rid ontology of its deity, what must Being be so that it can provide to Dasein a disclosive framework that excludes this possibility? In the final two of the fourfold reversals, *ananke stenai* and intentional presence, this becomes clear.

The intentional presence in the fourfold reflects the position or situatedness of the privileged finite being who participates in the formation of the meaning of Being. This does not mean that man constitutes being, but that he constitutes his knowledge of Being. But to constitute in knowledge the meaning of Being does not mean merely to read off a succession of events from a solely receptive position. To participate in the formation of the meaning of Being requires finitude as a dependency based on an actuality. Finitude is understood as limit, but to be the vehicle of transcendence, it mustn't be a deprivation rendered insurmountable. Finite need is realized in the act of to-be, and that act is grounded in the ever-actualization of man becoming the other as other in and toward the world. The structure of the intentional presence that forms but does not constitute Being can only exist when the act of to-be gives essence its existence rather than the reverse. In this capacity the intentional presence is a positive expression of finite need. Man is a complete ontological unity who has an active need to move knowingly toward its own completion. He does not constitute the being of the world nor is he stripped of the possibility of participating in Being nor relegated to a waiting for the world to inform him. This is St. Thomas. How the intentional presence can be both complete structurally and in need depends entirely on the structure of the act of to be.

There are two fundamental ways of looking at the problem of Being and essence where Being is understood as the act of to be. Either essence is a mode of to be or to be is a mode of essence. How one decides that priority will determine one's understanding of Thomistic intentional being-in-the-world. "Since they represent irreducibly distinct modes of causality, essence and existence are irreducibly distinct, but the reality of their distinction presupposes their composition, that is, it presupposes the actual reality of the thing. Existence is not distinct from essence as one being from another being; yet in any given being, that whereby a being both is and actually subsists is really other than that whereby it is definable as such a being in the order of substantiality."[49] Thomas holds essence as a mode of to be. If a being is understood only as a fully developed essence of a certain kind, for instance an individual, then there is no ontological, unifying, constitutive role for the act of being (actual existence) to play. If indeed being is a mode of essence everything that is necessary is already in place; existence then has no global role to play.

If everything that is necessary is already in place, the framework of existence would frustrate the meaning of and need for a genuine causality which not only allows but requires the cartographical mapping and detective tracking and tracing[50] of existential meaning by man. The intentional presence would be only at most/best a presence in a phenomenological thereness within what is always but only at-hand, the revelation of a self-supporting appearance. In a word, man could not be an *intentio*. He would be unable to participate meaningfully in the degrees of Being because these degrees would have no bearing on existence which is only phenomenologically "there" precisely because every essence is necessary and already in place. The intentional presence whose active need is fully active in the analogy of Being would disintegrate into the merely descriptive potentials of Being, or into an endless wait, or into a self-constituted actuality.

If on the other hand essence is a mode of to be, then to be plays the total role in the existence of any actually existing thing as the origin of its driving force or active need. St. Thomas' active need of the intentional presence is like the affinity of the soul for the body, "the need that the soul has to plunge itself into sensible matter by means of sensible organs in order to receive knowledge and truth from such a lowly source."[51] As it plunges it transcends by and through this active need, becoming the other as other. Only in the existential act of Being where everything is perhaps prefigured upon the act of to-be, but not already in place, can man be a complete ontological unity that is at the same time moving (*intentio*) toward his highest good. When existence became a realm to be intuited rather than the ground of knowledge, the last of the fourfold reversals (*ananke stenai*) is brought into light.

Ananke Stenai and the No-thing: A Response to the Self-caused Cause?

When the *Ananke stenai* and its uncaused cause were lost to the essentialist self-caused cause the degeneration of a genuine theological ontology was accomplished. We can understand the differences between these two original causes through the nature of their demonstrations. When the demonstration of the highest existence begins in the material order in something that can not account for itself, and ends in something (No-thing) that doesn't need to account for itself by means of the *ananke stenai*, it is the uncaused cause that is arrived at. The self-caused cause, while in some respects it begins in something that can't account for itself ends with something that does, namely the idea of a highest self. Beginning in Descartes, it blossoms in Spinoza and Schelling.

The subtlety of this shift from "un" to "self" by no means reflects a mild innocuous change. Because the latter ends in self, the existence of all things, from beginning to end, is bound up in the ego of consciousness, and thereby demands that the world ultimately be a product of consciousness. But when the origin doesn't need to account for itself, it first affirms the reality or existential independence of the world as distinct from man, and then further affirms the distinction or privilege of his being as the finite intentional presence who can participate in the formation of the meaning of Being because he does not constitute it. In a word, a self-caused cause, no matter how high or distant this "self" is postulated, is always possible to be immanentized into the domain of consciousness as its own or as its product and the move to Idealism is thus, if not inevitable, at least predictable.

All the reversals lead to the loss of the deity found most acutely in the meaning of *ananke stenai.* What is lost in this final reversal is the nature of an origin as outside the domain of explanation but not beyond thought, i.e., as the possibility for the origin to ground man's knowledge of his being and of Otherness. It points thought in its directional end *qua* origin. This differs fundamentally from the Heideggerian abyss. The former's No-thingness is teleological, the latter identifies concealment with the essential nature of Being leaving it sufficient for man to remain in the homelessness of dwelling in this unknown.

Heidegger does not outwardly purport a self-caused cause. But his rejection of the matrix of knowability of an uncaused cause reached as an end in the order of explanation and therefore of Being, leaves him, in the end, with little alternative. His primordial Idealism seeks not to find the cause but the fundamental thereness, an in-dwelling in the endlessness of concealment and unconcealment. This endlessness, when concretized or thematized cannot avoid the essentialist self-originating, self-contained cyclicity of an Idealistic self-caused cause.

Paradoxical as it may sound the essentialist structure wherein everything is already said and done does not require or permit an end in the order of explanation, rather it allows the thematization of the endlessness of the phenomena in terms of self-constituted knowability. The systematic Idealists are unlike Heidegger who, influenced by Nietzsche, still acknowledges the mystery of Being. Unfortunately his primal mode of inauthenticity doesn't recognize the "un" that allows the mystery to permeate existence and not be subsumed by the ego. Because concealment has no primacy over the unconcealed the two continually resolve themselves in each other, and thus concealment cannot be the equivalent of the mystery of the "un" that doesn't need to account for itself. Heidegger is in a unique position: in one sense he needed to claim a region of Being where everything is already said and done in order for the phenomena of appearances to suffice for being-in-the-world, but he also needed to retain the concealed as concealed. But rejecting the causality of Being that leads to the uncaused concealed cause, Heidegger cannot sustain the region of "already said and done" as the mysterious origin of the concealed-and-unconcealed. His rejection of causality (and his acceptance of the Husserlian phenomenon) inevitably lead to the concretized/systematic endlessness of the essentialist/Idealist self-caused cause.

The perpetual endlessness of the concealed and unconcealed when placed in a system speaks nothing more than that everything is done, everything is known, nothing can be placed as end. What was once concealed is nothing more than that which will become unconcealed and thereby known. In a word, within the essentialized structure where everything is already said and done, all that is left are projections of the self by the self that can never get outside the self. In this endless cyclicity of the self, there can be no end in the order of explanation.

If there is no *ananke stenai*, i.e., no uncaused cause, then there is no mystery *qua* positive finitude which is necessary in order to drive a genuine causality to its origins. That is why, in the endlessness of a phenomenologically self-centric projection, a "*theo*" inserted into the realm of ontology would indeed be a founded notion. "Un" is the crucial signate of man's existential direction, it reveals to man that for him something is always left undone or unfinished in his being-in-the-world. This sense of un-finished being is not a deficiency but his finitude as active need. The fourfold is the completed expression of man's twofold nature as (1) in knowledge, unfinished and (2) in Being, a complete unity. Man is un-finished and also paradoxically a complete unity precisely because of the intrinsic activity of this active need. This activity means man is prefigured upon a unity in Being that doesn't need to explain its existence and as such he is first in an ontological sense an actual being toward his completion, rather than a possible or potential this or that that is never complete but only at best contained as a self. In a word, man needs to "catch-up" to Being and must reach an end in the order of explanation, a reality which doesn't account for its existence, in order that he may know himself as existent. This is why all along ontology has had its deity.

Heidegger has by no means forsaken the mystery of Being; in fact he has done more to keep its reverence alive than most contemporary thinkers. If Heidegger's primordial Idealism has a self-caused cause at its origins it is by no means in Hegel's sense of the progress of mind or spirit consisting in the advance of self-consciousness.

And if he has confused his finitude with nothingness, collapsed the distinction between thinking and Being, and reduced existence to essence, the reasons for the implementation of these reversals at the core of our analysis can not easily be explained. The question of the possibility of Heidegger having a primordial pre-systematic Idealism must be phrased again as such: If Heidegger's goal is to rid ontology of its deity, what must Being be so that it can provide to Dasein a disclosive framework that excludes this possibility? And in a structure where everything is already said and done, wouldn't a phenomenological lived-world finally have its greatest freedom at the cost of reversing the meaning of freedom into resolve in the face of Nothingness?

These shifts are all there in the most original manner constituting the Heideggerian homelessness. Fundamentally, each reversal allows for the possibility of separating ontology from its theological foundation and direction and then making the appearance of the deity look as if it is an alien imposition. And yet, each reversal comes with the price of the thematized loss of otherness. But Heidegger himself is not looking for a thematic account of Being. Rather, he is striving for thought to resolve itself in the primordial thinking about Being before the advent of any such thematization, in a prelapsarian sense before philosophy. The essential confrontation with Heidegger is perhaps not played out in philosophy but in somewhere "other," somewhere else. Perhaps it is in Plato's thicket of nonbeing. Our confrontation with Heidegger, in order to be an essential confrontation must extend as far or as near to the end of philosophy and ask the questions at hand:

1. Is metaphysics like any other system because it is a conceptual thematization? Can there be a thematic understanding of Being that does not construct a system? Does every thematization of Being lead to the loss of Being because Being escapes all such possibility? Is the Christian God another mere God of the philosophers in Pascal's sense?
2. Has Heidegger reached the end of philosophy? Can he even remain in the pre-thematic pre-lapsarian dwelling of Being if he denies the possibility of a thematic movement in reference to man, who is the privileged being-in-the-world? Is this perpetual in-dwelling sans the theological retrieval a genuine mode of being-in-the-world for the finite intentional presence?

Heidegger sees in modern metaphysics its inevitable outcome in Idealism, but in truth his reversals lead to the same conclusion. In order to get to the problem of the deity within being-in-the-world an analysis of *Being and Time,* together with its companion treatise *Kant and the Problem of Metaphysics,* will provide us not only with the inevitable results of every thematization of Being but clarify the origin of Being in its relatedness to man as the possibility or impossibility of a thematic encounter as such.

Two Opposite Approaches to Finitude: Heidegger and St. Thomas Aquinas

St. Thomas and Heidegger both agree that finitude carries the privilege of fundamental intentional correlate because beneath all interrelations it is man's intimate essence as the necessary prerequisite allowing him to extend his being-in-and-to-the-world into knowledge. In a word, "the laying of the foundation of metaphysics is rooted in the question of finitude of man in such a way that this finitude itself can first become a problem."[52] But because the originary nature of man's intentional experience in-and-to-the-world is called into question as either phenomenologically noncausal or metaphysically causal, what it means to be finite, the what-it-is of finitude must first be examined.

For both St. Thomas and Heidegger, the meaning of Being *qua* Being for the finite being is grasped only through transcendence, so much so that the problem of finitude is equally the question of transcendence.[53] But the way in which finitude and transcendence are one movement of man's being is equally the problem-at-hand. For both St. Thomas and Heidegger it is true to say:

1. Finitude enjoys the privilege as the primary intentional signate of being-in-the-world-meaningfully and
2. finitude is primordially linked to transcendence; they are not two elements one of which overcomes the other in the process of knowledge but come-into-being as an original unity in order for man to have knowledge. *Transcendence is not a result but a precondition.*

These two points of agreement have uncovered also the chasm of difference, wherein lies the source of contention surrounding the fourfold intentional presupposition: if finitude is necessarily linked to transcendence, then finitude has an irreducible and inherent directionality. If ontology does have, as Thomas asserts and Heidegger denies, a fundamental theological calling or direction then the only way this is to be shown is by uncovering the way in which finitude is attached to transcendence. The way in which finitude is attached to transcendence prescribes the limit, parameter, framework and structure of man's being-in-the-world and thereby outlines the way of man as a teleological being: a way which is necessarily onto-theo-logical.

Heidegger has charged metaphysics with a neglectful passing over *ens finitum*. For him, this neglectful passing over of Dasein's possibilities fully to appropriate itself in-time results in the entrance of the deity as the distant-eternal reference point to which man must adhere in order to be a complete ontological unity.[54]

Without at this point challenging Heidegger's interpretation of Christian anthropology (which will have to await our reading of St. Thomas), we can say that for Christian Philosophy finitude is the vehicle of transcendence, whereas for Heidegger with his extrusion of the deity it must be conceived as and only as transcendence itself. If finitude is seen as transcendence, then transcendence itself is finite and not, as St. Thomas understands, open to the infinite.[55] To clarify this point, finitude and its relation to transcendence cannot be, for Heidegger, a unity that moves man beyond man, it cannot purport an end in the order of explanation that augurs the divine. The way in which finitude attaches itself to transcendence must, for Heidegger, preclude the possibility of a movement that injects the theological into the midst of the ontological. But this kind of onto-*noetic* movement invested in and delimited by the theological is the very stop in the order of explanation. For Heidegger, finitude can only exist finitely without any adherence to an *ananke stenai*.[56]

The endlessness of the phenomenon leads us to ask the question of how finitude adheres to Being unless Being itself is equally endless. The need to clarify the nature of man's attachment in-and-to-the-world for his knowledge has been problematic since the very beginnings of philosophy. In the *Poem of Parmenides* and in *Plato's Parmenides*, the presence of an infinite regress was indicative of this difficulty. The discussion of the nature of the Is as necessarily being something and not nothing gave rise to the meaning of attachment. That there must be "something" that is not within the natural order of things, in order for that order to be intelligible became of prime importance to our understanding of intentional-being-in-the-world. It was by virtue of man's finite-need, his ability to recognize the need for an end in the order of explanation, that things could be genuinely attached in the meaning-structure of existence. Only because man recognizes his finite need can he avoid an infinite regress as the annihilation of meaning, wherein the meaning-structure of language playing catch-up to Being loses sight of its end. We discovered that the One's primacy must be ontological; it is not the parts that determine the whole to be One or Whole. Rather, the parts must have a genuine dependency on some no-"thing" outside and independent of their composite whole that forces them both to be as many and yet to possess individual unity. Reaching this end, knowledge is achieved but attached with the radical understanding of our utter dependence on that end or formation or enclosure for our knowledge. *Implied both in Parmenides and Plato, as Heidegger well knows, is that Being cannot endure Otherness unless it is both self identical and causal.*

But with Heidegger there is a wholly different echelon of problems to be resolved with regard to man's adherence or attachment to Being. Heidegger, again, sees finitude as the core of man's correlative possibilities with and in the world. And because for him finitude is connected to transcendence, the latter thereby necessitates an involved adherence or attachment to something Other as irreducible. He understands most profoundly a kind of attachment or adherence belonging all the way down into the primordial depths of Dasein's existence. But he has secured his adherence and attachment in a noncausal Other, which has left him stranded in the same endlessness of the infinite regress and with an artificial Other.

The way in which finitude attaches itself to transcendence must, for Heidegger, preclude Dasein from the necessity of conjuring the theological out of fundamental ontology. For him, the "as" that connects or rather identifies finitude with transcendence purports a kind of primal "thereness" within the structure of Dasein. And "as" there, Dasein's finitude is then not based on a need for the deity but for a need to account for the primal manifestation of the Self in the face of Nothing, a need that moves him into his possibilities as Dasein.

Heidegger's Self cannot be reduced to the constructed self of any systematized deontology. He understands that it is precisely the Other's irreducibility which allows finitude "as" transcendence to be there in existence. Rather, it is the way in which his Other is irreducible that perhaps leads him down the road to primordial Idealism and into the endlessness of an infinite regress. The way of Dasein's existential Self is rooted in Care.[57] In Care, Dasein comes face-to-face with interrogating the whole constitution of its Being which is always "existing as the possibility of nullity."[58]

Dasein's finite need as transcendence adheres to an otherness that is not the causal No-thing of metaphysics: "The phenomenon of Care in its totality is essentially something that cannot be torn asunder, so any attempts to trace it back . . . will be unsuccessful."[59]

Ultimately, Heidegger's otherness *qua* nothingness is so irreducible, an abyss of such impenetrable endlessness, that through Dasein's attachment or adherence to it man cannot help but be situated in the thereness of his own Self as being-in-the-world wherein "finitude consists in the reception of that which offers itself."[60] Dasein seems to be constituted in its selfhood by the other but is in fact self-constituted.

"The laying of the foundation as the projection of the intrinsic possibility of metaphysics is necessarily a letting become effective of the supporting power of the established ground,"[61] and at this stage we must not lose sight of the serious possibility that traditional metaphysics has become so rigid in its "correctness" over *a-letheia* that it has suppressed or missed the meaning of finitude. The difference between finitude in the face of Nullity or of the No-thing will demonstrate the true fullness of the fourfold presupposition in its tradition and in its reversals.

Finitude: Nullity or No-thing?

The onto-logical directionality of Dasein's finitude as transcendence is best described as an implanting in the "there" which is already "there." This notion of implanting the Being of the Self in the "there" that is already "there" explains the other reversals within the fourfold. This "implanting" is made possible by the appeal of Otherness as nullity which finite transcendence adheres to or attaches itself to for its knowledge as Self:

> The appeal calls back by calling forth: it calls Dasein forth to the possibility of taking over, in existing, even that thrown entity which it is; it calls Dasein back to its throwness so as to understand this throwness as the null basis which it has to take up into existence. This calling-back in which conscience calls forth, gives Dasein to understand that Dasein itself—the null basis for its null projection, standing in the possibility of its Being—is to bring itself back to itself.[62]

This appeal is not a mere projection of the self that returns to the self; in such a system everything is openly reducible to the self. But is it this nonreciprocal abyss of the unknown, particularly in its unrelenting irreducibility, that possibly annihilates Heidegger's finitude, making him the most meaningful Idealist? The irreducibility of Heideggerian Nullity is not the same as the irreducibility of the *ananke stenai;* the latter's irreducibility doesn't leave it outside the penetration of knowledge. It is the precondition of knowledge and the end in the order of explanation that allows for thinking to "catch-up" to Being. This metaphysical irreducibility enables a fundamental reciprocity between man and Otherness: this reciprocity invites man to exercise his active need for the divine by his becoming the other as other. For Heidegger, what makes the nullity irreducible and its irreducibility existentially null is that it offers nothing to Dasein but the Fact that Dasein is "there." With this Fact, can Dasein become the other as other? Can Being tolerate or endure let alone enjoy Otherness without causality?

Heidegger's nullity is not mere privation, but nor is it causal. What it is is utterly non-relational, something like the compounded weight of Dasein's Being-towards-Death. "As the non-relational, death individualizes, but only in such a manner that, as the possibility which is not to be outstripped, it makes Dasein, as Being-with, have some understanding of the potentiality-for-Being of Others. . . . The certain possibility of death, however, discloses Dasein as a possibility, but does so only in such a way that in anticipating this possibility, Dasein makes this possibility possible for itself as its ownmost potentiality-for-Being."[63] The nullity of Being is most acutely manifested in the nullity of Death, which must be taken up as the finitude of being-in-the-world.

Can this non-relational origin offer man a genuine otherness or does it, through Dasein's anticipation of this non-relational possibility, only make possible its ownmost potentiality-for-Being and Nothing more? To detect the presence of Idealism, when what is presented so far is both without a system and with an adherence to something Other, seems at first absurd. But if we examine what it means to have otherness and what Heidegger intends by fundamental ontology, the possibility of such a primordial Idealism comes to the forefront of our discussion. Heidegger's predicament was to identify Being *qua* Being with otherness, but only if this otherness was divested of any theological implications. The problem is, what kind of otherness sustains itself as irreducible but isn't theological? Furthermore, what kind of irreducibility gives man the reciprocity of being-in-and-to-the-world meaningfully? Whereas the *ananke stenai* maintained the fundamental distinction between thinking and Being because the same is for thinking and for Being, and because in and through it thinking follows upon the trail of Being, can a Null basis possibly provide the same framework? Can there even be a "catch-up" without causality?

Dasein's finitude as transcendence situates man in-the-world but not in such a way that he must navigate degrees of Being outside himself in order to know. As being-in-the-world, Dasein is rather "there" in its-Self.

Heidegger has recognized that by wresting away from finitude the idea of it as a "vehicle" and replacing it with the notion of a Factical thereness, he has placed upon Dasein the disclosure of its own *solus ipse*. For him this reversal of finitude as compounded by nullity, rather than a reaching to-the-end as No-thing, is not a concession to any kind of Idealism, but this is not enough to satisfy us. We must see if he can maintain, via the Null basis, the meaning-structure wherein otherness and finitude thrive together primordially. This first reversal has laid the predicate for understanding

the other three reversals and the reason why Heidegger has imple-
mented them. In sum, this first reversal is as such: for St. Thomas,
through finite transcendence, man as intentional presence must reach the
end in the order of explanation, i.e., the No-thing or *ananke stenai* in order
to attain knowledge of Being as knowledge of the divine. For Heidegger,
Nullity confronts and overwhelms the Being-of-Dasein to remain within
the "thereness" of its finite Factical Self.[64]

In our earlier discussion of intentionality, the problem of the meaning of "truth" in relation to causality was essential to understanding
Heidegger's rejection of metaphysics. Causality, for him, illegitimately
springs from and toward a counterfeit idea of the meaning of "truth."
Heidegger sees the Latin "*veritas*" not only to be fundamentally at odds with
the Greek *a-letheia* but its command over all of Western thought has
resulted in a systematic restriction/dilution of being-at-hand to mere
present-at-hand, ultimately undermining man's relatedness in-and-to-the-
world. For Heidegger, when *a-letheia* became *veritas* the possibility of systematic Idealism grew out of it: *veritas* became *metron* then *meson* and then
mensura and man became *mens*. And is he not correct? Didn't this entire
apparatus of causality, correctness, rectitude and exactness conform and
deform the meaning of Being into a system of certitudes which annihilated
the very origins of Being where Dasein must dwell?[65]

> Why was the phenomenon of the world passed over at the beginning of
> the ontological tradition which has been decisive for us (explicitly in the
> case of Parmenides) and why has this passing-over kept constantly
> recurring?[66]

The "Catch-up" of Thinking into Being

Heidegger's rejection of metaphysics is most vehemently directed against
its causal structure. Is the intentional structure of causality, as Heidegger
claims, the denigration of Dasein into mere *mens*, or has he placed his rejection of causality on a metaphysics of causality that was already degenerate,
wherein it becomes a prop or crutch by which, as in Descartes, to build and
cross the bridge between *mens* to world?

The causality of the fourfold intentional presupposition is not only
not trapped in immanence and thus does not intend to build a bridge
from thought to things, but rather this causality is involved in the most
serious play, in the "catch-up" of thinking into Being. This "catch-up"
thereby understands the primacy of Being and of being-in-the-world; it

understands that Being is the fundamental prerequisite and ground of all knowledge.

Heidegger most certainly has not failed to notice the vast differences between a modern and a medieval metaphysics! But there are of course subtle changes from St. Thomas to Descartes that have created more havoc than the most obvious of differences. The problem of causality, the collapse of the "catch-up," will lay bare these subtle shifts in the fourfold, e.g., the primacy of essence over existence, and from the uncaused cause to self-caused cause. But paradoxically, these subtle shifts have not their greatest development in Descartes or Leibniz or Spinoza or Fichte or Schelling or even Hegel. Rather, their most primordial possibilities are realized outside metaphysics in Heideggerian ontology.

Heidegger sees in these reversals an end to metaphysics by means of its culmination. If metaphysical transcendence is maintained but undermined by these reversals which annihilate the deity, then Heidegger's claim that metaphysics leads to a systematized deontology is quite correct. But, on the other hand, what if one such thinker, like Heidegger, were to implement these reversals without futilely attempting, like Descartes, to uphold the finite transcendence that links *ens finitum* with *ens infinitum*, what would it prescribe or make possible for Dasein's being-in-the-world? These subtle but by no means innocuous shifts are utilized by Heidegger in the most original manner. Through them, Heidegger has created a fundamental ontology that is finally rid of its deity. But at what cost?

How does the causal reversal which leads to the systems of Kant, Schelling and Hegel lead to Heideggerian fundamental ontology? Once the "catch-up" is reversed, there are several levels to the loss of the Being *qua* deity that will lead to Heidegger.

How this reversal leads to Heidegger is not a simple step-by-step process of inevitability. Heidegger's thought is not the final result of the reversal as if he is the highest point or nucleus of some architectonic Idealism. Exactly how this causal reversal leads to Heidegger requires an examination into how Heidegger draws from this reversal; how he plucks from it what he understands to be fundamental truth about Being and then attempts to discard the problematic aspects of the reversal that would land him in an Idealism. Heidegger attempted to steal away the endlessness of the phenomenon which reflects the anti-onto-theo-logic "thereness" of Dasein, without dragging with it the trappings of Idealism.

By rejecting the causal structure of the "catch-up," has Heidegger accepted the dissolution of the existential independence of Being? Or have we missed the point of Dasein? Doesn't the "thereness" of Dasein have no need for the idea of the Real?:

> But it has been long held that the way to grasp the Real is by a kind of knowing which is characterized by beholding [*das anschauende Erkennen*]. Such knowing is as a way in which the soul—or consciousness—behaves. Insofar as Reality has the character of something independent in itself, the question of the meaning of 'Reality' becomes linked with that of whether the Real can be independent of consciousness or whether there can be a transcendence of consciousness into the sphere of the Real. The possibility of an adequate ontological analysis of Reality depends upon how far that of which the Real is to be thus independent—how far that which is to be transcended—has itself been clarified with regard to its Being. Only thus can even the kind of Being which belongs to transcendence be ontologically grasped. And finally we must make sure what kind of primary access we have to the Real, by deciding the question of whether knowing can take over this function at all. These investigations, which take precedence over any possible ontological question about Reality, have been carried out in the foregoing existential analytic. According to this analytic, knowing is a founded mode of access to the Real. The Real is essentially accessible only as entities within-the-world. All access to such entities is founded ontologically upon the basic state of Dasein, Being-in-the-world; and this in turn has Care as its even more primordial state of Being (ahead of itself—Being already in a world—as Being alongside entities within-the-world). The question of whether there is a world at all and whether its Being can be proved, makes no sense if it is raised by Dasein as Being-in-the-world; and who else would raise it? . . . the world is disclosed essentially along with the Being of Dasein; with the disclosedness of the world, the world has in each case been discovered too. . . . The question of the Reality of the external world gets raised without any previous clarification of the phenomenon of the world as such.[67]

St. Thomas would agree but Heidegger confuses realism with a need to prove the independent existence of the world. Causal knowledge for Heidegger is merely the founded means to overcome a founded "space" or Reality between man and Being. The Real is for him an overemphasized and founded category, and as the contrast to man, it purports to him a "space" outside his being that he must transcend into in order to know. This notion of leaping forth augurs the "need" for something like a deity. Dasein there-fore loses the reality of its "thereness" in this "need" for the Real, becoming just another being present-at-hand among entities-at-hand. For Heidegger, the metaphysical "catch-up" confuses the meaning of the "same" is for thinking as for Being as the need for the soul in knowledge to exteriorize itself in order to become the "same" as Being in knowledge.[68]

Rather, the "same," divested of any metaphysical confusion, simply means adherence to the primordial region of Being which is always "there" in-and-to Dasein and to the utter irreducibility of the nullity with which finitude must adhere.

Heidegger's rejection of causality is far more than a disagreement over the existential Reality of Being. Arguing over the ability of causality to lead man to the existential independence *qua* truth of Being would be, not only for Heidegger, but for St. Thomas, entirely founded on a false presupposi-tion. For St. Thomas, the Reality of Being is not something that thought arrives at or needs to be proved. St. Thomas is by no means what mod-ern thought including Heidegger understands by "realist."

Heidegger executes the causal reversal in order to succeed where system-atic idealism failed and clarify the fact that Being cannot be explained through entities. The causal reversal does not reflect merely a disagree-ment over an epistemological judgment, rather, it makes the "same" between thinking and Being a matter of equiprimordial identity rather than of causal difference. Heidegger sought to reveal the intentional pre-suppositions, the same is for thinking as for being and the soul is in a way all things, as an identification of the ontological difference over and against the metaphysical difference, in a sense to preserve the identity (to auto) of Being and thinking in the "thereness" of Dasein. Causality does exactly the opposite; it finds identity only in the adherence to its *telos*, the *ananke stenai* or No-Thing. The meaning of "catch-up" reflects the specifically metaphysi-cal goal and the paradox of its self-transcendence: the same is for thinking as for being—the known enters in the form of the knower only insofar as the knower belongs in and in reference to a higher Being, and while I con-stitute my knowledge of Being, by no means do I constitute Being.

"Thereness" as Dasein's Beinghood

Heidegger's causal reversal reflects the core of his fundamental ontology. The meaning of Being *qua* Being is found beyond the debate over the primacy of either Being or thought. This competition, either from the side of realism or of idealism, occurs only on the level of entities-at-hand, and misses the entire point of Dasein's Beinghood. On the level of entities-at-hand, realism is merely the obverse of idealism: a restriction of Dasein. Neither idealism nor metaphysical realism accepts the fundamental nature of Dasein as ontologically "there." As structurally "there" Dasein can call itself to face its-Self without being reducible either to a need for metaphysical otherness or to the self *qua* system. Even the primordial experience of conscience is loosed from any metaphysical or theological dependence or relation.[69]

When Kant initially grounds pure knowledge and pure intuition in the transcendental imagination, Heidegger sees this as a decisive reclamation of finitude: a recovering of finitude, absent any degenerate metaphysical causality. This finitude "as" transcendence is frustrated if it attempts to "get outside" Dasein's Selfhood. Rather as "there" it is Dasein's Selfhood. Heidegger considers what is commonly labeled a negative finitude, if traced to the fullest meaning of its possibilities, to be the only genuine positivity. In a word, only because it is incompatible with the theological, because it cannot move beyond the "thereness" of Dasein's own *entelechy*, it can reveal the real possibilities of Dasein.

Because Kant was still heavily invested in the metaphysical enterprise he inevitably, according to Heidegger, retreated from this understanding that proved antithetical to the possibility of metaphysical transcendence. This anti-theological finitude, situated in the transcendental imagination, placed man at the primordial origin of Being; in this thereness, there is Nothing (and Nothing more) which faces Dasein at the event of his being-in-the-world:

> But with the revelation of the subjectivity of the subject, Kant recoils from the ground which he himself established . . . Kant's profound study of the subjectivity of the subject, "the subjective deduction," leads us into obscurity. . . . It now appears that Kant's recoil from the ground which he himself revealed, namely the transcendental imagination, is—relative to his intention of preserving pure reason, i.e., holding fast to the base proper to it—that movement of philosophical thought which makes manifest the destruction of this base and this places us before the abyss [*Abgrund*] of metaphysics.[70]

The preliminary characterization of the essential structure [*Wesenbau*] of finite knowledge has already revealed a wealth of supplementary substructures which function as modes of synthesis . . . the indications given to us concerning the field of origin of fundamental sources of finite knowledge lead into the unknown.[71]

The possibility of finite knowledge is posed as such: "how must this finite being be constituted with respect to its own ontological structure if, without the aid of experience, it is able to bring forth the ontological structure of the *essent*, i.e., effect an ontological synthesis?"[72] The Kantian synthetic a priori is a response to the Humean problematic: with the rationalist and empiricist divorce between reason and sense knowledge, between relations of reason and matters of fact, the world had become inarticulate, it could not voice its own intelligible structure. Through the a priori ontological synthesis, Kant was attempting to rebuild the bridge between reason and sense. The idea that causality is precisely an *a posteriori* synthetic judgment whose terms are synthetically united in the sense experience of efficient causality was entirely lost with the modern loss of the intentional presence. The idea that sense has its own evidence and that sensations are principles is long gone.[73] But Heidegger is not coming out of the Humean problematic; he has intentionality and the world for him is by no means an inarticulate mass. What, therefore, does Heidegger find in Kant's a priori ontological synthesis that is essential for Dasein's finite transcendence? Is he conceding too much to Kant?

This need to articulate the constitution of the finite being so that it may bring forth the ontological structure of the essent, if taken beyond the limitations of a "systematic" a priori synthesis, opens up the possibility of uncovering a noncausal and non-theological transcendence. Let us take the liberty and rephrase the earlier Kantian question in terms of Heideggerian ontology: How must Dasein be constituted in its ontological structure, so that this structure shows Dasein as "there" and yet this "there" (the being of the world and the world of being) is not reducible to Dasein? How must Dasein, while being its own "there," also provide the Self of Dasein with its finite need to move toward its "there"? What makes the "thereness" dynamic enough to be the "is" equiprimordially uniting Being and thinking and yet also to maintain the irreducibility of Being? How is Dasein's need to submit itself to Being, essential to any genuine ontology, maintained in the face of Dasein's ontic-ontological priority understood in a Kantian way? What protects Heidegger from taking the last steps into Kantian Idealism? How is this paradox maintained?

If, for Heidegger, "Dasein, in so far as it already is, has always submitted itself already to a 'world' which it encounters, and this submission belongs

essentially to its Being,"[74] then there must be for him a preconceptual constitution of Dasein's meaning-structure that allows it to be the privileged
being-in-the-world:

> We are raising the question of comprehending that which we already
> understand and have always understood. The question of Being as a
> question of the possibility of the concept of Being arises from the precon-
> ceptual comprehension of Being. . . . The elaboration of the question
> of Being thus conceived first enables us to decide if, and in what way,
> the problem of Being in itself bears an intrinsic relation to the finitude
> of man.[75]

Heidegger continues where Kant recoiled, and utilizes the primordial
possibilities of a noncausal non-theological finite transcendence, that only
an a priori synthesis could furnish to a fundamental ontology:

> The "possibility of experience" denotes primarily the unified totality of
> that which makes finite knowledge essentially possible. The possibility of
> experience is, then, what gives objective reality to all our a priori modes
> of knowledge. Consequently, the possibility of experience is identical
> with transcendence. To delimit the latter in its full essence means to
> determine "the conditions of the possibility of experience."[76]

Heidegger's use of an a priori synthesis within his fundamental
ontology which recognizes the intentional structure of existence is, at
first, perplexing. The a priori is commonly understood as a necessarily non-
experiential judgment. But if we are to uncover Heidegger's incipient
primordial Idealism, it is essential to trace the possibility of an a priori
ontological synthesis into its originating pre-systematic primordiality as
possibility or endlessness.

Through Kant's shift from an *a posteriori* synthetic to an a priori synthetic,
the causal reversal is finally realized. While in the *a posteriori* ontological
synthesis the terms were synthetically united in the sense experience of
efficient causality, in the a priori ontological synthesis the terms are preconceptually prescribed outside the sense. For the former, the way in which
these terms unite is through the "catch up" of thinking into Being. Traced
to its most primordial reality, the *a posteriori* synthesis reflects the metaphysical *entelechy* of man's existence as satisfied only in the *ananke stenai*, while in
the a priori ontological synthesis, only in the Self. Because there is no "catch-
up" Dasein's "thereness" is confirmed. And finally, without any possible

"catch-up" there is then no end in the order of explanation, and finite transcendence becomes endless in and toward its Self as "there." Explanation is dislodged in favor of description; the phenomenological reduction is complete.

"Thereness" and the Endlessness of Dasein

Endlessness is the Self-of-Dasein's finite transcendence within the fundamental thereness of its being-in-the-world. Endlessness is realized in Dasein because Dasein is the privileged being who announces its own "thereness" in its endless possibilities. Dasein is "the entity which in every case we ourselves are, is ontologically that which is the farthest."[77] Within its "thereness," Dasein is in every case what it can be. Utilizing the primordial possibilities of the Kantian ontological synthesis, Dasein is shown in its authenticity: it is not something entitatively present-at-hand that must extend outside itself to become what it is in reference to another higher Other. Its very nature, its what it is or its actuality, is possibility. This possibility is no metaphysical potentiality that needs to be actualized in order to be. Rather this possibility as endlessness is the actual state of the Self-toward within the "thereness" of Dasein's being-in-and-to-the-world:

> The kind of Being which Dasein has, as potentiality-for-Being, lies existentially in the understanding. Dasein is not something present-at-hand which possesses competence for something by way of an extra; it is primarily Being-possible. Dasein is in every case what it can be, and in the way in which it is its possibility. . . . Possibility, as an existentiale, does not signify a free-floating potentiality-for-Being in the sense of the 'liberty of indifference' (libertas indifferentiae). In every case Dasein, as essentially having a state-of-mind, has already got itself into definite possibilities.[78]

While the endlessness of its transcendence is reflected in the finite Self-of-Dasein, its "thereness" has been alluded to throughout as its goal or dwelling-place, as the Factical Being-of-Dasein which the Self-of-Dasein comes toward through uncovering its own authenticity.[79]

Because Dasein is structurally antithetical to the metaphysical onto-theo-logical "catch-up," these two aspects (endlessness and "thereness") present the fullness of the causal collapse. There is no difference as difference between them that calls to mind the theological. And neither are they simply reducible one to the other. Their unity is not a synthesis formed in knowledge, but a synthesis as an originating synthesizing unity. Their unity is not a present-at-hand identification of two identical things, wherein, as two, they are also different. These two aspects originate as one in the mode of their distinction. Dasein, in itself, is this originating unity and is found "there" because it has already gotten itself into its definite and "endless" possibilities. Therefore, Kant's negative finitude and his a priori causal reversal can be viewed in what Heidegger understands to be their full potential. If in the very structure of Dasein these two aspects originate as Dasein's Being but originate as distinct, outside the causal difference as difference that must be "caught-up," then there is no worry of an Idealist reduction of Being into self-thinking: "knowing does not first arise from an immanent self-perception, but belongs to the Being of the 'there', which is essentially understanding";[80] nor is there a need to build a bridge from thought to Being or Being to thought.[81]

Finally what was once conceived as a negative finitude, because it was attached to the causal reversal still adhering to the theological otherness of metaphysics, is no longer considered as such. Heidegger's finitude situates man in his "thereness" with no causal possibility of reaching the highest possible Other and doesn't need to be overcome, precisely because Dasein originates in it-Self, its own endless possibilities, but originates them as distinct from its Factical "thereness." "The comprehension of Being which dominates human existence, although man is unaware of its breadth, constancy, and indeterminateness, is thus manifest as the innermost ground of human finitude."[82]

The first two reversals have dramatically altered man's ontological commerce in-and-with-the-world. Neither finitude in the face of its own null basis, nor the causal reversal that brings into the unconcealed the utter "thereness" of Dasein can represent the metaphysical intentional presence. In a word, the intentionality that pertains to Dasein cannot be reconciled with classical intentionality: the "throwness" of the former is not compatible with the *intentio* of the latter.[83]

For both St. Thomas and Heidegger, intentionality is the onto-*noetic* act of becoming, in knowledge, the other as other. But for Heidegger, the sameness which is accomplished in becoming the other "as" other is not prefigured upon the *ananke stenai*. The "as" which connects the other as other, or thinking and Being, or finitude and transcendence, is not understood as the vehicle of transcendence. If it were, it could not possibly reconcile endlessness with "thereness." The "as" residing in the primal structure of Dasein's facticity in its-Self-originating-unity means, "in every essent 'there is' what-being and that-being, essentia and existentia, possibility and reality."[84]

Dasein's intentionality is not grounded on becoming the other as other because there is a need for the deity, but because there is a need to account for the primal manifestation of the Self toward the Factical "thereness" of its Dasein—over and against the deity: "the establishment of the intrinsic possibility of ontology is accomplished as the disclosure of transcendence, i.e., the subjectivity of the subject."[85]

Note Heidegger's ontological structure: the Self-of-Dasein "is" the Fact-of-Dasein; the endlessness "is" the thereness of Dasein, but in such a way that they are born into the world "as" an original unity of difference. They are one ontological unity housed in Dasein's preconceptual primordial temporality. But when the projection or horizon or emergence of Dasein's possibilities unfolds conceptually its "thereness" withdraws in order for the projection to be made possible as possibility:

> Can Dasein's Being be brought out in such a unitary manner that in terms of it the essential equiprimordiality of the structures we have pointed out, as well as their existential possibilities of modification, will become intelligible. . . . The Being of Dasein, upon which the structural whole as such is ontologically supported, becomes accessible to us when we look all the way through this whole to a single primordially unitary phenomenon (time) which is already in this whole in such a way that it provides the ontological foundation for each structural item in its structural possibility.[86]

Dasein's possibilities reveal themselves in the horizon of its Being, its "thereness": "what is most closely ready-to-hand within-the-world possesses the character of holding-itself-in and not emerging."[87] For Heidegger, this unitary onto-temporal structure renders the two aspects of Dasein's Being irreducible to each other while preconceptually being the "same-as" or the identity of the other in Being. While this structure might avert both Idealism and metaphysical transcendence, it is quite possibly the very weakness that leads him into the heart of a primordial Idealism.

Starting with the Intentional presence reversal and ending with the *ananke stenai* reversal, the decisive moves that leave Heidegger in the impasse of Idealism emerge. Until now, it hasn't been shown that the deity is at all necessary. It seems that finitude and causality are altered in its absence, but can be originated, maintained and satisfied in Dasein's temporal mode. But through the meaning of the intentional presence the question of man's privileged access in-and-to-the-world is at stake. Can man be the intentional presence, a participant in the formation of the meaning of

Being, if the delicate balance between the knower and the known is not grounded upon the No-thing? Can Dasein participate in the formation of the meaning of Being if, for Heidegger, the unity of endlessness and thereness is grounded only in a preconceptual throwness that cannot further issue in the very formation of knowledge?

Intentional Presence: The Meaning of Formational Being-in-the-World

Because knowing is founded, the two aspects of Dasein, endlessness and "thereness," are a unity only in the preconceptual act of being-in-the-world and thereby are not reducible to thought. For St. Thomas knowing is founded as well, but the way in which knowing originates as founded consti- tutes the difference "as" difference between Thomistic and Heideggerian notions of being-in-the-world. For Heidegger, to presume that knowing as founded can participate in the distant eternal is absurd. There is for him no genuine reciprocity between what is founded and what is not (abyss); there is, rather, knowing in the face of its own nullity, that offers nothing more than that it is:

> A finite cognitive being is able to relate itself to an essent which it itself is not and which it has not created, only if this essent can by itself come forward to be met. However, in order that this essent be encountered as the essent that it is, it must be "recognized" in advance as essent, i.e., with respect to the structure of its Being. But this implies that ontological knowledge, which in this circumstance is always pre-ontological, is the condition of the possibility that an essent as such can, in general become an ob-ject for a finite being. All finite beings must have this basic ability, which can be described as a turning toward (. . .) [orientation toward] which lets something become an ob-ject. In this primordial act of orienta- tion, the finite being first pro-poses to itself a free-space [Spielraum] within which something can "correspond" to it. To hold oneself in advance in such a free-space and to form it originally is nothing other than tran- scendence which marks all finite comportment [Verhalten] with regard to the essent. If the possibility of ontological knowledge is based upon the pure synthesis, and if it is ontological knowledge which makes the act of objectification possible, then the pure synthesis must manifest itself as that which organizes and supports the unified totality of the intrinsic, essential structure of transcendence. Through the elucidation of the

structure of the pure synthesis the inmost essence of the finitude of reason is revealed.[88]

But St. Thomas understands knowing in causal degrees of Being, and through them thought engages beyond thought as it must if it is to-be thought intentionally understood. Thought as founded begins in the un-founded, in the *ananke stenai*, the radical other. This understanding of the intentional presence allows for a genuine reciprocity within the enclosure of Being and knowing which is no vicious systematic circle negating the mystery of Being, but the genuine hermeneutic circle codifying "the Same is for thinking as for Being."

The intentional presence's "un-foundation" allows man to participate in the formation of the meaning of Being, i.e., move beyond thought and into its origins, Being itself. In a word, thinking can and must "catch-up" to Being because the way their unity is grounded in the preconceptual "un-foundation" allows for it also to be grasped in the act of knowledge "after" the descriptive facticity of being-in-the-world. This is not a reduction of Being into thought. When man participates in the formation of the meaning of Being, he recognizes his utter dependency on Being for his knowledge (of meaning). Only then, when thought can "catch-up" to Being, is the world not alien. And through this similitude or *adaequatio* between man and world, thinking and being, man is the intentional presence. Being-in-the-world *qua* the same between thinking and Being because the soul is in a way all things, is, all along, an onto-theo-logic identifi-cation—a progressive *revelation* of Being into consciousness.

Dasein cannot participate in the formation of the meaning of Being; if it did, the need for the deity couldn't be averted. The core of difference between Dasein and the intentional presence is that for the former Being is understood as a fully developed essence of a certain kind. There is no ontological, unifying, constitutive role for the act of the Self-in-knowledge to play except for unconcealing what has been concealed. Dasein's "thereness," the Fact-of-its-Being, ultimately reveals an Essentialized/Factical structure over the Existence of its-Self as potentiality-for-Being. In a word, because Dasein's essence is its Factical null basis, essence enjoys a kind of primacy over existence as Self.[89]

As existent, Dasein is flung or thrown as a Self into its own possibilities. Dasein's only privilege is that as Self it can think through its possibilities, possibilities that have already been pre-understood. The Fact that Dasein throws and calls its-Self into its possibilities which are projected from its own null basis. This call calls nothing but nullity to its-Self. It must not allow the

Fact-of-Being, its "thereness," to be reduced to its-Self as "thinking" through its possibilities. If it did, given its Essence/Factical structure, Heidegger's ontology would be reduced to a product of thought. The problem with Heidegger's fundamental ontology is not that Being cannot be reducible to thought; it cannot. Rather, this ontology is unable to become a unity in thought, and thus the question of the unity of man, so critical in the philosophical/theological anthropology of Aquinas, cannot be resolved. Despite Heidegger's repeated disclaimers of the title "existentialist" we can more than detect their lineage from him.

What is the reason for this Essence structure, and why would Heidegger, with such a robust accounting of an existential fundamental ontology, accept the Intentional Presence Reversal of essence over existence? Because for him the meaning of Being *qua* Being mustn't leave room for the entrance of the deity and because he ultimately accepted conditions which altered the meaning of Being he desired to uncover.

Heidegger's Essence structure is far more original then a debate over priority. For him, the common interpretation of *essentia* and *existentia* does not and cannot have the ontologically logical signification of their traditional terms, which reduce Dasein to Being-present-at-hand.[90] The appearance of Heidegger's Essence structure results from his view of this metaphysical distinction as essentially inappropriate to entities of Dasein's character. He then proceeds to articulate Dasein's actual being-in-and-to-the-world as a fundamental "thereness" outside or beyond this distinction through temporality;[91] and while *essentia* is recast so *existentia* is reduced, and *esse* ignored.

In this phenomeno-temporal "thereness" wherein Being has already been delivered over to itself, man for Heidegger needn't recognize the metaphysical distinction (essence and existence) in knowledge. But has this temporal position "outside" the need for the metaphysical distinction forced Heidegger to accept elements of an essentialized understanding of existence wherein Being cannot endure genuine otherness outside Dasein's Being-constitution?:

> Not only is Being towards Others an autonomous, irreducible relationship of Being: this relationship, as Being-with, is one which, with Dasein's Being, already is. . . . So far as Dasein is at all, it has Being-with-one-another as its kind of Being.[92]

At the center of the medieval debates over the primacy of essence or existence is the problem of man's finitude in relation to God's infinite Being.

With Heidegger the meaning of man's finitude in the face of nullity explains why Being is encapsulated in a deeply primordial Essence structure. For Heidegger finitude "as" transcendence must situate Dasein in the thrown "thereness" of its own Being. Dasein arrives at this thrown "thereness" because nullity confronts the Self-of-Dasein to invest it-Self in its own-most possibilities.[93]

Heidegger's ontology has utilized the errant possibilities invested in an essence structure but outside metaphysics to satisfy and maintain a phenomenological existence.[94] Within this phenomeno-temporal essence structure the possibility of engaging nullity frustrates onto-theo-logical causality and resituates Dasein's totality of Being as ahead-of-itself-already-being-in-a-world as Being-alongside entities encountered within-the-world.[95] For Heidegger, Kant, Descartes and Schelling must be commended for inaugurating these reversals.[96] But because, for Heidegger, they remained within metaphysics, they failed to follow these reversals to their necessary conclusions as the end of metaphysics and the embracing of a fundamental ontology. Whereas he sees their failure to move beyond metaphysics as the emergence of Idealism, it is in accepting these reversals whether "inside" or "outside" metaphysics that leads to it. And because Heidegger does not cleave even to the most feeble metaphysical transcendence, his Idealism is more far reaching, and perhaps its most original and primordial manifestation. The Self-of-Dasein through its endless possibilities entered an alien world where everything is said and done. Because everything necessary is already in place, thought is placed at odds by its own possibilities that cannot lead to something genuinely Other. The Self-of-Dasein can only continue into its endless possibilities which itself already is. Because the Essence-Fact-of-Dasein is primal, every possibility is already "there," everything is already, in a way, said and done.[97]

Because Heidegger's concessions have been made outside the metaphysical *telos*, he is unable to employ these reversals to his advantage without serious repercussions. Heidegger has taken the a priori essence structure of Kant but left behind its metaphysical intentions. Without metaphysics he can take the a priori ontological identity and firmly resituate it within the phenomeno-temporal "thereness" of being-in-the-world.

> We must lay bare the fundamental structure in Dasein:
> Being-in-the-world. In the interpretation of Dasein, this structure is something "a priori;" it is not pieced together, but is primordially and constantly a whole. It affords us however, various ways of looking at the items which are constitutive to it.[98]

This a priori essence structure has rid ontology of its need for the deity. In this complete ontological identity "the world is therefore something 'wherein' Dasein as an entity already was, and if in any manner it explicitly comes away with anything, it can never do more than come back to the world."[99]

A genuine metaphysics must prove that this conflict over essence and existence to be appropriate even to entities such as Dasein. It must show that the primacy of existence not only brings the Deity closer, but uncovers it to be the fundamental factor in man's commerce in-and-with-the-world.

In one way, there is an infinite ontological distance between man and God, but if this distance is not measured in terms of essence, its identity is not bound up in man's Factical thereness-in-the-world. If that distance were bound up in the essence of man, then finitude would indeed be the negative finitude that Heidegger advocates, i.e., a limitation that cannot connect to the deity, unable to go beyond the Factical "thereness" of the constitution of Dasein, whose totality is as ahead-of-itself-already-in is primordially a whole existing as always factical wherein existentiality is essentially determined by facticity.[100]

For St. Thomas, within any Being, existence must necessarily have primacy because existentiality is not essentially determined by facticity. Because the distance between man and God is prescribed by existence, it is an irreducible component of man's teleological being-in-the-world. This distance is not an impediment to the metaphysical intentional presence, rather, it constitutes the essential difference as difference which houses the unity between man and God. This distance is the longer way, the way that allows finitude to be a "vehicle" of transcendence. Through it there is always something more and Other, something not yet said and done, and thinking must indeed "catch-up" to Being.

The privilege of the intentional presence, to participate in the formation of the meaning of Being, seems at first glance closer to Idealism than what we have deemed to be Heidegger's fatal flaw, the loss of formation. Does not the lack of formation mean that man has less "impact" regarding the way of Being, and with less "impact" doesn't he have a greater adherence to Being? Without formation man becomes, at first, a participant in the "meaning" of Being, but absent formation what is he participating in but the production of a meaning-structure? Either man assumes the role of reading off the appearances of Being as they engage him or he takes one small but logically fatal step, and assumes the role of sole meaning-giver in such a way that Being is essentially the same as the meaning man prescribes. In order to understand the necessity of formation we must uncover the special kind of temporal structure corresponding to man's privileged access in-and-to-the-world.

Formation is at the heart of the intentional presence as the "catch-up" between thinking and Being, as the temporal structure appropriate to man's privileged access in-and-to-the-world. This kind of time is not an a priori essence structure converted into Heidegger's phenomenological "thereness," nor is it the loss of finitude in favor of a kind of self-projected systematic Idealism. This time neither denies the intelligibility of the world nor relegates man's privilege to merely reading off the appearances of Being in the world; both these errant positions amount to the loss of otherness. Rather this time, or what St. Thomas calls aeviternity,[101] forms the intentional presence; its temporality is an onto-theo-logical identification that becomes fully temporal only at the *telos*-of time at the end in the order of explanation in and as the "un"-caused foundation of Being.

Man's privilege depends upon not forsaking otherness. This means that man can recognize something truly other than himself, even though in-the-world man cannot separate Being and the meaning he gives it. In a word, there must be something (or No-thing) within man's very ontological constitution that is not reducible to it, so that man can understand the same is for thinking as for being in terms of their difference as difference.

Man is a being that proceeds from and turns-toward his origin. He does not accomplish this because he is susceptible to corruption and change.[102] Man to be man must not corrupt and change with each degree away from the beginning *qua* end. Such a position undermines man as a complete ontological unity and mistakes causality as his failed attempt to return to his whole and original ontological constitution. Rather, proceeding from and returning to the origin is the act of participating in the formation of the meaning of Being. As a being in time, man in-forms Being that he needs to "catch-up" in order to know. When man is at the "end-of-time," i.e., the end in the order of explanation, Being in-forms man that all along it has provided the ground in which the soul is in a way all things because the same is for thinking as for Being. This twofold structure of formation fundamentally distinguishes the intentional presence from Dasein.

In *aeviternal* formation, the "sameness" in which his soul is in a way all things is an onto-theo-logical way and identification. Because this kind of identification is housed in man's constitution but not reducible to it, man comes to understand his Being only in the face of otherness and, as such, otherness is not merely endured but celebrated. In a word, *aeviternal* formation or onto-theo-logical identification (unlike Heidegger's onto-logical identity) is discovered only at the end-of-time (*telos*) *qua* end-of-explanation. Because Heidegger denies Being *qua* Being its necessary onto-theo-logical identity, Being is inevitably reduced to that which is sole meaning giver, i.e., Dasein. Even if temporality is invested with the qualities of otherness, even if "thereness" and "endlessness" are born as a unity of difference, still because there is no end in the order of explanation (because Dasein does not have something, i.e., No-thing, within its ontological constitution) Dasein cannot endure genuine Otherness. While both Dasein and the intentional presence face the inseparability of thinking and Being, Dasein does not have irreducibility as part of its onto-temporal constitution. Ultimately, Dasein cannot help but resolve thinking and Being in to its own temporal structure. And if we gave Heidegger the existentialist reading he deplores, one might say with Sartre that Dasein is repelled by the gaze of the Other.

St. Thomas' Prima Via: A Brief Discursus on the *Ananke Stenai*

Synopsis

We have been arguing that the entire enterprise of metaphysics rests upon the fourfold unity of finitude, intentionality, causality and the *ananke stenai*, and in their supporting presuppositions: that the Same is for thinking as for Being, and that the soul is, in a way, all things. As we approach the critical distinction between an uncaused and a self-caused cause, it is necessary to consider in more depth the nature of the necessity to come to a stop in the order of explanation, and of just what that stop augurs for being-in-the-world. The *ananke stenai* is the linchpin, the trigger mechanism of St. Thomas' famous *quinque viae*, explicitly in the first three, implicitly in the fourth and fifth: with this principle or presupposition the deity enters philosophy. About this Heidegger is absolutely correct. Further, the idea of a noncausal metaphysics is the idea of something that is not metaphysics. It may be, for the sake of argument, the idea of something better, but it is not metaphysics. Heidegger is correct about this too. Thus some comments on the *ananke stenai* are here called for.

Within the order of meaning or essence there can be no regress to infinity. Why? For if it were not necessary to come to a stop in the order of explanation we could not even ask the question of the meaning (the what-it-is) of Being. And yet this is precisely the question that philosophy as philosophy asks. Thus to ask the question of meaning or essence is to presuppose a meaningful or essential "answer." This involves a causal tracking that cannot, in principle, go on to infinity. Or again: the philosophical question of the meaning of Being is asked precisely because we are already in the presence of Being and its meaning is at issue: What-is It? If this is a presupposition, it is nevertheless one with which we must begin! That Being is meaningful is implied in and by its presence. Thus, because essence is already and in advance the primary question that necessitates the existence of an "answer," there can be no regress to infinity—for this would deny the existence of an "answer" and thus of the question and thus of the meaning and thus of the presence and thus of Being. But this is where we started from. In other words, if we could not or need not come to a stop in the order of meaning or explanation this would be to deny what we began by affirming and which gave rise to our questioning: Being as present. If on the other hand we must come to a stop in the order of explanation, then there must be such a "stop" or foundation in the order of Being. Why? Because the Same is for thinking as for Being, and because the soul is, in a way, all things. If by the necessity of thought itself I must reach a foundation in the order of meaning, then there must be such an ontological, indeed metaphysical foundation, that announces itself, when reached, as "first," as ontologically, not necessarily chronologically, first *qua* foundation. Thus the "end" in the order of explanation is the "first" in the order of Being.

To illustrate this better, a look at St. Thomas' (and Aristotle's) prima via, the demonstration from change, motion or becoming will be helpful.

Prima autem et manifestior via est quae sumitur ex parte motus. Certum est enim et sensu constat aliqua moveri in hoc mundo. Omne autem quod movetur ab alio movetur. Nihil enim movitur nisi secundum quod est in potentia as illud as quod movetur. Movet autem aliquid secundum quod est actu; movere enim nihil aliud est quam educere aliquid de potentia in actum, de potentia autem non potest aliquid reduci in actum nisi per aliquid ens actu: sicut calidum in actu ut ignis facit lignum quod est calidum in potentia esse calidum in actu et per hoc movet et alterat ipsum. Non autem est possibile quod idem sit simul in actu et in potentia secundum idem sed solum secundum diversa: quod enim est calidum in actu non potest simul esse calidum in potentia sed est simul frigidum in potentia. Impossibilis est ergo quod idem et eodem motu aliquid sit movens et motum vel quod moveat seipsum. Oportet ergo omne quod movetur ab alio moveri. Si ergo id a quo movetur moveatur, oportet et ipsum ab alio moveri, et illo ab alio. Hoc autem non est procedere in infinitum, quia sic non esset aliquod primum movens et per consequens nec aliquod aliud movens, quia moventia secunda non movent nisi per hoc quod sunt mota a primo movente, sicut baculus non movet nisi per hoc quod est motus a manu. Ergo necesse est devenire ad aliquod primum movens quod a nullo movetur, est hoc omnes intelligunt Deum.[103]

Clearly, the essential move in the demonstration, the one which if legitimate renders the argument conclusive but which if illegitimate negates the entire operation, is contained in that brief phrase "*hoc autem non est procedere in infinitum.*" Let us follow the argument and then analyze it.

St. Thomas looks at the world and sees in it motion, change, becoming. This is certain and obvious and indubitable. He starts from where he is and not from where he is not. And where is he? In a world of becoming. Another presupposition? Of course. Naive? Not at all, not if I must begin with this presupposition because there is no other place to begin. This is no more and no less than, in its own way, the Parmenidian presupposition. Becoming undeniably exists: now note the implicit question: what is it? What is change or becoming? Well it implies a lack or a need or an imperfection which things in a state or condition of becoming naturally tend to overcoming in a completion of which they are naturally capable. Or, becoming is the transformation or reduction from a state of potentiality to a state or condition of actuality. Not possessing (yet) that perfection, completion or actuality, closing the gap (temporal yes, but more so ontologically!) between potentiality and actuality requires that anything in the process of becoming be changed by something other. That is why it can be said that nothing changes of itself. Now this something other or else causing change must be itself actual: "*de potentia autem non potest aliquid reduci in autem nisi per aliquid ens actu.*" Thus for example, the acorn becomes the oak. In order to be-come the oak, it must be brought to a state of actuality by something in a state of actuality. Thus, the sun must not merely potentially shine; it must actually shine. The rain must not merely potentially fall; it must actually fall, and so on. But the sunshine and the rain are, if you will, in the same boat as the acorn, and they must be carried from potentiality to actuality by something(s) else in a state of actuality, but these are also in the same boat as the acorn, and on and on. But: "*hoc autem non est procedere in infinitum*"! Why?

Because we cannot continue explaining one thing that cannot account for itself by another entity that cannot account for itself, by a third thing that cannot account for itself and on to infinity. Why? Because then I will not have accounted for or explained the meaning of becoming! So I must come to a stop in the order of explanation or meaning which says: there is a foundation of becoming in the order of Being! Why, once again? Because the Same is for thinking as for Being and because the soul is, in a way, all things. Now when we have reached this stop, this "first" (and again, and never too many times, this is not a chronological first but an ontological first), we have reached something different in kind from beings-in-becoming. It is something that causes change but does not change, something outside of but intimately related to, causally speaking, the order of change. It is beyond (meta) the order of physics as the cause and meaning and explanation of that order. It is the famous uncaused cause as un-changed changer; just as in the second demonstration it is the uncaused cause as un-made maker; and in the third proof the uncaused cause as the Being that cannot Not-Be. In each instance we move not from what cannot account for itself to something that can account for itself, but from something that cannot account for itself to something that does not need to account for itself. We shall see soon the difference between the two.

Now, as a final remark, note the language: un-caused, un-changed, un-made: we are not saying too much about this Cause other than that it is and must be and that it is not (like) that, i.e., that of which it is the cause, for if it were we would be back on the treadmill of the regress and never reach an explanation. The caused is not thereby diminished, rather it is elevated as the means by which I get to God for Aquinas. If I cannot get to God through the world, then I cannot get to God. But if there were no way for things to be, then there would be no things—but there are things: therefore there must be a way for things to be. This way is the world's intelligible meaning revealed in the Necessity to come to a stop. It itself may be mysterious and bottomless and even infinite, but what we know from the *ananke stenai* is that it is the Cause and therefore the meaning of the world of change or efficiency or possibility. In other words, we ask the question of essence: what-is it? Now the answer may not itself be an essence. This foundation may be, as it is for St. Thomas, Pure To-Be. But still the question of meaning is always posed as a question of essence, otherwise such non-metaphysical, natural answers as scientific ones would be satisfactory. If I wanted to know how an acorn becomes an oak I would ask a botanist, not a metaphysician. But this is to miss the point by confusing a "how" question, even a "why" question with the metaphysical "what" question.

The deity has thus entered philosophy, and it would require the reversal of the entire fourfold, but especially of the principle of the necessity to come to a stop, to extrude Him.

Heidegger's primordial Idealism has its roots in failing to distinguish the genuine metaphysical *arché* from its modern permutation. By failing to distinguish the Thomistic "un" caused cause from something like the Spinozistic self-caused cause, he is led to the conclusion that metaphysics naturally ends in the immanentization of the self-caused cause within the world as an idealistic constitution of consciousness.[104] If he had recognized the fundamental differences between these two alternative origins perhaps he would not have rejected in advance the fourfold intentional presupposition. Heidegger proceeds not to discard the self-caused cause but to utilize this misappropriated reversal in two ways: (1) to defend his claim that metaphysics is a founded and deficient study of Being leading to systematic Idealism, and (2) to take these elements (the fourfold reversals) that contribute to the failure of metaphysics as the crucial signates of fundamental ontology if resituated outside the theological metaphysical architectonic. Because these reversals culminating in an immanentized self-caused cause cannot reconcile the world with the deity, his primordial Idealism is not just the result of his anti onto-theo-logical ontology but in fact an integral source of its very development. We shall examine several things: (1) how Heidegger fails to distinguish the "un"caused cause from the self-caused cause, (2) how he utilizes elements in the reversal to his advantage and, finally, (3) whether his attempt to separate his ontology from systematic Idealism is at all possible given what he has conceded.

Uncaused Cause versus Self-caused Cause

There is indeed a subtle but decisive shift in philosophy regarding the nature of the deity. The uncaused cause and the self-caused cause are by no means innocuous synonyms but rather reflect the very divide between such thinkers as St. Thomas Aquinas and Spinoza. For the former the effort of thought ends, as a requirement of thought, in something (Nothing) that doesn't need to account for itself: the *ananke stenai* stops at the uncaused cause. For the idealist it ends in the idea of a highest self as that which first accounts for itself because it needs to account for itself. We have shown how the uncaused cause can truly exist at the end of the order of explanation as the irreducible, onto-theo-logical origin of all thinking about Being and, as such, how it affirms the distinction between thinking and Being. But the self-caused cause, from its very beginning to its end makes the entrance of the deity into philosophy a founded failure, leaving it susceptible to idealistic indeed a-theistic interpretations.

When Heidegger attempts to "explain how the deity enters philosophy,"[105] he has failed to notice this difference as difference between these two origins, and because of it he has lost entirely the meaning of thinking as "catching-up" to the ground of Being:

> To what extent is an explanation [of the entrance of the deity] successful? To the extent that we take heed of the following: that matter of thinking is beings, as such, that is Being. Being shows itself in the nature of the ground. Accordingly, the matter of thinking, Being as the ground, is thought out fully only when the ground is represented as the first ground, prote arché. The original matter of thinking presents itself as the first

cause, the causa prima that corresponds to the reason-giving path back to the ultima ratio, the final accounting. The Being of beings is represented fundamentally, in the sense of the ground, only as causa sui. This is the metaphysical concept of God. Metaphysics must think in the direction of the deity.[106]

For Heidegger, in metaphysics all Being has its "final accounting" at the first ground as *causa sui*. In a word, all beings are "brought up" and accounted for in the first self-accounting. To account for is to be "named." If the ground which accounts or names all being is itself a Self-caused self, its privilege is to be that which accounts or names itself first. What then really distinguishes the privilege of *causa sui* from the privilege of man? Naming is the spoken unity of thinking and being, this privilege extends both to *causa sui* and to man, the only difference is that the former is, again, the first to be able to account or name itself. But can this kind of "first" really sustain itself as an ontological first, or is it inevitably reducible to man's accounting?

In the *Poem of Parmenides*, the goddess represents the end in the order of explanation, the *ananke stenai*, the No-thing. She is the *prote arché* in which all things are accounted for, all names are spoken. But the goddess herself is unnamed. For Aristotle and St. Thomas when thinking "catches-up" to Being it adheres to a "first" which must be irreducibly different from man; it is the difference as difference that houses their unity. If man is the privileged being who announces or names or predicates that which is the "same" between thinking and Being, then his origin must be in something more, something Other than a mere higher version of his own privilege, i.e., his own Self-accounting. This first must be the ground of the possibility of man's privilege, it must be that which doesn't need to account for or name itself, i.e., it is the uncaused cause.

Heidegger has unfortunately and inexplicably overlooked the distinction between an uncaused cause and a self-caused cause, and has rejected all of metaphysics on the weight of the latter, that indeed passes over the lived-world. He wants man to adhere to being-in-the-world and this adherence must be so irreducible that man cannot even think to pass over the world. The problem is what must Dasein adhere to, if Heidegger has overlooked and rejected the uncaused cause that provides man's irreducible adherence to being-in-the-world? For Heidegger, the metaphysical first cause artificially reorders beings in terms of a first accounting passing over the possibility of Dasein to account for itself. This reordering goes against Dasein's way in that existing is that which "in it, out of it, and against it, all genuine understanding, interpreting, and communicating, all rediscovering as appropriating anew, are performed."[107] For him, Dasein's is possible only because "Dasein's Self-hood has been defined formally as a way of existing, and therefore not as an entity present-at-hand," which has no privileged access-in-and-to-the-world.[108]

If Heidegger hadn't overlooked the uncaused cause, he might have noticed that man is a complete ontological unity who accounts for himself only because the nature of the uncaused cause is to provide the ground of the possibility for man's accounting, and not to be an example of the highest accounting. There is a fundamental incommensurability between man and the uncaused cause, which sustains man as a being-in-the-world. Man needn't pass over the world to account for himself, rather, through the "un"-caused cause he seeks to embed himself in his privileged access to be the other as other, in-and-to-the-world. Man's dwelling upon the "un" caused cause is an in-dwelling into his special kind of being-in-the-world.

Only within the uncaused cause can man's and the world's ability to account for themselves not enclose them in a pure essence structure. When man accounts for himself in the face of the "un," everything isn't already said and done. By accounting, he is a complete ontological unity, a participant in the formation of the meaning of Being. Through formation he is informed of the irreducible distinction between his need to account for himself in knowledge and that which doesn't need to account for itself in Being. This irreducible difference as difference means that there is something more, something left over, something Other. Man, dwelling on the uncaused cause, reflects his Being in ever intensifying degrees toward the core of Being itself.

But in reference to a self-caused cause, man is never a complete ontological unity when he accounts for himself. There is something else with a higher accounting of itself and of man; man in reference to this higher and fuller accounting cannot be complete. He resides, incomplete, alien and at odds, in an essentialized system, where everything is already said and done. In this system, there is a fundamental reducibility, between man and the self-caused cause—cannot man assume the role of highest being in the order of explanation? Wouldn't then man's entire meaning-structure be already said and done, consisting in an endless projection of the self? Isn't this the entire project of modern, particularly Hegelian Idealism?

By virtue of overlooking the distinction, Heidegger's understanding of the origin became a confused melding of the two opposing first causes ultimately making the deity a formidable but impossible figure. In this fused view, he came to several decisive conclusions. (1) The idealistic move was inevitable for metaphysics; all that needed to occur was for man to assume the role of highest cause; this possibility reflects the first cause already interpreted as self-caused cause. But for Heidegger man wasn't rid of the deity if his thinking still adhered to the metaphysical transcendent scaffolding. Heidegger saw even in the metaphysical Idealism of Kant the illicit otherness which the deity provided.[109] Therefore, (2) the structure of metaphysics still pointed toward the uncaused cause's irreducibility or adherence to something irreducibly distinct from Dasein. When Heidegger rejects the metaphysical first cause, he is really rejecting the remnants of an uncaused cause's irreducibility as founded, within the reducible structure of the self-caused cause. Understanding how this rejection unfolds is necessary if one wants to see how Heidegger arrives at the primacy of the Self-of-Dasein, how he attempts to distinguish it from Idealism and, finally, why Dasein is unable to endure genuine otherness.

For Heidegger, the vestiges of the "un" caused within *causa sui* would dramatically alter Dasein's being-in-the-world. Heidegger understands that it is not merely the self-caused cause's reordering of beings that is problematic, for this kind of accounting is subject to an idealistic reduction. Rather, what he sees, even without differentiating the two opposing first causes, is the irreducibility factor of the uncaused cause as the greatest offense against Dasein's ownmost possibilities.

Beyond Heidegger's rejection of the self-caused cause's artificial reordering of beings in terms of a highest accounting, he has rejected its metaphysical structure as the real culprit against Being *qua* Being. For Heidegger, the primacy of Self is appropriate to entities like Dasein who have so much more than Being present-at-hand as their access in-and-to-the-world.[110] The problem is that the metaphysical structure, even as it degenerates in modernity, still cleaves to something that is for Heidegger inappropriately irreducible. The metaphysical structure may become an empty edifice for Idealism, but its framework is itself the last vestige of the uncaused cause, pointing man toward the Otherness of the deity. In a confused way, Heidegger sees through the self-caused cause to the irreducibility of the "un." He sees the violence it could commit against Dasein's phenomeno-temporal priority and structure. Because the uncaused cause does not need to prove itself, it augurs an adherence to the divine.

For Heidegger, Dasein's phenomeno-temporal structure directs itself toward its ownmost potentiality-for-being and then discloses its own "thereness" within these possibilities. As a fully temporal structure, its futurity comes out of its past, and it temporalizes its "now-ness" precisely because its being-in is futural.[111]

But if the irreducibility of the uncaused cause were to enter Dasein's phenomeno-temporal horizon, Dasein's totality of involvements within its being-in-the-world would not return to itself where there are no further involvements but would redirect itself in a teleological causality. With this "un" there would be one further, one "un"-accounted for irreducible involvement that would redirect Dasein's whole temporal structure to the end-of-time, to the end in the order of explanation.[112]

This emerging uncaused cause takes away Dasein's primordial familiarity *qua* identity with the world. For Heidegger, Dasein must already be familiar with what he encounters. This familiarity is essential to its onto-logical identity and necessary if Dasein is to remain ontologically planted within the world over and against the deity. Dasein may enter the inauthentic or the uncanny, he may experience the most primal dread but ultimately because Dasein's ownmost potentiality-for-being is housed within its own essence structure, all of these moods are primordially familiar to Dasein and therefore have already been seized by him in the most primordial manner as "there."[113]

Heidegger rejects these remnants of the uncaused cause in order to liberate the self-caused cause from its metaphysical transcendent scaffolding. Heidegger takes the self-caused cause, and brings it outside of the problematic metaphysical transcendence. He then places this "self" within phenomenological "thereness." For him, what was once problematic to the metaphysical self, i.e., its reducibility in the face of the errant irreducibility of the "un" is no more. For Heidegger, the reducibility of the metaphysical self leads to Idealism when placed in polarity to the distant eternal. But outside the metaphysical transcendence it becomes the genuine phenomeno-temporal Self-of-Dasein. The Self is now liberated to uncover its endless finite possibilities within its ownmost phenomenologically Thrown "thereness."

For Heidegger, the Self-of-Dasein cannot lead to Idealism; what was once reducible within the metaphysical scaffolding in the face of the distant eternal is liberated and given its own irreducibility within phenomenology:

When the they-self is appealed to, it gets called to the Self. But it does not get called to that Self which can become for itself an "object" on which to pass judgment, nor to that Self which inertly dissects its "inner life" with fussy curiosity, nor to that Self which one has in mind when one gazes "analytically" at psychical conditions and what lies behind them. The appeal to the Self in the they-self does not force it inwards upon itself, that it can close itself off from the "external world". The call passes over everything like this and disperses it, so as to appeal solely to that Self which, notwithstanding, is in no way other that Being-in-the-world. . . . What does the conscience call to him to whom it appeals? Taken strictly, nothing. The call asserts nothing, gives no information about world-events, has nothing to tell. Least of all does it try to get going a "soliloquy" in the Self to which it has appealed. "Nothing"]gets called to [*zu-gerufen*] this Self, but it has been summoned [*aufgerufen*] to itself— that is, to its onwmost potentiality-for-Being. The tendency of the call is not such as to put up for "trial" the Self to which the appeal is made; but it calls Dasein forth (and "forward") into its ownmost possibilities, as a summons to its ownmost potentiality-for Being-its-Self.[114]

The Self-of-Dasein in its endless possibilities is now irreducible or irreducibly "towards its own thereness, within Being-in-the-world." Endlessness and "thereness" constitute Dasein's being-in-the-world, and are born equiprimordially as an original difference in-the-world. This phenomeno-temporal structure allows for Dasein to be its own self-caused cause without reducing it-Self to a systematic self, or transcendental Ego. The phenomenological Self becomes the ontological identification of Dasein's Factical being-in-the-world, but cannot reduce this facticity to it-Self.[115] The endlessness of the Self-of-Dasein prohibits it from crossing over into its ownmost Factical being-in-the-world, rather the Self takes or identifies its "thereness" along with it and keeps doing so constantly.[116]

Heidegger utilizes the self-caused cause because it collapses any meaningful dependency on deity, and believes that the phenomenological structure has safely liberated the Self from any transcendental Idealism. The Self-of-Dasein's way of being-in-the-world—toward its own phenomenological "thereness"—is outside the possibility of entering a systematic self-centric Idealism. In sum, these are the two fundamental points that Heidegger believes separate his Phenomenological Self from any idealistic imputations:

1. Dasein isn't understood in terms of metaphysical transcendence, because it doesn't need to extend outside of itself into an "external reality";[117] the problem of reality reduced to the self in systematic Idealism cannot apply to the kind of Self-of-Dasein.

2. What further separates Dasein from Idealism is that the Self-of-Dasein by virtue of its endlessness provides enough "distance" between it-Self and its own Factical thereness that the Self can for him remain the same as its basis as "there" and yet distinct from it.[118]

Unfortunately, these two distinctions are not sufficient to allow the phenomenological structure to endure and tolerate otherness. Two factors enter into maintaining genuine otherness : (1) irreducibility and (2) a fundamental difference as difference between the ground of Being and beings.

Heidegger recognized the first factor. He recognized the need for an irreducible adherence to being-in-the-world after having stripped man of his illicit adherence to the "un" within *causa sui*. He resituates irreducibility within Dasein's being-in-the-world structure. Through the relationship between Dasein's endlessness and its ownmost factical "thereness," he believes the problems of reducing Being to thought are not only averted, but uncovered to be an unnecessary distinction. In a word, if Dasein is understood as irreducible being-in-the-world and not as an entity within an external world, the problems of the existential independence of Being in the face of thought are resolved.

But Heidegger overlooked the most essential component in maintaining man's irreducible adherence to being-in-the-world, the factor of maintaining a genuine otherness. This component lies beneath and beyond the conceptual problems between thinking and Being, and lies at the heart of the meaning of Self and what it is the Self adheres to. Even if Dasein's phenomeno-temporal structure seems to take over that irreducibility by placing it with it-Self as unable to cross over its facticity, Heidegger still hasn't overcome one final obstacle needed in order really to differentiate the phenomenological Self from systematic Idealism. Heidegger is unable to show how Dasein's privilege unfolds ultimately any differently from how the privilege of the idealistic transcendental self unfolds. Heidegger cannot convert Dasein's ability to account for itself to the ability not to need to account for itself, nor would he want to. Nor would St. Thomas want to convert the intentional presence either. But how this privilege unfolds, i.e., in reference to what it adheres really determines the authenticity of the privilege.

Although Heidegger grasps what systematic Idealism could not, the irreducibility of being-in-the-world, this only makes him the more primordial Idealist. Paradoxically, the problem was what Dasein could not and should not overcome—the very privilege of all men! Heidegger couldn't change this privilege, it would undermine the meaning of Dasein. But because he rejected adherence as irreducible only in the face of the ground which doesn't need to account for itself, Dasein, even with all the null distance between it-self and the Fact that it is, still must account for that distance by constituting its own irreducibility in and to the world. Even nullity in the face of Dasein's ownmost potentiality-for-Being isn't outside the need to account for itself. In Dasein, Nullity actually accounts for itself more than anything else. It accounts for itself again and again, as impenetrable "there-ness" in order to keep finitude in its place "as" finite closing Dasein off from the possibilities of the infinite.

Without the deity there is no adherence that is not reducible to the self. No matter how high or distant this self-caused cause is postulated or even if irreducibility is fundamental to Dasein's constitution, the only way Being is not reduced to consciousness is if there is something outside the Self that doesn't need to account for itself. But man cannot ask of himself not to account for himself; even such an asking is still an accounting.[119] The self is that which in order to be-the-self must account for itself, the possibility of epistemology resides in that act. But in order for man to have a meaningful ontological understanding of the world, i.e., for epistemology to recognize its rooted dependency on ontology, for language to play "catch-up" to Being, ontology must be recognized in its distinction as onto-theo-logic from its start and that requires accepting the longer way.

Chapter 4

The Fourfold Intensities

When scholasticism degenerated into a method of disputation, the stress was put on a certain acquired cleverness in the use of dialectical argument, which, although it was very useful in itself, invited its students to start from the first principles rather than to dwell upon them in view of deepening their interpretation. The time has now come for minds still interested in the acquisition of metaphysical wisdom to recapture the meaning of a fruitful method of philosophical investigation.

Etienne Gilson, The Elements of Christian Philosophy

Up to this point, we have sought to elaborate the meaning-structure of the fourfold intentional presupposition as a kind of catch-up and adherence of thinking into Being. The question remains as to the what it is of the very catch-up point? As we have insisted, this point is not merely an end but the beginning *qua* end of being-in-the-world, as that which gives Being its worldhood and the world its beinghood. Thereness is perhaps what best describes this point; its proximity or nearness to man accompanies and coinheres in every single one of his acts, structuring them as the very structure of his becoming. And yet, at the same time, this thereness is of the strangest sort, for its closeness is unlike anything else that accompanies man; it cannot be put aside, it is in a sense beyond or before his being-in. This point is the only closeness or thereness within his being-in-the-world that is also seen as a distance, and it augurs the uncanny; it is the essential distance between man and Otherness that allows or obligates him to ask about his surroundings. Not so much is the question asked "Why is there something rather than nothing?" (Heidegger's question)[1] but "what does it mean that there is something and not nothing?"

We have said that man's being-in-the-world is onto-theo-logic from its very start to its very end, and the catch-up is the confirmation of that structure. Now we must ask into the meaning of this catch-up in terms of the point of catch-up and its essential relatedness in, to and with man. How do we inquire into and evaluate the unfamiliar familiarity of this thereness—of this point that seems to be right beside us and yet at an essential distance—so that we may speak of it?

Man looks around at all the thereness of his surroundings. He sees the innocence and beauty and indifference and terror of becoming, and the order that seems to exist in its own perfect pitch, even in its discordance and strife, as if we were not even involved, as if we were the unnoticed and unwanted stranger outside the gates of the polis. We ask ourselves, "isn't this (the world of becoming) enough?" That is to say, whether seen in its Heracliteian fieriness or in its Parmenedian effulgence, isn't this mystery enough, isn't this awe sufficient? Does it need or deserve to be denigrated in favor of some distant divine transcendence? Is this not only Nietzsche's serious question[2] but, following Nietzsche even as early as *Being and Time*, Heidegger's question, and it is serious indeed. And the answer is "yes and no." This answer is not indecisive, nor does it waver between affirmation and rejection. The answer is both "yes and no," at the same time, in time, for all time. Why? Because the question itself is of a different order, precisely because we can and must ask it. Because I can ask "isn't this, this thereness enough?" it is enough. I am there and it has elicited from me such awe and reverence in the very question; it has brought me to the door of the question. And yet, at the same time, precisely because I can form the question, because I am at its door, it is not enough. In a way, I am fully embedded within the temporal order of this there and yet the fullness or plenitude of it is of such a sort that it overflows and brings me "outside" or "beyond" while always within it. Moreover, there resides a distance, the difference as difference, within my temporal structure precisely because I can mouth this question within the always particular time in which I reside. The question and the answer reflect the vast extent of man's historical relationship with the catch-up point this strange thereness coinhering with man-and-Being-in-time.

"Isn't this enough?" The answer "yes and no" reveals not only the longer way of St. Thomas, but exactly where the way becomes a way. In the structure of the catch-up, where thinking must adhere to Being, I am somewhere distinct; the essence of my thereness is an up-bringing (and turning), a unique kind of temporal formation. To understand man's being-in-the-world as onto-theo-logical from the start is to answer "yes and no." To remain within the tension of that answer is to understand the meaning, length and limits of philosophy. One might be reminded here of those famous passages in the Confessions wherein Augustine questions the world of becoming in all of its beauty and terror, and is told in response that it is not God but that it is God who made it.[3] The *plenitudo essendi* for St. Thomas is precisely that which preeminently contains and grounds all finite participation.[4] The grandeur of God, to speak poetically with Hopkins, is the existential charge running throughout the world: "it will flame out, like shining from shook foil."[5] Thus the question "is not this enough?" is the question of the possibility of Christian Philosophy. When it is asked whether there can be a Christian Philosophy (and we are about to see Heidegger ask it), we might ask in return whether there can be, at this time, any other? And so the question of metaphysics in its fourfold presuppositional structure is also the question of the possibility, the necessity, of Christian Philosophy. The "Christian" in Christian Philosophy, does not merely specify a philosophical field of study like "modern" is to Modern Philosophy. What "Christian" adds to Philosophy is outside and beyond adjectival or even adverbial modifications; as a whole it embodies the actual necessity of Being as transcendent-in-and-to-the-world and man as the transcending. Christian Philosophy does not describe or conditionalize philosophy but is the very fulfillment of form of the philosophical life.

The fourfold intensities show that just as ontology is irreducibly onto-theo-logical, so philosophy "in se" is inherently, implicitly Christian. That is to say, the "Christian" in "Christian Philosophy" is neither adjectival nor even adverbial: it betokens not merely a state or condition but a precondition; so much so that it is to be found even in the pre-Christian wait situation, about which we will speak briefly below. The task is intellectually perilous, and to secure the authenticity of this task, the questions and problems we shall soon face must arise from and remain in historical philosophical thinking. To accomplish this we will discuss the meaning of the catch-up in this order:

1. first with regard to the necessity of the causal structure and how it extends its influence ontologically;
2. then in reference to finitude as the precondition of being-knowingly-in this catch-up structure;
3. the intensification of the intentional presence will reveal the specific *aeviternal* historical temporality that corresponds to the act of being-in-the-world as being-knowingly-in the catch-up structure;
4. and finally, through the *ananke stenai*, the what it is of the point that allows for all the four constituents to have a formational role in the catch-up structure.

Our analysis will find itself necessarily entrenched even more in the supreme confrontation between Martin Heidegger and St. Thomas Aquinas. This confrontation will be compounded with a new and necessarily greater weight; this pressure will insure the necessary violence essential to any productive advance.

The Necessity of the Causal Structure

Causality is more often than not greatly misunderstood. These misunderstandings are exhibited as often as not by its greatest supporters. One of Heidegger's many contributions to metaphysics has been to expose this misconstrued causality and its infectious hold over the understanding of existence. It is time to return to the beginnings and lay bare, quite simply, the structures or parameters or laws of thinking that allow for the catch-up into Being. Why the catch-up is necessary, how it reflects the inseparability of thinking and Being as an inseparability prefigured upon our utter recognition of their difference as difference within metaphysics is the fundamental point. Why is it necessary to say that Being and thinking are distinct, when in our own acts we know it is impossible to separate thinking from Being? This uncanny structure is coinherence or the inseparability factor.

The paradoxical nature of the inseparability factor is this: thinking is distinct from Being, but that distinction is understood by man only through those very acts which cannot separate thinking from Being. Man lives his exteriorized existence, coming to knowledge even of the self only reflexively through knowledge of otherness. He cannot think without Being, he cannot separate thinking from Being. By knowing this, by virtue of his inability to separate thinking from Being, he recognizes the order of the catch-up, the primacy and distinction of existential Being from thought. Causal dependency understood as such is the natural progression of man's thinking about Being. All around man's familiar thereness is this uncanny reasoning, this inseparability factor; he recognizes the difference as difference of Being from thinking through his inability to separate it in his acts. On the one hand, causality is a directional movement, moving man in time; the distinction of thought catching-up to Being in knowledge confirms this. Causality thus is not so much a relation from Being to man, as it would be in some naive objectivism or realism, but from man to Being: it is man's relation to Being. On the other hand, causality is also a kind of thereness in its genuine manifestation. Causality cannot pass over, even as it passes through and with, the beings of the world precisely because the privileged being whose involvement is to move within this causal structure cannot in his acts separate thinking from Being. This inseparability factor carries causality as a thereness, a progressive movement that remains embedded and engages itself in that embedding, situating us ever more deeply in the act of to-be. Everything must be referred to Being and, as we shall see, Being must be referred to God.

The maintenance or recognition of this paradoxical coinherence factor is essential to any genuine thinking about Being. The forgetfulness of Being is evidenced in the forgetfulness of this structure. To recognize this coinherence or inseparability factor means asking, "isn't this enough," and answering "yes and no." By answering "yes and no," what has been understood is that the soul is in a way all things, because the same is for thinking as for being only because in my knowledge I am the other as other. Each of these presuppositions recognizes the uncanny essence of mutual transcendences[6] within causality that we call the inseparability factor. The relationship between thinking and Being is not formed by simple composition and division but preformed by something else, something other, happening in the now within our thereness. So much so that our knowledge of this coinherent unity is prefigured on a unique kind of historical temporal structure.

Causality versus Sufficient Reason

While Heidegger more than others recognizes the uncanny unfamiliar structure of existence, he denies it to be an event of the causal structure.[7] In fact he sees in causality the very antithesis of the strange nature of Being to be concealed. What Heidegger understands to be causality is not causality but a founded form of understanding the relational way of being-in-the-world. This form of causality is not the genuine causal catch-up structure. Just as Heidegger conflated the uncaused into the self-caused and then employed this conflation to explain how the deity entered philosophy, so here we shall see he has conflated or identified causality with the principle of sufficient reason with the same purpose in mind. But we have seen how different is the uncaused cause from the self-caused cause; and we shall presently see how different is the causal principle from the principle of sufficient reason, which is rather a direct and even deterministic causality and it is by no means compatible with maintaining the inseparability factor as the difference as difference. Furthermore, this direct deterministic causality is the culprit behind the problems faced when attempting to understand the possibility of a Christian Philosophy, as well as the modern debacle over free will and determinism.[8]

There is a frightfully long lineage in the history of philosophy that lends credence to Heidegger's critique. Because finitude is conceived as negative limitation, man cannot be a complete ontological unity that yet needs otherness in the systems of Descartes or Leibniz or Spinoza. Man is for them a partial being subsumed under a systematized structure in which Being is power, and his deficient beinghood is revealed in his inability to live within the difference as difference: to live up to his privilege and maintain the twofold paradox of the inseparability factor; to know the world in its effulgent otherness except through some reductive mechanism that substitutes for the intentional presence and by doing so empties the world of its causal effulgence, leaving behind a deterministic chain of sufficient reasons.

Historically, the more self-enclosed thinking became, the more appendage-like the body, and therefore the world, became, and the causal structure was converted into a form of accountability for man's polarity, or an epistemological doctrine utilized to overcome this polarity. But to coinhere as a being-meaningfully-in-the-world requires that while thinking and being are distinct, this distinction is based on an essential unity without which man could not exist. If the inseparability factor is lost, then the role of the highest Being is reduced to solely accounting for and/or compelling the beinghood of man and world, as for instance in Spinoza.[9]

And what then is the highest Being, if His role is merely to account for and/or compel the reconvergence of those aspects of our being which man unnecessarily drove apart? The effects of this direct causality are far-reaching. By subverting the catch-up, cheapening it into some kind of well-timed system superimposed over and against the dynamic and appropriative act of thinking participating in Being, God became what Heidegger has understood all along. And again, if this is the God of Christian Philosophy, then, isn't such a philosophy a radical makeshift that is neither Christian nor philosophical?[10] In direct causality man cannot adhere or respond to or participate in Being, precisely because the mystery, the essential unknowability, of the highest Being cannot be reconciled into the systems of accountability. But it is this very mystery at the heart of Being that allows causality not to be a vicious deterministic system. This mystery comes in many forms, in the uncanniness of the paradoxical structure of the inseparability factor and in the fact that, as Parmenides affirmed, man acts and thinks only within the structure of Being-is. But in his actions and in his thoughts there is still the backdrop of the possibility of something like nonbeing, even if only as an illegitimate no-way, though it is so much more than that, for it is only in alternative to Is-Not that the Is stands in numinous, even divine contrast. And of course with Heidegger even more than that:

> Ever since the question about the essent began, the question of the non-essent, about nothing, has gone side by side with it. And not only outwardly, in the manner of a by-product. Rather the question about nothing has been asked with the same breath. The manner of asking about nothing may be regarded as a gauge and hallmark for the manner of asking about the essent.[11]

A genuine Christian Philosophy depends upon a notion of causality that allows man genuinely to answer "yes-and-no" to the question "isn't this enough?" By answering "yes and no" Christian man recognizes what Heidegger denies to Christian Philosophy, namely the real possibility of the *Nihil.*

Heidegger sees the onto-theo-logic structure of the catch-up as a kind of direct causality that falls under the more specific category of the principle of sufficient reason. The principle of sufficient reason is readily utilized across the philosophic spectrum to support as well as to reinterpret demonstrations for the existence of God. It is quite easy, this day and age, to argue St. Thomas' "*quinque viae*" as logical proofs through the eyes of sufficient reason.[12] Man no longer is aware of the difference between the notion of a "way" and a "proof." The former is the signate of something more and mysterious, and gives us the direction in which we may turn toward it. The path or the way is existence itself. It is a progressive relationship within existence as existence. A proof, on the other hand, has laid the conceptual concrete over and against an unwieldy existence so that man has a clear and distinct path to the origin which will account for all things, and allow a deformed reason to dominate Being.

St. Thomas' prime concern is not directly to account for the things within the world. The intent of his demonstrations was to point to the extent in which we are in a relationship with the divine. Thomistic man understands that yes we can account for natural things by natural causes, but a more primal question is implied: "isn't this enough?" And here he must say no because the entire order of the natural is shot through with and depends upon the order of the supernatural relationship. For St. Thomas, man is involved in a relationship of his thinking catching up to being-with-the-divine; this is the intent of the *quinque viae.* Man is a complete ontological unity that still needs, but not as something that needs something else merely to account for himself and the things around him. What he needs is the truly relational response that speaks to him, why and wherein his thinking catches up to Being, to answer him when he asks why he himself is not indifferent, why unlike everything else he recognizes the inseparability factor, this utter uncanny unity within his being-in-the-world. And however much we may pit St. Thomas against St. Anselm, it is here we can see their convergence; not in the development of proofs, cosmological or ontological, but as meditating and explicating not only the so-called givens of the faith, but those givens as themselves articulations of man's primal being in the world, or, in Voegelin's sense, within the *metaxy*. [13]

Again: man looks around at his surroundings, at the beauty and becoming of the world, a world which has a perfect order that does not itself inquire into the reason of its order; the order is indifferent to him and indifferent to its own order. He sees the beauty, the becoming and the indifference because of the painstaking privilege situated solely in his being-in-time. Causality is the natural ontological asking into man's privileged being, a natural structure that brings man to the door of the divine. For St. Thomas, man is a fully relational being-in-the-world. But to be fully relational requires that he has entered the world already as an asking-being, as a being already in a relationship. Causality is not onto-theo-logical because it lights up clearly and distinctly a direct path to God. It is onto-theo-logical because its structure continuously reveals to us the uncanny familiarity of our already existing relationship with the divine.

When articulating the structure of causality, what is at stake, therefore, is the possibility of being-with and moving-toward the genuine affirmation of man's being-in-God. What is at stake is the possibility of Christian Philosophy: man comes to God not only in faith but in his being-meaningfully-in-and-to-the-world.[14] But when man seeks to account for his world with something like the principle of sufficient reason, what is lost is the meaning of relational-being-in-God as relational-being-in-the-world; what is lost is Christian Philosophy. Causality points toward the reason of or in the world; the point of sufficient reason goes looking for the reason the world. It is an incipiently idealistic attempt to overcome, absorb and reduce *for* the world to a product of reason. To understand truly Heidegger's rejection of causality and the deity and to reap the reward of his insights, we must see the principle of sufficient reason as irreconcilable with classical intentionality.

For Leibniz, there must be a "sufficient reason for the contingent truths and truths of facts."[15] At first glance, such a statement seems not only innocuous but true. It is neither one nor the other. Such a statement has ratified the already established divide between the universal and the particular, deeming the latter to be a lack, a partiality. In this way, the particular can in no way house the universal but at best be a mere effect of it. In the classical vision, intentional presuppositions such as the "same is for thinking as for Being" or "the soul is in a way all things" are not separate or divided from the reasoning needed for "contingent truths and truths of fact . . . for the connexion of the things which are dispersed throughout the universe."[16] Moreover, these presuppositions are the stop in the order of the explanation within these very contingent truths and truths of fact. And as the stop within the order of contingent truths that allows them to be what they are, these stops are arrived at within and through the order of these "contingencies" and truths of fact. Because the stop is arrived at within the order of these truths, and not in spite of them, the meaning or integrity of these truths is very much different from the Leibnizian understanding. Because these truths are, in the classical vision, able to point to their origin, reflecting their origin through their dependency, their contingency is not based on an inability to be truly what they are; rather, their contingency reflects an essential part of being-in-the-world. In classical intentionality, these contingent truths or truths of fact have the role of necessary signate, signifying that there is always something more, something left unsaid and undone in existence. This more, this unsaid, this undone is only further realized at the origin of their dependency, at the end of the order of explanation, in the intentional presuppositions that speak of the universal housed in the particular. And while Leibniz recognized the need for the stop in the order of explanation, it could not be the kind of stop representative of classical intentionality, for it denied any genuine relation with the things in the world in favor of a process of rationalist accountability.

Beyond Causality as Sufficient Reason

How can Christian Philosophy and its causal principle accomplish the task of a genuine philosophy aimed at the first and last grounds of the *essent*, if these grounds have already been, and in advance, accounted for? How can man let thinking "break the paths and open the perspectives of the knowledge that set the norms and hierarchies"?[17] How can man "restore to things, to *essents*, their weight" if the stop in the order of explanation has relieved man of that privilege and obligation by giving him either through faith or reason a roadmap of where thinking must resolve itself? But again, the Leibnizian stop is not the intentional presuppositional stop of

Plato, Aristotle or St. Thomas Aquinas. The principle of sufficient reason doesn't distinguish the presupposition from its constituents in order to highlight their relationship in its unique unity as the difference as difference. Rather, the Leibnizian stop is built on the denial of any relatability between itself and the things within the world. Modern man enters the world as a self-thinking thought chasing Being, as if Being were outside or alien to him, and then, in order to gain control of Being, he exiles out of it any meaningful contingent existence. The problem with the principle of sufficient reason, as Heidegger notes, is its inability to understand the ground relationship between thinking and Being:

> The question we are faced with by the principle of reason is this: to what extent are being and ratio the same? To what extent do grounds and Reason (ratio) on the one side, and being on the other belong together? . . . If we ask to what extent being and bifurcated ratio "might be" the same, that is belong together, then it seems the only thing worth asking about has to do with the accommodation of being on the one side and, on the other side in the averred belonging-together, bifurcated ratio. If one has something like this in mind, then the belonging-together in question appears as though it were some third thing, like a roof, a vault that stands ready, as it were to accommodate. To think this would be cockeyed. Rather, the belonging-together must already light up from what has its abode in it and therefore what also already speaks for itself: being speaks to us . . . "together" means something else and something different than the welding together of two otherwise separate pieces.
>
> Accordingly being qua being must belong to ratio, as well as the reverse.[18]

As we know well, for St. Thomas the relationship between thinking and Being is rooted in and as the analogy of Being, in the inseparability factor of the catch-up. For him, the same within thinking and Being is based on a fundamental difference as difference, on a catch-up that reflects an uncanny unity with distinction, but without division, from otherness, and without alienation. Man enters the world as fully relational being, as an exteriorized existence, so much so that his being is to move in terms of the causal catch-up. For St. Thomas, the catch-up involves thinking adhering to Being and the will adhering to thought. When thinking catches-up to Being, the will rejoices in what it had desired thought to understand.[19] But in the principle of sufficient reason the non-relational stop in the order of explanation, this distant "account-taking" eternal, drove the relationship among created things, between thinking and Being, into a constructed belonging-together, a bifurcated ratio. This rationalist bifurcation led to measuring the things in reality in terms of their power to exist or potential not to exist and then placing them within a hierarchical structure of a will to-power-dominated direct causality.[20]

What were once intentional presuppositions became the remnant sign-posts of a distant eternal, and this distant deity had no reasonable relatability to the things in the world. And how could it? The things within the world were not competent for a relationship precisely because they were not complete ontologically. Man could at first, in Modern philosophy, only reach far enough to account for himself. The distant eternal made up the difference for the incomplete being-ness by accounting for whatever could not be accounted for by the ego such as other extended things dispersed throughout the universe. I don't get to God through the world, as I do for St. Thomas; instead I get to the world through God.

To give an account of something is a genuine duty of thought. But blind continual accounting wherein "reason as such demands to be given back as reasons," in order for the cognizing subject to eliminate a lack in being that seems un-fitting to reason yet very much present in creation is to degrade the whole process of causality, as well as its corresponding Highest Being, into a system.[21]

Through the hierarchical levels of accounting, sufficient reason reverses the adherence structure of the catch-up. This especially includes the elevation of the will over the intellect. In this elevation, as Heidegger notes, "God exists only insofar as the principle of reason holds."[22] When the elevation and dominance of the will infiltrated and degraded the act of the catch-up, the meaning of God, as we have shown, was reduced to the role of accounting for the otherwise unaccountable. Here the rationalist answer to "isn't this enough" is a clear and distinct "No," but one which will historically lead to an equally clear and distinct "Yes." And finally, as the "cognizing subject" begins to realize that the demands for reason can in a sense be answered by his own will to power, it is then in man's will that he finds the last proof for the existence of God. Paradoxically the intellect ends in infallibility before the floodgates of skepticism and nihilism wash it away.

The need for the catch-up is best seen in the aftermath of its reversal by the elevation of will over intellect. In this reversal, not only does the relationship between God and man become diminished, it becomes alienated. To keep God as a necessary element in the system of man's existence becomes ever more strained. In the catch-up there are parameters, a structure. The structure is existence itself and man announces that structure. The causal catch-up thus provides man with the framework of his being-there; as existing, he is fully there but his thereness requires an essential distance. In the principle of sufficient reason this distance is at odds with the framework of existence. This is why modern philosophy in its rational idealistic shape was a system. Man is dislodged from any understanding of being-in the inseparability factor and all that comes across is that which cannot not be caught-up. Without existence as the causal matrix of the catch-up there are no limits, no genuine fully relational stop in the order of explanation except that which man imposes upon himself and the world. If he could, he would be, as reason is, infallible. The transcendental Ego would be king.

The principle of sufficient reason cannot demonstrate the way in which man and God are fully relational. Rather it proves the existence of God in such a way that the existence of God depends upon man leaving something left over for God to account for, something like Kant's *noumenon*. Again, as Heidegger notes, God exists only insofar as the principle of sufficient reason holds; in a word, only insofar as man leaves him something extra or unaccounted for. In the end, the distant eternal becomes even further and higher, and in that sense, impotent. He is greater in that His Will is more comprehensive. And after the historical collapse of Hegelian idealism, there is no longer any role for Him to play other than religious. He may as well not exist even if he does exist.

At odds with himself and the world in the dissolution of the catch-up structure, man comes to identify the origin of that alienation as God himself (Feuerbach & Marx). Being-in-the-world as Being-in-God was no longer reasonable. After Descartes, it was only a few short steps into Idealism: why restrain the will when it can leap forth and account for all things? God was not even needed to account for the unaccountable, nothing was outside the purview of the will. Heidegger is in a sense the final word on the principle of sufficient reason. For the moderns, the irreconcilability or unrelatability between the truths of reason and the contingent things (the world) needed to be explained or swept up into the region of clear and distinct ideas, either situated in the distant eternal or in man, or finally to be swept aside altogether.[23]

For Heidegger, the only stop left was to rid ontology of its causal structure once and for all, and to allow for the endlessness of the phenomenon to arrive at the real non-onto-theo-logical meaning of "Nothing is without reason." In that principle, the will resolves the problem of the origin of the essent as Nothing. For Heidegger, the will needn't find itself restrained in a causal apparatus, needn't embrace clear and distinct ideas, needn't eliminate contradiction but seize it as the very bulwark against the divine. Because the will never stops, it continues in the face of nothing, freeing itself for the event of its ownmost historical destiny.[24]

Both Heidegger and St. Thomas would agree that the desire to overcome what seemed unaccountable in Being (a desire that undoubtedly changes the face of the nature of the stop) by explaining it away dilutes the meaning of Being. While the Leibnizian principle is very much an attempt to rid existence of the uncanny it leaves behind the trace evidence of it. Heidegger seeks to salvage the uncanny from the principle of sufficient reason. For him, the problem with sufficient reason is precisely that causality suppresses Being, forcing it to resign its nonbeing for a theological scaffolding. If the causality were stripped from the principle, then it would evoke the fundamental question about Being, the question why there is something rather than nothing. For St. Thomas, the problem is that this sufficient reason is not causality but the very antithesis of the catch-up. The "causality" of sufficient reason denies the mystery and reduces the meaning of the divine to something like an essentialist will-based self-caused cause. For Heidegger and St. Thomas, sufficient reason doesn't leave man enough room to be genuinely open to the infinite. For Heidegger, we must strip the last vestiges of causality and close off the door to the divine once and for all. For St. Thomas, causality must be returned to its genuine adherence in the inseparability factor.

The meaning of the nondemonstrability within the intentional presuppositions is the key difference between St. Thomas and Heidegger on the one hand and someone like Leibniz or even Husserl on the other. For St. Thomas the nondemonstrability of an intentional presupposition cannot, and does not, enclose its truth in an apodictically abstracted autonomy outside any referential aspect to the things or *essents* within the world, and neither does it for Heidegger. The intentional presuppositions are completely immersed in being-in-the-world, entering into the language of the traditional everyday, often as the uncanny. We start from being-in-the-world, and experience the stop in the order of explanation within it. Heidegger reinterprets the principle of sufficient reason as a referent to the nullity that would prohibit man from straying from being-in-the-world and into a founded ontotheologism.[25] Why there is something rather than nothing eliminates causality and the divine; the Nothing rushes in to take their places.

Causality and Christian Philosophy

Heidegger sees in the principle of reason the possibility of the reclamation of nonbeing the non-*essent*, at the core of genuine philosophical asking, but in this he sees the im-possibility of Christian Philosophy:

> Abstract thinking a feast? The highest form of human existence? Indeed. But at the same time we must observe how Nietzsche views the essence of the feast, in such a way that he can think of it only on the basis if his fundamental conception of all being, will to power. "The feast implies: pride, exuberance, frivolity; mockery of all earnestness and respectability; a divine affirmation of oneself, out of animal plenitude and perfection: all obvious states to which the Christian may not honestly say Yes. The feast is paganism par excellence." For that reason, we might add, the feast of thinking never takes place in Christianity. That is to say, there is no Christian philosophy. There is no true philosophy that could be determined anywhere else than from within itself.[26]
>
> A "Christian Philosophy" is a round square and a misunderstanding. There is, to be sure, a thinking and questioning elaboration of the world of Christian experience, i.e., of faith. That is theology. . . . For the original Christian faith philosophy is foolishness. To philosophize is to ask: "Why are there essents rather than nothing?" Really to ask the question signifies: a daring attempt to fathom this unfathomable question by disclosing what it summons us to ask, to push our question to the very end.[27]

Is he right? Doesn't the certainty of the kind of Being that theology hands over to its Christian Philosophy destroy the whole process of thinking and being within Being-is? Philosophers come to say that "Being-is" from a transformational standpoint, from the dark and uncanny. Parmenides must enter the gates of Night and Day, in order to speak meaningfully of Being. How can the uncanny sense that something lurks within the shadows of becoming, i.e., the possibility of nonbeing, survive in the light of a theologically dominated philosophy, even if that theologically saturated philosophy claims to have its origin not in accountability but in the relational act of being-in-the-world? Does such a distinction really make a difference?

Let us begin with the abbreviated, seemingly simpler, and ostensibly stricter form of the question: "Why are there essents?" When we inquire in this way, we start from the essent. The essent-is. It is given, it confronts us; accordingly, it is to be found at any time, and it is, in certain realms, known to us. Now this essent from which we start, is immediately questioned as to its ground. The question advances immediately toward a ground. . . . Tacitly we are asking after another and higher kind of essent. But here the question is not by any means concerned with the essent as such and as a whole. But if we put the question in the form of our original interrogative sentence: "Why are there essents rather than nothing?" This addition prevents us in our questioning from beginning directly with an unquestionably given essent and, having scarcely begun, from continuing to another expected essent as a ground. Instead this essent, through questioning, is held out into the possibility of nonbeing. . . . Why is the essent torn away from the possibility of nonbeing? . . . This "rather than nothing" is no superfluous appendage to the real question, but is an essential component of the whole interrogative sentence, which as a whole states an entirely different question from that intended in the question "Why are there essents?" With our question we place ourselves in the essent in such a way that it loses its self-evident character as the essent. The essent begins to waver between the broadest and most drastic extremes: either essents—or nothing—and thereby the questioning itself loses all solid foundation. Our questioning being-there is suspended, and in this suspense is nevertheless self-sustained.[28]

Is the structure of Christian Philosophy grounded upon, or does it lead to, the same kind of self-evident certainty of the moderns? Has Christianity emphasized the chain of command among the differences as differences in the world so much so that the unity of difference is dependent on a highest Being rid of all sense of nothingness? Does the causality of St. Thomas Aquinas end in the same certainty as Descartes', if Christianity is the prime force behind both? On a more radical level, this means that because, according to Heidegger, Christian Philosophy presumes to know the answer before it even asks the question, there is no real asking and thus no real thinking and thus no real philosophy in Christianity.

Because Christian Philosophy and its causal structure are inseparably involved in the coinherence factor, it more than merely retains or accommodates the possibility of the uncanny or the backdrop of the possibility of nonbeing when it says Being-is. Of necessity, it has the greatest involvement in the recognition of reverence for and deference to the uncanny. For St. Thomas, a relation is based on dependency, but because of the primacy of existence, the dependents in this relationship are not partial realities needing something else or something other to complete or account for their being-ness. The principle of sufficient reason brought forth an essentialist will-based self-caused cause. The uncaused cause of St. Thomas has none of the problems of direct causality; for him, man is complete ontologically as an originatingly relational completion. The key is the notion of man as an originatingly relational completion.

Christian Philosophy is implicitly evidenced in the causal structure of all the early thinkers who have, when at the edge of the uncanny, asked "isn't this enough" and have answered "yes and no." And because genuine causality is not a direct or deterministic search for a vulgar accountability but rather the very maintenance of the strange as divine, we can show how the causal structure of the early thinkers reflects something essential to Christian Philosophy. The strange must become through history either the alienation of its unfulfillment or the ratification of its divinity.

But, Heidegger is not an early thinker; he has become rather that man of the forest who has stayed within the strange too long, outlasting its becoming as the strange by denying its emergence into the divine. He has not recognized the length and limit of philosophy, of the *essent*. He has waited too long and did not answer "yes and no," and as such the strange became alien. He left himself in the forest unable to accept the No-thing. In nullity, he waited too long, unaware that he had already left the movement of being-in-the-world, forgetting the privileged access of our being to participate in the formation of the meaning of Being.

The inseparability factor, the linchpin of causality, is the existential recognition of the causal structure of being as mysterious, it allows us to see our ownmost being-in-time in its unique temporality as a thereness and a movement. Man's thereness and movement are not composed of two different temporalities but are one unitary act-in-time. As such, causality is not a superficial glance across the back of Being, it is the very existential-temporal way of the kind of being that man is; it is inseparable from him as a knowing historical being. Causality, as seen in its intensity, is the very structure or framework in which being-in-the-world is what it is. Its framework comprises the beginning *qua* end of philosophy.

As the act of inquiry most prized by the privileged being, philosophy is the first seeking into Being, the first herald of the catch-up structure. To enter the structure or nature of philosophy is undoubtedly to engage the causal catch-up of thinking into Being. It is the template by which we gauge and return to, again and again, the question, "isn't this enough?"[29]

Thus understood, philosophy is inseparable from the causal intensity. Through it, man's historical becoming in being is given its name or form: to locate, announce and participate in the causal intensity is the e-vent of philosophy. Philosophical inquiry/asking situates us more than anything else in our ownmost being-in-the-world. As the accentuated manifestation of our nature, it is the paradigm of who we are: the fully participating non-participating spectator in-and-to-the-world. Here we have the larger meaning of the midwifery simile: the essential distance required for *noetic* involvement. The philosophical enterprise is thus the emphatic annunciation of that essential distance in which we reside. It understands that this spectatorship position corresponds to our ownmost thereness within being-in-the-world, because it lays open for all time the uncanny nature of the catch-up.

As a special kind of asking, philosophy is able to grasp the temporality involved in the inseparability factor. As a being-in-the-world, man is fully in time when he inquires into being-in-the-world, but the what it is of what he asks about points toward a unified historical being-in-and-to-the-world; a unique kind of eternality in which man is a participant. Man is a fully relational being, a philosophical being within this balance between his temporal becoming and his ownmost historical eternality. Neither the temporal becoming nor the uncanny sense of eternality can be forsaken when one seeks to understand the event of the catch-up, the event of man as the event of philosophy. Heidegger, to a certain degree, understands this balance:

> We ask the question "How does it stand with being?" "What is the meaning of being?" not in order to set up an ontology on the traditional style, much less to criticize the past mistakes of ontology. We are concerned with something totally different: to restore man's being-there—and that always includes our own future being-there in the totality of history allotted to us—to the domain of being, which it was originally incumbent on man to open up for himself. All this, to be sure, in the limits within which philosophy can accomplish anything. . . . Philosophy is historical only insofar as it—like every work of the spirit—realizes itself in time.[30]

But for Heidegger this balance maintained in philosophy stands within the historical as historical, as if the historical could maintain itself without adherence to an end. The balance is for him an endless event, an event of thereness without any causal movement. It is only a "happening for the sake of a happening."[31]

Our difference with Heidegger stands in the ground roots of philosophy, in what philosophy demands of its privileged being. Philosophy requires that man recognize the event of the causal structure he alone apprehends. Because philosophy is inherently causal its temporal balance is not (and cannot maintain itself as) "happening for the sake of happening." It is rather for the sake of an end, and without that end, philosophy itself could not be named as the essential inquiry into man's being; it would not have the length and limits to be the essential guiding force through which man understands the event of his being as a participant in the formation of the meaning of Being.

The unity of man's temporal progression and the mysterious *aeviternality* within his historical being-there are embedded in the very structure of existence as the kind of temporality of the privileged being. Philosophy is the herald of that structure. All philosophical inquiry (particularly the demonstrations of the existence of God) are a form of the question, "isn't this enough?" And because philosophical asking is the kind of inquiry that possesses the balance of man's unique temporality it can lay open the tradition or the structure of our ownmost being in the catch-up. We look at this clearing, and begin to understand what we are. As Heidegger remarks, "the tradition will open up to us only if we bring into view what it brings to us."[32]

The Wait and Christian Philosophy

Philosophy is already onto-theo-logical in its asking, housing the universal in the particular, in the historical tradition, so much so that the eternality of its asking unfolds only in its temporal becoming. If philosophy is inherently Christian there will be evidence of a "waiting" within the tradition for the answer to the asking. The asking of such questions as "isn't this enough" can be formed because of this unique kind of eternality that persists through time. But the answer must wait in time to be resolved because man's kind of eternality unfolds only within the temporal structure. This balance within the inseparability factor, within the movement toward the historical articulation of the causal intensity, we call the "wait." If causality is a "catch-up" structure of thinking into Being, then thinking has a "waitfulness" to it in its desire to know the sameness it has with Being. The same is for thinking and for Being is based on a difference as difference: that difference resides in the way Being comes to be known in the temporality of the privileged being, and that way requires something like a "wait"; to be along the way is to be involved in a process-of-being and processes take time. To understand the causal intensity as the very way in which man exists as a participant in the formation of the meaning of Being means that man doesn't merely traverse the path of Being, nor is he situated in a solely absolutized essentialized existence. For man there is always something more, something left over, something uncanny, and his eternality moves toward this in the form of a catch-up or a historical "waiting" within the particular.

The issue of the "wait" as the embodiment of the causal catch-up that would link Christianity *essentially* with philosophy is delicate and easily misunderstood, and so before proceeding, a few comments are in order. It will be objected from what some consider to be the side of ratio that the notion of the Wait is so purely theological, indeed so soteriological, that it is the illegitimate imposition of alien religious categories upon philosophical phenomena in a sort of facile retrodiction. From the side of a particular conception of fides, on the other hand, it will be objected that to consider such a notion as the Wait to be philosophical at all dilutes, even negates the unique and irreducible necessity of freely given grace, making what cannot even be expected to be indeed predictable. Either, therefore, it is too Christian to be philosophical or too philosophical to be Christian; if it is not one or the other it must needs be neither the one nor the other. But our point is far different.

The idea of the Wait as an existential-ontological component of finite existence is the unsaid but implicit category running throughout Greek tragedy and philosophy, most dramatically discoverable in Plato and Aristotle. It is not a case of baptizing the Greeks. Rather is it a case of seeing what is there to be seen. And what is there to be seen is the philosophical elaboration of a philosophical problem whose only philosophical resolution philosophically requires a theological possibility. If the idea of the Wait therefore is a critical descriptive indicator of finite human existence it would be more strange not to find it deeply embedded yet struggling to be articulated, than to find it. And so the objections ring false and fail. It is not an attempt to rationalize religious concepts along the lines of Hegel, although it is not a denial of their ontic rootedness and rational intelligibility. Nor is it that kind of patronizing and vulgar dismissal of the Greeks as merely pre-Christian, unlucky enough to be born before the "Truth" was revealed to all with the kind of pseudo-certitude that would make even a Cartesian's jaw drop.

Aristotle perhaps best articulates the causal catch-up "wait" structure or the uncanny sense of the inseparability factor when in his *Nichomachean Ethics* he entered the deepest *aporia* as he began to describe the way to beatitude. He refined the natures of virtue, knowledge, friendship and pleasure into a unified perfection, so much so that virtually no man on this side of eternity could achieve it, insisting and encouraging man to try to immortalize himself while admitting its impossibility for man as man to achieve. After having identified, sought and exhausted the candidates for the good life, he has settled on the philosophic life as the paradigm of happiness. But now in that famous passage in Book X he admits, if not defeat, at least a recognition of his, and our, embarrassing predicament.

> But such a life would be too high for man; for it is not insofar as he is man that he will live so, but in so far as something divine is present within him; and by so much as this is superior to our composite nature is its activity superior to that which is the exercise of the other kind of virtue. If reason is divine, then, in comparison with man, the life according to it is divine in comparison with human life. But we must not follow those who advise us, being men, to think of human things, and, being mortal, of mortal things, but must, so far as we can, make ourselves immortal, and strain every nerve to live in accordance with the best thing in us; for even if it be small in bulk, much more does it in power and worth surpass everything.[33]

Aristotle here lays the predicate for a natural beatitude and then confesses a solely divine element as its procurer. This paradox can be maintained only within the framework of Christianity. Without Christ, not only would Aristotle have leapt into an epistemological absurdity, but his paradox having become a contradiction would fail to gain any historical ontic validity; so much so that the philosopher would become fully man only at the price of becoming philosophically not merely meta-physica but meta-cosmos and finally *contra mundum.* Plato's non-participating spectator would not be able to step away and still be within the *noetic* world. A world in Wait without its *telos* carries no meaning: it is an empty Form. The historical path of being-in-the-world has always been a happening for the sake of an end.

Intentional Presence *qua* Finitude

When Descartes remarks "We must in the end acknowledge the infirmity of our nature,"[34] he has summarily conveyed the utter collapse in man's philosophical understanding of finitude. Man no longer considers himself in an originary relationship with the divine, and no longer senses how that relationship with Being must necessarily be a dependency based on a radical activity. Rather he only sees the distance as distance: the theoretical imbalance or disproportion that Husserl knew had to be corrected. Modern man is rootlessly rooted in the divine but has forgotten the ancient vision which recognized that the difference as difference is prefigured on a unity.

The very reason negative causality has the appearance of a prolonged or endless ladder of accountability with none of the essential distance *qua* unity of the causal inseparability factor can be traced to the degradation of finitude from an active need to a passive limitation. Man lives in a state of forgetfulness, neglecting finitude as the way or activity of existence which makes man's being to be privileged.

The prerequisite for the causal catch-up depends entirely upon finitude as an original activity, so much so that finitude is the precondition of the existential structure of the catch-up. It is in the very nature of finitude to have limits and dependency. But if finitude's original in-dwelling is seen as a mere potential or a limiting lack, its limitations demand that man be bound to a world he cannot know, leaving him not only naturally un-open to the infinite but open only to the possibility of nihilating Being by moving toward its ownmost quality as an originating lack. This takes us back to our earlier point about the substitutes for intentionality. What is ushered out the front door of thought must somehow be smuggled through a back door, and so God and world must be reached by: innate ideas, the a priori, engagement. Finitude is reduced to that which inescapably distances ourselves from God as a limit or imperfection or lack instead of the binding reminder of the originary relationship. In a word, rather than being created by God as the very difference as difference upon which we actively know of our union with the divine, finitude becomes the null basis to divide man from God. As such the ladder of sufficient reason must be lengthy if it is to overcome a finitude far closer to saying that Being-Is-Not.

Finitude in its intensity is an original activity, an activity based on a relationship wherein man is ontologically involved in the way for things to be. By active need we understand that for man to be a fully relational being-in-the-world finitude must begin in actuality, in an activity. Therefore his need is not based on a lack or privation but rather on a plenitude. How could finitude be based on anything else, if Being really Is? How can man participate in Being, if his central defining factor is contrary to that relationship as a partial being that moves more in terms of Being Is-Not? Isn't this the heart of St. Thomas' doctrine of the intimate union of soul and body, and of his criticisms of Platonic dualism?

This need rooted in plenitude overflows man and places him not outside Being, but in a spectatorship position in which he can actively and meaningfully participate. Isn't this knowledge in the Thomistic sense? That activity, that actuality is situated wholly in our being-in-the-world beginning in the nondemonstrable descriptive fact of existence, in an intentionality that already knows that Being-Is. We begin in and never leave the house of Being, it is our kind of thereness. Finitude is the source of the *noetic* activity that springs from the intentional ground of the mutual acts of to be.[35] The privilege of playing in the house of Being-Is requires that we ourselves are complete ontological unities. Man cannot possibly know that Being-Is from Being Is-Not. He may indeed say Being-Is-Not, but that annihilation is possible only on the very basis of Being-Is.

Man is always being-in, as a fundamentally and inseparably a relational being and intentionality is the critical indicator of the origin and extent of his relationship. In the structure of thinking catching-up to Being, man desires to understand what intentionality already pre-knows: that Being-Is. As an originatingly relational Being-in, his finitude is the active need, the driving force of his *noetic* act to turn toward what he is: a being-in-the-world, a being-in-otherness, a being-in-the-divine, thus coming to know himself only in knowing the Other.

Man is a being-in-the-world and a being-in-otherness, and a being-in-the-divine, all at the same time because this nondemonstrable descriptive fact of existence is onto-theo-logical. The intentional ground of man's active need places him in the uncanny, in the midst of his unique kind of temporality, for finitude is the vehicle of transcendence. The finite intensity is the original activity of his being-in-time, in its temporal becoming and its unique eternality, it is why he answers "yes and no."[36] Therefore, finitude is from its beginning open to the infinite. Our complete involvement in being-in-the-world requires this activity and ability to turn toward and be open to the infinite: to recognize through our finitude the difference as difference, and speak the very fact of existence that Being-Is.

The activity of finite need can never fall into a meager passive limitation constrained within a mere temporal progression. It is the bringing into view of intentionality which can only mean Being-Is: the nature of the relationship says Being-Is. We cannot have intentionality as a fact and not have Being-Is. I am the Other as Other (not as myself) because finitude is the assimilation of my being in-and-to-the-world that doesn't begin or end in alienation. Yes, indeed, finitude is a "throwness" into the uncanny of the intentional ground, but it does not and cannot resolve itself in limit or lack or nullity. Heidegger's finitude denies its relationship with the onto-theo-logical and cannot bring into view its *telos*, nor is it competent to hold in view in any kind of permanence of Being precisely because, for Heidegger, finitude is driven by the null basis of existence.[37]

Man's relationship with Being-Is is and will always be a fully relational activity. It only degrades into a form of accountability when Being-Is is

denied or diluted. Man not only endures this activity, this kind of temporality, this otherness, but participates in bringing into view Being-Is. Thinking
cannot be caught-up to Being-Is if finitude is in any way a signate of Being
Is-Not. When finitude is lost, man becomes alienated from his world and
from the possibility of genuine transcendence. Man lives nihilation becoming the very dis-embodied signate of Being Is-Not when he becomes constrained to limited things.

Aristotle, on the other hand, having entered his *aporia* in Bk. X of
the *Nichomachean Ethics* understood quite well the criterion of perfection, the
paradox of existence, that to be finite means to be open to the infinite. In
a word, if finitude were only a passive limitation, intentionality would
not be basic. To say that the soul is, in a way, all things presupposes that
there is a way for each thing to be. The lost logic of the classics is again this:
if there were no way for things to be there would be no things. But there are
things, therefore there must be a way for things to be. And this is the presuppositional logic of the five ways.

The privileged being's ownmost being-in is itself a way for things to be.
There is one Being that agrees with all.[38] Because finite being is a way or
a relationship based on the causal catch-up activity in and to and with
Being-Is, man understands himself only by becoming the other as other in
being-in-the-world. Therefore only in finite being as active need can man
really have Being-Is: Being-Is has its self-identity but as causally creative not
only endures but rejoices in otherness. If finite being were not an originating activity deeply active in the intentional structure of existence, we
could not come in any way to the existence of Being-Is or God-Is.

In objection three to St. Thomas' famous demonstrations for the existence
of God, the objector remarks: "if the existence of God were demonstrated,
this could only be from His effects. But His effects are not proportioned to
Him, since he is infinite and His effects are finite, and between the infinite
and the finite there is no proportion."[39] St. Thomas' response to the objector shows us that the *quinque viae* depend upon finitude as the prime motive
of existence, as the vehicle of transcendence that retains the mystery of
Being:

> From effects not proportioned to the cause no perfect knowledge of that
> cause can be obtained. Yet from every effect the existence of the cause
> can be clearly demonstrated, and so we can demonstrate the existence of
> God from his effects; though from them we cannot know God perfectly as
> He is in His essence.[40]

Finite being gives us the existence of the cause, it gives us Being-Is, but the what it is of Being-Is retains its mysteriousness as the uncaused cause. This mystery is at the core of man's active need, it plunges him into an ever deeper intensity with Being-Is. As the vehicle of transcendence, finitude directs or informs the causal catch-up of its direction as a thereness and a movement. Finitude and causality may be given a conceptual distinction but in the act of to-be their movement is one unified phenomenon becoming the intentional presence in tension to the ground of Being.

The intentional presence has asked, "isn't this enough?" He has recognized the exteriority of his soul, the necessity of a fundamental activity within his need for otherness and he has answered neither "yes" nor "no," but "yes and no." Everything he has done so far points toward his unique temporal being-in, his *aeviternal* structure.

Grounded in existence, his privilege is to be in-formed by and in existence to the extent to which there is something more, something left over, something left unsaid. To be in-formed requires that man's own temporality be of such a capacity it can be both fully in the world and in a distance from it as a spectator, so that he may name his being-in. He does not and can not merely choose to be in the world at one moment and deny its efficacy in the next. As the non-participating participating spectator, his being-in is formed with each of his acts so that he may speak the fact that Being-is. He is a revelatory being, taking in at each turn the fact of Being-is.

To be in-formed is to accept the ground of existence as onto-theo-logical, to recognize the super-sensible in the midst of the phenomenon. But the side effects of direct causality reduced man's relationship within the world to a scientifically objectivized stance. Man effectively lost any sense of being formed by the world (at most he is determined by it) and replaced that lost notion with a process of representation. He denied the factical existence of Being-is, favoring an essence structure that contained only what he could ascertain in representation. He effectively moved Being-is toward Being Is-Not, toward ideas and conceptions and abstractions far away from the formation of the things themselves.

Modern man, with Descartes as the supreme representative, is at odds with existence because the modern's God is at odds with His creation. Because He has been reduced to the source of accountability, His participation in His creation is also reduced to a bare laying forth of the possibility of representation for man, rather than giving him a world in which man is formed in the degrees of Being-Is as a participant in the formation of the meaning of Being. There is no integrity in this "onto-theo-logical" structure, if man's relationship to God is based solely on representation. In this impasse, modern man came to realize it would be just as easy to take over this structure, as the producer of these representations. In the modern decline, man is utterly annihilated from his activity to be in-formed in existence and existence is subsumed by thought.

Modern man is two things, and two things at the same time: he is cogito, that is an unbounded unit with no need for otherness. But at the same time, when he takes the extra step and seeks to affirm his attachment to a body he becomes an incomplete bounded unit with total need for the God of the accounting and representation process.

In this struggle of Modernity between man as an unbounded unit with no real ontological or formational need for God, and man as needing God to account, represent and cosign for corporeal existence, the former position has prevailed. After God has gotten man back into the world, what is the point of actively keeping Him around? Once we have reentered existence, are we not able to take over the accounting and representing necessary to live as objectively-subjectively as possible?

Summation of Finitude: Revisiting the Wait

The loss of the meaning of man's privilege as a formational being has far-reaching repercussions: now man thinks his privilege is to say Being Is-Not. If man is to grasp Being-Is, if he is to gather in-time something other than either the mere chronological progression of events or the absolutism of his representational ego, if he is to be a meaningful happening for the sake of an end, then his historical beinghood depends entirely on the onto-theo-logic/catch-up/wait structure of existence.

The meaning of the wait is the most critical aspect of man's genuine activity in the world. The wait houses man's unique temporality. The wait structure is the historical evocation of man's adherence to existence for his knowledge. In-time man is most fully in-the-world, but his being-in is prefigured on an essential distance that allows him to understand his active need as the privileged being. As a being-in-wait, man's eternality comes to-be-in-time, in his temporal *aeviternal* becoming. The wait accomplishes this because it is the temporal existence that befits man. It is the process of the super-sensible unfolding in the midst of the phenomenon, the uncanny emerging as divine, so much so that it is the historical movement of the privileged being. The wait over and in-time is the historical articulation of the formation of the intentional presence.

Modernity unfortunately must deny anything like a wait structure, for something like waiting leaves open questions un-accounted for. He cannot accept that he must wait by becoming the other as other, accomplished in an exteriorized temporal existence; instead, it becomes certain that the knowledge of our existence taken in its precise meaning cannot depend on things whose existence is not yet known to us. He accepts that all knowledge is within the domain and power of consciousness, and in due time (as if time is nothing) he will account for what he desires to know by constituting the world.

Nevertheless, to be the access way requires that man be formed by what he comes to know. Being-Is demands from its privileged beings the greatest dependency and involvement in being-in-the-world. Man's knowledge of Being-Is is prefigured on his being-in-formed. This act of being-in-formed, this intensity of the intentional presence, this non-participating fully participating spectator as wayfarer on the *confinium* of Being, we will call *aeviternal formation*. To know the meaning of being-in in its original evocation is not merely to say what is seen or encountered. Man's being-in at the core of Being-Is cannot mean that he merely reads off appearances as they come. Such a conception is an impossibility that fails to recognize that what comes to be at the very core of Being-Is is man himself! Man is a being-toward, in the midst of the very activity of Being-Is, through his own formation as being-in-formed.

Heidegger has also leveled this same charge, that modern man's being-in-the-world is reduced to mere representation and he has leveled it against the entire metaphysical enterprise as such .[41]

But he has filed this charge based on the same misinterpretations that led him to misread the metaphysical God as self-caused cause and causality as sufficient reason. And by doing so, Heidegger is at an impasse regarding man's being-in-formed and being-in-wait. His thought, straddling both his categorical rejection of a metaphysics already in decline and his acceptance and refurbishing of modern, particularly Kantian concepts unable to replace genuine intentional being-in-the-world, left him susceptible himself to a somewhat representational way of being-in-knowing.

Heidegger has recognized, in spite of his ontological difficulties, that man can never place himself in a scientized objective position. For him, man cannot engage the phenomenon if he neglects to realize that the horizon of Being includes the total involvement of his being. Heidegger senses the importance of something like the intentional presence.[42]

Heidegger has also returned to modern man a kind of waitingness[43] as an essential aspect of man's historical Dasein.[44] He understands more than most the involvement required for man's being-in-the-world. And from his noble fight against the historicists and the absolutists alike, he has returned to man a sense of waiting in being-in-time. In modern day, he is perhaps the sole figure to recognize historical being-in-time in its integrity, its irreplaceability and its irreducibility.[45]

Undoubtedly, Heidegger has also recognized the strange, the uncanny. The world for him is *novitas mundi*, full of risk and project. The beauty, terror and becoming of existence, the uncanniness of man as an asking being are safeguarded by him.[46]

Unfortunately, he could not have a fully involved Dasein because he could not envision an *aeviternal* formation for Dasein. Heidegger would not root this uncanny in anything that allows it to emerge as divine. He accepted its untimeliness as a descriptive fact over and against the world of Being-Is. Unable to recognize that what makes a fact factical is its onto-theo-logical ground, he failed to allow the causal catch-up structure to emerge at all, let alone emerge as divine. The uncanny could not wait any longer and plummeted into alienation. For him, man as philosophical being remains and will always remain untimely, and at odds with Being itself.[47]

Heidegger chose to remain in the forest of something like a wait. But having denied that a wait is waiting for something else, Dasein could not genuinely adhere to anything other; he waited in the forest until he became stranded in the thicket of nonbeing of Being-Is-Not. Because he denied the uncanny as the signate of the onto-the-logical fact of existence, Being could not be for him both self-identical and enjoy or even endure otherness.[48] Instead, he bound this uncanny to remain un-timely within the free activity that pertains to Dasein:

> The passage from the ordinary tonality of the principle into the unusual one stands, as a leap, under no compulsion. The leap remains a free and open possibility of thinking; this so decisively so that in fact the essential province of freedom and openness first opens up with the realm of the leap.[49]

This kind of deontological freedom was based upon man's unopenness to the infinite, his proximity to the null-basis, a freedom secured *against* the divine, a freedom to say and become Being Is-Not. For Heidegger, only at the edge of the abyss could man be free for a full existence situated fully in the world. Is this not the meaning of Resolve (Entschliessen)?

This fundamental irreconcilability between Dasein and the *aeviternal* formation of intentional presence finds its source in the possibility of Christian Philosophy. Heidegger's acceptance of an essence structure, and his utilization of it in phenomenology went the greatest distance to deny any genuine onto-theo-logic relatability between man and God, and as such severed any meaningful ties between Christianity and Philosophy. The essence structure has always had its serious problems, it is not merely that Heidegger has perverted it. Rather he has taken what is there to be seen and has brought it to its own inevitability, to a freedom born out of skirting the edge of existential nullity.

In such a structure, nullity is the central defining factor of man's being-in because Being cannot be both self-identical and endure otherness unless it is causally creative, which he denies a priori. And if it cannot endure otherness, there can be nothing like the inseparability factor that points toward pure Being-Is, or a finitude as active need based on plenitude and an openness to the infinite. And finally there can be no ontological support for the Christian God. Why? Because in an essence structure, "the distance from nothing to being is no greater than being itself makes it."[50]

The meaning of the fourfold as the active recognition of the inseparability factor, of the difference as difference between man and God as prefigured on an original unity is at stake. In the essence structure there is no catch-up possible, there is nothing in man's existence that genuinely gives him any united activity or any relatability to God; the distance between man and God is confounding in all ways. Why? Because, man is far closer to Being Is-Not, and for this reason is he free. In such a structure, God is the distant eternal, at best the God of accountability and representation. Man is situated on the very edge of formlessness rather than being a being-in-formed.

But when existence has a real role to play, the unity at the ground of the difference as difference between man and God is not only maintained but thrives: Being can be both self-identical and enjoy otherness. Man recognizes the difference between his creaturehood and God as creator, but not because it is a chasmic divide, and not somehow in spite of his being-in on the verge of total annihilation. Yes, the difference between man and God is infinite, but that difference is not a distance frustrated at its beginnings with every attempt to overcome it. It is not a distance as Heidegger understands it to be, through which metaphysics has set up a partition between the sensible and the nonsensible in hope that the endless length to God might be lessened.[51]

It isn't a difference that needs to be overcome or accounted for; it is rather what places man in the adherence structure. How? Because, "although to create a finite effect does not point toward an infinite power, to create out of nothing does point toward an infinite power. And indeed it must be so, if what is at stake is existence, because, between to be and not to be, the distance is infinite."[52] In a word, man recognizes his unity with God because he himself in his very existence has an infinite distance from nothingness, an infinite distance from nullity. That distance, that infinity situates him in his likeness in the image of the divine. His being-in-time is onto-theological from the start.

The *Aeviternal* Structure of the Intentional Presence

Man, says St. Thomas, by virtue of his intellectual soul stands on the borderline, "the horizon or *confinium* between eternity and time."[53] It would do no violence to his understanding to say even more: man is the horizon between time and eternity, and this betokens a uniquely human temporal structure or mode of existence. As a unified being it is an embodied soul or incarnate spirit: "its action, in respect of which it comes into conjunction with lower and temporal things, is itself temporal . . . its action, by reason which it comes into conjunction with higher things that are above time partakes of eternity."[54] Standing behind this conclusion, of course, is the entire doctrine of the union of soul and body[55] and the problem of the unity of man.[56]

Our immediate concern, however, is the uniquely human temporal structure that follows upon the understanding of man as a unified embodied soul, as the very horizon or *confinium* between time and eternity. This uniquely human temporal structure is called by St. Thomas *aeviternity* and it is the key to man's intentional presence and to the onto-theo-logic direction of being-in-the-world.

In ST. I, Q85, ad 4, St. Thomas presents himself with the seemingly abstract, even innocuous question: whether man can understand many things at the same time. Proceeding to the first objection, however, we see that his entire anthropology is at stake:

> It would seem that we can understand many things at the same time. For the intellect is above time, whereas the succession of before and after belongs to time. Therefore the intellect does not understand different things in succession, but at the same time.[57]

Such an understanding would render man's "longior via" superfluous and thus strike at the heart of the unity of man's being-in-the-world. St. Thomas' response is as compact as it is decisive:

> The intellect is above that time which is the measure of the movement of corporeal things. But the multitude itself of intelligible species causes a

certain succession of intelligible operations, according as one operation is prior to another. And this succession is called time by Augustine, who says that God moves the spiritual creatures through time.[58]

What does this mean? First, it means that the human soul is not divine, otherwise why be united to a body and a material world?[59]. More importantly it implies a kind of temporality not merely reducible to the measure of the movement of corporeal things. In relation to that time the intellect stands above. And yet, it stands below that mode of temporality we call eternity! While there is no change or movement or, therefore, "time" attributed to the intellectual soul, there is succession, as there is not in eternity, a succession irreducible to the movement of before and after in material things. This succession of intellectual operations is caused by the multitude of intelligible species, of meanings and implications, embedded in the material world and meaningfully open to an intellectual soul immersed in sensibility but not reducible to material change or time. Is this not the longer way appropriate to an embodied soul: an incarnate spirit who comes to know the world gradually in-time, over-time in successive stages of understanding, who comes to be the world more and more the more he understands? But then this is a unique kind of temporality, is it not?

The long-standing, perennial common distinction between time and eternity is too narrow to capture the difference in man. It is Heidegger in *Being and Time* who struggles to do thematic justice to Dasein's unique temporal structure. But St. Thomas, much less thematically, and encoded in a philosophical vocabulary that is inarticulate to modern and postmodern man, is more than aware of this temporal structure, and in ST. I, Q10, a5 he calls it *aeviternity*, and goes to great lengths to distinguish it, against the objector, both from the time of material change, as well as from the temporal structure we call eternity: "*aeviternity* differs from time, and from eternity, as the mean between them both."[60]

> The being that is measured by eternity is not changeable, nor is it joined to changeability. In this way, time has a before and after, *aeviternity* in itself has no before and after, which can, however, be joined to it; while eternity has neither before nor after, nor is it compatible with such at all.[61]

Spiritual substances, therefore, are measured by a special temporal-*aeviternal* mode appropriate to their unique status. Thus man and angel share one genus, spiritual being, comprising, so to speak, two species, embodied and non-embodied spiritual beings. This is astonishing because it belies the generally existentialist critique of the ancient/medieval philosophical anthropology in terms of rational animal. Heidegger is particularly harsh in this regard.[62] However, the critique certainly misfires when directed at St. Thomas. Note the remarkable complementarity between first Heidegger and then Gilson on this point:

> Presumably, animals are the most difficult of all beings for us to think of, because we are, on the one hand, most akin to them, and on the other hand, they are, at the same time separated from our existential essence by an abyss. And against this it might seem that the essence of the divine is much nearer us than the strangeness of animals, nearer in an essential distance, which as distance is much more familiar to our existential essence than the barely conceivable abysmal corporeal kinship to the animal.[63]
>
> From the intellectual substances to the spiritual substances the distance is considerable, yet it is a small one compared with the distance there is from man to brute . . . man is much farther removed from beasts than from angels.[64]

And so the fourfold intentional presence that we call man occupies a unique and not always comfortable position in existence. As *homo viator* he is always already embarked across time and history to his unique destiny. His life does not quite pass as the years pass given his *aeviternal* measure and his embodied status, with all the risk implied in both. Fully immersed in yet above time, man is structurally the non-participating spectator because fully participating actor in the dramatic history of his existence. Just as his *aeviternal* structure is irreducible to mere change, so his historical presence is not reducible to mere chronology, but has, or rather is, its own unique temporality co-extensive with human presence in relation to its divine origin and end.

Because man's distance from nothingness is infinite, his finitude is more than open to the divine, it is a veritable communion with the divine. For the infinite distance to God situates man in the world, in otherness, in his difference from God, in his temporal waitingness, and in his need to be an exteriorized existence; while the infinite distance from nullity situates him in the image of the divine in his activity as a being whose privilege is to know the eternal in the particular and to be a being-in Being-Is. Together, these distances are one indivisible difference as difference that make up the unitary activity of man's privileged to-be. The causally creative act of pure To-Be, the very font of the difference as difference, indeed made the *aeviternally* in-formed intentional presence a complete ontological unity that needs the other in order to be what it is. Metaphysics has not, as Heidegger contends, set up a partition between the sensible and the non-sensible in order to grasp a distant theological abstraction over and against the temporal. Rather, metaphysics has recognized that by answering "yes and no" man's kind of time must be the most unique kind of time, a time that hints at the strange eternality of such an answer, a time that captures his coinherence/inseparability, a time unlike that enjoyed by all the other things around him which cannot and need not ask "isn't this enough?"[65]

Being-in as being-spectator requires a seamless unity that is almost in two places at one time. In knowing I become the world as world while maintaining my self-hood. With the understanding of his ability to turn in a world where nothing else needs or requires or asks for such an involvement, man is in one place, but because he can turn and look around, he can grasp Being's otherness. Man lives as spectator among the prerequisites or preconditions for being-in. He grasps this only from the fact that he is in, being-in, in all time. The *aeviternally* in-formed intentional presence recognizes the difference as difference, the longer way of existence: that he is infinitely closer to Being-Is than to Being Is-Not, that he is a complete ontological unity that needs. In the catch-up structure his being is already there onto-theo-logically but his being in knowing is a movement toward. This is the privilege of his temporality. His freedom is to be the openness or way to the infinite through his being-finite. Freedom is a fundamentally Christian movement. From the waiting to the articulation of the wait, man's movement is based on freely turning toward what he is in Being-Is, and not some contrived freedom based on saying Being Is-Not and which seeks to deny Christian Philosophy.

Man can know that Being-Is is self-identical and that it can endure otherness, because the structure of existence, the causal catch-up, invites man to be the other as other so that he may grasp that the same is for thinking and for Being, and that the soul is in a way all things. In his difference as difference, in otherness alone he grasps unity and the extent to which Being is self-identical.

For man to understand that Being endures him is for him to be in the wait structure, like Parmenides, Plato and Aristotle. For the catch-up to be complete, for man's historical waiting to find its waiting not a contradiction but a happening for the sake of an end requires the creative causality exemplified in Christianity. The intentional presence in its intensification as the *aeviternally* in-formed knows that Being not only endures but causes and therefore enjoys otherness. Being enjoys the relationship, a relationship situated in man's unique temporal structure which is a waiting to be *aeviternally* in-formed of the extent to which man is a participant in the formation of the meaning of Being.

For the intentional presence to know this relationship will require man's upbringing in Being-in-time. The catch-up configures man's upbringing as a being-in-the-world that asks "isn't this enough?" He is a primarily historical or philosophical or formational being. Man is not at his core a representational being who can only say Being-Is as self-identity, who thinks that Being is encountered only immediately or intuitively in his knowledge as representations which he must endlessly wait for (Heidegger), or representations that he considers himself author of (Idealism). Representations ultimately do not allow the participation in otherness. In representation, Being cannot endure the gaze of the other, and so it freezes into a concept.

But if man understands himself to be at his core a formational being, a being who answers both "yes and no," at the same time, for all time, he sees that his active need based on a plenitude and that his temporal becoming are thus an eternality unfolding in-time. Man is an *aeviternal* being-in-the-world.

Because man's existence comes to be out of nothing, he is situated at an infinite distance from nothingness. Existence is thus not a path upon which we trample and then forsake for something else but a kind of ground that is onto-theo-logical from the very start. It is a presupposition yes, but never to be taken for granted, and always to be dwelt in and upon: this is the true nature of thought. And as onto-theo-logical from its very information, man as philosophical, as historical, as privileged is so bound up in this existence that as he acts as a being-in-time, at the same time, he acts in all time by being formed in Being-Is. This is indeed the intensification of the intentional presence, his participation in the formation of the meaning of Being.[66]

For Heidegger, the intentional presence never sees the light of day, the full historical unfolding of man's historical being-in. Heidegger cannot accept that Dasein has a waitingness which is at its beginning onto-theo-logical, that it will lay bare the eternal within historical becoming. He attempts to return and return, again and again, to the beginning, to the strange, the uncanny, the origins of the wait.[67] But Heidegger cannot go home again. He has rejected the very onto-theo-logical grounds on which the house of Being stands. His pre-lapsarian yearning misses that the crucial form of history is in truth the cruciform of history. [68]

Conclusion: The Plenitude of the *Ananke Stenai*

Rationalist and fideist man has asked, "what does Athens have to do with Jerusalem?" To engage the possibility of Christian Philosophy we must look at its central defining point, the nature of the catch-up as caught, as housed and as originated. What is the what-it-is of this beginning *qua* end? How must the house of Being be, what is the nature of it as original ground, if its inhabitants can be seen genuinely in their final intensity?

The *ananke stenai* is the originating stop in the order of explanation and in Being. As such, among the fourfold it is the convocation point that lays open the criterion of perfection for such a fourfold structure in the first place. If Christian Philosophy is not only possible, but the most essential philosophical realization of Being, then its legitimacy rests entirely upon seeing what is to be seen at its ground or stop. The connection between Athens and Jerusalem is neither facile nor founded, but deeply united in the wait structure of existence. The fourfold have been the defining parameters of our analysis. Their intensifications have brought into view the movement toward beginning *qua* end. Each constituent has spoken what the stop has allowed it to be:

1. causality is not deterministic but the natural directionality of man's super-sensible being-in-the-world;
2. finitude as finite being is not a privation but a plenitude or active need;
3. the intentional presence is not merely a representational being, but the very embodiment of a historical wait structure as an *aeviternally* formational being;
4. the fact of existence is onto-theo-logic from its very start to its very end.

Each aspect of the fourfold points toward one kind of original unity. As we have stressed, causality cannot be deterministic. Why? Because it is grounded and directed by an "un"caused cause. That "un" points toward something that naturally and of necessity leaves man open to the uncanny and mysterious. Finitude cannot be a privation. Why? To engage Being-Is man must be a complete ontological unity that needs to fulfill itself in the other. Finitude is based on a plenitude or an active need. This ever intensifying activity discloses that the requirement of man's being-in-Being-Is is not based on a self-evident ground he begins in only by passing it over. Rather, the ground is there as the sole provider for man's progressive thinking about Being. The most primordial activity of intentional presence cannot be representation. Why? Because representation loses all sense of a historical wait structure and of man's privilege as a formational being, effectively alienating him from being-in-the-world and Being-in-the-divine. The wait has pointed toward our own factical unfolding, that existence is onto-theo-logic from its very start. The fourfold speaks from the point of the unsaid, the undone: that there is something more and something left undone. With every movement into the thereness of this Ground, man finds himself invited into the mystery of this "un." The more man is *aeviternally* informed, embedded into the very body of Being-Is, the more the constituents of the fourfold disclose their stop in the order of explanation. Man begins to realize something strange, something along the lines of the great Heideggerian insight: that the Ground might just be groundless! [69] For Heidegger, this possibility of is-not leads him to reject not only the inauthenticity of scientific positivism[70] but the possibility of Christian Philosophy.

But again, that his rejection of the onto-theo-logic grounds of Being (the very grounds that would permit him to arrive at the genuine understanding of nonbeing), his placement of metaphysics along the same lines of a "merely logical science," comes from his conflation of several key metaphysical concepts: the reductionist self-caused cause, the determinist principle of sufficient reason, and finally mis-seeing the *ananke stenai* as something like a trans-phenomenological illegitimate foundation rather than the unique kind of ground that it is. What Heidegger looks toward but cannot accomplish is the genuine speaking of nonbeing, the philosophical consideration of nullity as the fundamental aspect to be acknowledged when metaphysically asking into the meaning of Being-Is.

The criterion of perfection in which the fourfold adheres must in some way point to a kind of foundationlessness/groundlessness so that the intensities can be what they are. This groundlessness keeps the fourfold out of the vicious domain of self-evident certitudes that reduce causality to a ladder of chainlink determinism, and finitude to privation, and the intentional presence to a representational function. The Christian Philosophical fourfold is at its core an onto-theo-logical recognition of a unique kind of groundlessness. As a unity, the fourfold is an ever intensifying contemplation of this uncanny quality of Being-Is within existence, and this is confirmed by the historical waitingness in Plato and Aristotle and through the articulation of the wait by St. Thomas. So critically is this true that groundlessness is what each constituent of the fourfold is directed toward and has been for all time. Whatever this groundlessness is, it is inseparable from Christian Philosophy as its essential criterion. For St. Thomas, the ground of being-in is not a self-evident foundation but the presupposition of all thought; it is something more because it is something irreducible, and if were not irreducibly distinct it would not be the end in the order of explanation and of Being. If there were no way for things to be there would be no things. But there are things, therefore there is a way, and that way requires a stop unlike any other mere foundation. It requires a stop that is a beginning, an opening to something other that has always been, and no mere foundation can do this.

The Christian philosophical *ananke stenai* is the only stop that is an opening or a clearing, that requires us to stop in our tracks in the order of Being and explanation, and wait to come to know the extent of Being-Is in our being-in, the extent of the universal housed in the particular, the extent to which we are becoming *aeviternally* in-formed. Aristotle, in his time, adhered to the meaning of Being and to what the wait gave him. And St. Thomas, at his time, adhered to Being and recognized the meaning of that wait. Both understood that to be in waiting meant that man can never place a foundation of certitude over this hidden region of Being-Is and still think he has the privileged access in-and-to-the-world.[71]

The catch-up point has revealed the ground to be an utter indemonstrability, an existence of a Primal Truth not self-evident to us but presupposed by us: a region concealed, a kind of anti-foundation or essential groundlessness. And yet all along haven't we seen repeatedly the necessity to come to a stop, a stop in man's being-in-the-world, so that he may have knowledge? Haven't we seen this to be the fundamental defining metaphysical point? Hasn't this need to stop at the ground of Being become the irreconcilable difference between Heidegger and metaphysics? This is where Heidegger is so important. His efforts to give proper deference to the ground or meaning of Being have gone a long way to reveal the true nature of the metaphysical stop. The metaphysical stop is not and never could be, as he understands, a foundation bound by self-evidence. It is instead, what St. Anselm understood, when he argued that than which nothing greater can be conceived cannot be conceived except as without a beginning.[72] The origin, the uncaused cause, must necessarily be, by its nature, without beginning, thus groundless.

What kind of stop is this, in which the "un" gives us nothing like a self-evident, self-caused foundation, but more like an opening or clearing into something other? What kind of stop is this, where finitude hasn't stopped, impotent in its privations and limitations, but rather where it has overflowed in its relational activities with Being-Is? What kind of stop is this where the intentional presence seems to be more and more *aeviternally* in-formed in its historical becoming? What is the nature of this stop wherein every aspect of the fourfold points toward an end where *nothing* seems final, accounted for or self-evident?

Christian man is not stopping at a modern foundation in which there is nothing but his own self-evident *cogitata*. The metaphysical stop is actually very close to Heidegger's understanding of groundlessness, but in the end it is so very far from it. Christian man stops at the onto-theo-logical fact of his existence, at the opening of the strange into the divine. Man has stopped at the most original groundlessness, the formational fact of his creation *ex nihilo*. That kind of stop is progressive and intensifying. It has elicited from him a numinous awe, in a waiting for his thinking to catch up to this most radical Being-Is that brings forth everything out of nothing.

St. Thomas understands the difference between a foundation whose primary duty is to account and the stop-as-origin that must be something more. As uncaused cause, God has created man in such a way, that their union is an original and historically recurrent originating formation. Because of the radical act of creating *ex nihilo*, God's primary activity with man isn't to bring into account completely formed essences, and then when they are in existence maintaining or conserving their existential accountability. Out of nothing He forms man's existence. Thus in every act of man's existence he is being in-formed by and through that existence. That is why man can be a complete ontological unity that needs, an originally relational being and an exteriorized soul. Man doesn't enter the world and "add" on relationships with the divine or with others, his relationships are inseparable from his being, grounded on an original having-a-formational-relationship with the divine. As such, a cogito is radically impossible. Because man's existence came out of nothing he is in-formed to be an inseparably relational/formational being-in-existence. God's core activity with man is this formation, in every act of man's existence, and by that existence he is in-formed of the extent to which he is in union with God. Being-in existence discloses to man that the universal saturates the particular. In man's unique kind of *aeviternal* time, as a being being-formed in and through every act of his existence, he comes to the meaning of this universal, the nature of the Ground, in his temporal becoming. When coming toward the Ground, when contemplating God, man naturally contemplates in and through and by his very formation the possibility of *ex nihilo*, of nothing, of nullity, of nonbeing. The more he understands God, the more Christian man has entered the most serious involvement with the possibility of nonbeing. This is man's necessary and therefore essential encounter with nothingness.

Epilogue: The Metaphysics of Tragedy

I will tell you that I am a child of the century, a child of disbelief and doubt.

I am that today and will remain so until the grave. How much terrible torture this thirst for faith has cost me even now, which is all the stronger in my soul the more arguments I can find against it. And yet, God sends me sometimes instants when I am completely calm; at those instants I love and I feel loved by others, and it is at these instants that I have shaped for myself a Credo *where everything is clear and sacred for me. This* Credo *is very simple, here it is: to believe that nothing is more beautiful, profound, sympathetic, reasonable, manly, and more perfect than Christ; and I tell myself with a jealous love not only that there is nothing but that there cannot be anything. Even more: if someone proved to me that Christ is outside the truth, and that in reality the truth were outside of Christ, then I would prefer to remain with Christ rather than with the truth.*

Dostoyevsky

Sanctity is an adventure; it is indeed the only adventure. Those who have once realized this have found their way to the very heart of the Catholic faith; they have felt in their mortal flesh the shuddering of another terror than the terror of death: the shudder of supernatural hope.

Bernanos

The Elusive Tragic Essence

There are those who deny the possibility of Christian tragedy because what is tragic is finite, the tragic act resounding with the distinctive thud of the end. The tragic lances man with the stigma of irretrievability, underlining all his acts and exposing them as fully human. What made life tragic for the Greeks was the earnest recognition of man's specifically finite end. The Greek *telos* was a true finitude—*unopen* to the infinite and one that orders every act and outcome in terms of the unrepeatable, irretrievable, irrevocable fatalism that alone engages the truth of Being.

In the Greek tragic vision man's encounter with nothingness is further confounded and elevated by the meaning of truth. Within *a-letheia*, man is at the whim of Being, Being without notice appears and pulls him toward his own-most possibilities. In its appearance we see the birth of the tragic hero. Without notice, *a-letheia* retreats into its union with hiddenness, distancing man from his acts and resituating him in his only possibility, as fully situated in the world seemingly unopen to the infinite. This return to finitude is the birth of tragedy.

The rejection of the possibility of Christian tragedy is rooted in the relationship of truth to finitude. For the Greeks, *a-letheia* was the handmaiden of finitude; it delivered man into his earthly bonds. The problem of Christianity is in the nature of its truth: wasn't it infinitized into *veritas* and transformed into an onto-theo-logical *entelechy* that reduced the tragic to a mere developmental attitude, and the finite to excess baggage to be shed in the move from pre-Christian to Christian? Again, how can there be tragedy if it is to compete with the possibility of Christian transcendence?

Tragedy is something unique; it echoes the irretrievable and delivers the fatal blow of finitude. It is rejected as irrelevant if this irretrievability cannot compete with the presumed happy ending of Christ. But what exactly is tragedy? If something is lost or done away with, what was it, in its nature or in its essence before it went missing? If the tragic vision was intact prior to Christ and lost after the Resurrection, what kind of essence could not persist in the face of the risen Lord? And yet, doesn't it seem *contra naturam* that Christ the giver of life would extinguish any genuine Form, especially if it be the Form of tragedy? This is Nietzsche's problem and it must be confronted: the problem of the meaning of suffering: whether a Christian meaning or a tragic meaning: Dionysius or the Crucified One?

It is hardly accidental that the long sought "essence of tragedy" has escaped the dust storm of theories designed to extort it. Not a single one of those theories has done justice to the essence of tragedy and could not in principle do so because tragedy was without final essence. Tragedy is the *not-yet-there* essence.

Terror, dread and suffering are not in themselves tragic. Their very essences preclude them from being unleashed or open to the full and endless possibilities of *tragic distance*. To name things as "dreadful" or "terrible" is to have a presence or an essence to describe. This presential being-thereness frames suffering, dread and terror as distinct modes of being, as ends that can point toward the tragic but never capture it.

Tragedy is not the thud of the end so often ascribed to it. The end or frame is in all essences, by and through the limit that distinguishes one essence from another. If tragedy contained its essence, it would be reducible to knowledge and categorically resemble its descriptions; there would be no *real* distinction from other essences that has prompted so many to dwell on tragedy without satisfaction. Because the tragic does not yet have an essence, it is the only "thing" that man does not and cannot *own* or *take in*, in the act of knowledge. Tragedy's not yet there essence reverses the terms of knowledge, taking man by the throat and reconstituting him *noetically*. Perhaps, it is this real distinction that Nietzsche sensed when he distinguished tragic and Christian suffering.

The Tragic Wager

Man can no longer accept his place in the eternal through the death of tragedy. Nor is it possible to claim that its death opens the possibility of transcendence. Christian transcendence exists and persists only through our engagement with existence in its tragic form. The reality of salvation depends upon the tragic just as the tragic derives its *distance*, the spanning lengths and depths of its confounding there-less-ness, from the patterns of salvation.

To claim that Christ abolishes tragedy, that tragedy existed, Christ came and it disappeared is to whitewash the meaning of His death. Christ is rather the fulfillment of tragedy because as Savior he *takes on* the burden of the tragic hero, a burden of sin that until now could not be *taken on*. As tragedy's existential fulfillment, Christ's action and meaning are uncovered only in the tragic. Otherwise Christ would subvert our encounter with nothingness so essential to salvation and thereby so essential to understanding Him.

Christianity disappears the moment it relegates tragedy to an alien category. Without the tragic vision who needs a savior? Without the *tragic distance*, faith is no longer faith but a neat collection of clear and distinct ideas. Only in the *tragic distance* can faith maintain and engage its most critical paradox: faith, as Dostoyevsky and Pascal knew, carries the greatest risk. Man is certain only that Christ can save him, but equally certain of all the risks in loving him; and by love, we surrender ourselves to that *tragic distance*, that waiting-ness for Christ where we are certain we can do nothing to save ourselves. Faith does not exist outside this *tragic distance*. To put it another way, man is certain that all he owns is his own nothingness; this certitude is realized in the crucifixion and in the agony of Christ by taking on our nothingness and becoming sin itself in the total absolute abandonment and self-knowledge that the Greek tragic hero prefigured but not complete.

The long-held, perennial conclusion that Christ negates the possibility of tragedy is found, in different forms, across the philosophic spectrum. For Jaspers, Nietzsche and Heidegger, the meaning of Christ strips man of his tragic sense of life. Christ places the power of salvation over and against the finality of mortality. His death ratifies the decisive shift from good and evil ordered only by their free primal confluence to a good diametrically opposed to evil, where each is further reduced to corresponding degrees of truth and falsity. His Resurrection injects an illicit desire for other-worldly transcendence. Christ has undone the tragic; He has made the irretrievable, the irrevocable, the unattainable that permeates all human life subordinate to His Human/Divine Form. When the tragic becomes secondary it is no longer tragic!

Is Christian transcendence this vast labyrinth of smoke and mirrors? Has Christ derailed our encounter with nothingness and the tragic, and thus denied in advance what Christianity requires most, being-in-the-faith? This claim is serious, and if true undoes the faith. But perhaps both sides have missed the meaning of tragedy.

Where do we see the tragic? We see it roused in the basement of Being where nails are driven clear to their source. Its happening is always uncaptured and as it eludes possession it leaves each man in the strangest of ways, un-possessed of himself. This strange rapture augurs the faith: because the tragic ground knows not its *distance* or its limits it alone can carry man into the most serious of mortal acts, the wager of faith.

The Act of Knowledge within the Tragic

The tragic is not that which forces the end, delivering man over to utter negative finitude. As the not-yet-there essence, tragedy does not possess the limit, proportion and distinction of other essences; thus, by its strange nature, it could not possibly dictate or outline or direct an end. Without an essence, it does not have its *telos* or directionality, and even though man may sense it and speak about it in terms of an end-ness, he does so only because man knows in terms of ends. This is what confounds man about the tragic, man's activity as a knower is always directed toward an end or a good or an essence or a form or an intelligible species, but this is not the case with tragedy. Without the properties of essence, tragedy cannot direct us to an end to be known. In fact, the tragic, if it directs us at all, directs us by its not-yet-thereness which places man against himself into an endlessness, a homeless and timeless place.

What happens to man when confronted with the endlessness of the tragic? In knowledge, man *takes on* or becomes the other; he names things because he becomes the thing and articulates it as what it is, in its *quiddity* or its essence and its relational being-in-the-world. When man names or knows the essence, knowledge reaches its terminus, and this is the finite good. Knowledge is an immanent act beginning in otherness, and through this relationship man exteriorizes himself in-and-to-the-world. As St. Thomas understood, knowledge for the embodied soul requires the longer way, a way in which man knows himself only reflexively. The otherness that man desires to know lays bare its givenness and gives man over to his most essential knowledge, his role as a knower in the world.

If the world does not present end-ness, then I do not have the *telos* necessary to know myself. Tragedy eludes all capture precisely because man cannot complete the act of knowledge within it. Because it is not yet there, by entering the tragic man enters his own undoing. What constitutes the essence of man is his status as knower; his ability to embrace *noetically* the end of each being-in-the-world. Only when he takes in an act's particular end can he know himself and know his world. Man deconstructs himself in trying to know the tragic. When he enters the no-ground where reflexivity is at its brink and has fallen off, man is at his brink and has fallen away from his *noetic* distance and *leapt ahead* into the beginning and the beyond. This is not the beginning and the end of the spectator who has the *noetic* distance necessary to see the horizon and to frame it as such. The man in *tragic distance* is truly inside the horizon because he knows not where he is and the lengths he ascends and descends preclude in advance any possible thought of beginning and end. Man knows himself only reflexively through the world as other: and this, existentially, implies and requires suffering through the engagement in action by means of the always delayed catch-up into the meaning of action *and* the other. This is how man fulfills the Greek injunction: Know Thyself, which reaches its acme in the tragic hero's and the philosopher's painful ascent and fatal but immortalizing descent through the dialectic of stripping the soul of all that is in-essential.

Man actualizes himself when he becomes more than himself *noetically*. By becoming the other as other, man has *leapt ahead* into otherness. This strange act of knowledge, this *leaping ahead* reveals the extent of his relationship in the world: man is only man when he is more than himself. Why must man be more than himself in order to fulfill himself? Because man's privileged status as a knower can only be acted out in-between time and eternity in the struggle for godlikeness, not only the tragedies but in Plato.

As *aeviternal*, man throws himself to the ends in his anticipation and desire for the eternal discoverable within the temporal. And perhaps man goes so far in his anticipation that he throws himself to the edge of time, the brink of finitude and into the horizon of transcendence. This leap that pushes past the ground of temporality is the horizon not only of transcendence but also of tragedy. In this inseparable horizon of the tragic and the transcendent lies the real possibility of faith.

If man possesses the privileged access to the eternal then he is ontologically familiar with what is *not-yet-there* temporally. As he throws himself to the edge, to what has not-yet-appeared on the horizon of time, he strands himself in the core of the *wait*. Man may leap so far as to overstep his *noetic* recognition, to hurl past the limitations of the longer way of a reflexive being. If the eternal is appropriated only in the temporal, then, if the temporal is not present it is as if the eternal is not there in the only form commensurate with man's nature.

If man throws himself to the brink of his ownmost ontological familiarity he has entered an irretrievable *wait*. What can he not retrieve? Himself: he has thrown himself to what is not-yet-there temporally and has entered a *wait* that is without end. What is without end precludes the possibility of knowledge: man is so confounded he cannot even know he is *waiting* for the manifestation of the eternal. Because he has leapt ahead beyond end-ness, there is no ground, no particularity, no temporality where his knowledge can actualize itself.

Because knowledge is reflexive, the most profound waitingness would undue his *noetic distance*, his spectatorship position where man knows he is *in-wait*. This kind of leaping into the horizon of transcendence would in turn throw man into the *tragic distance*, where man knows not the other nor knows himself, nor his own wait. Isn't this the meaning of surrender?

Man's *noetic* formation, activity and privileged status as a knower *begins* in surrender. As the nondemonstrable fact of existence, intentionality is the irreducible starting point I must surrender to in order to know. Man must surrender himself to the totality of Being and its irreducibility invested in all things; he must surrender himself to his own dependency on Being. Man knows nothing without the irreducibility of Being in-forming his actions. The greater surrender is the openness to Being's primacy and to the origin of genuine knowledge. And what is the full surrender but to enter the *tragic distance* in its totality? When man throws himself into what hasn't completed itself, man can no longer participate in the formation of the meaning of Being because the meaning is not yet there.

This is the tragic vision: the hero leaps ahead to participate in the meaning of Being but something confounds him. It is not radical finitude or embracing the end. Tragedy has a distinction that cannot be articulated or named. The hero leaps past his *noetic* requirement, of knowing the eternal through the temporal, and into the brink or horizon of his ontological familiarity. While the hero's intention was to know and reconcile the end, he reaches so far in his protagonistic stance, in his being-full-of-possibilities urged on by the transcendent Good, by the appearance of truth, that he goes to where myth is made, to the beginning and to the beyond and so undoes himself. In his undoing we may see the appearance or the effects of tragedy's eternally non-apparent not-yet-there essence; we see despair and pessimism, and a *telos* interrupted by grief overflowing with banality, dread and an intense longing without description that finally folds into death. Yet the tragic cannot be captured, its endlessness surrenders the hero outside himself, outside all *noetic* distance, beyond the comfort of regret, grief, dread and despair, beyond the categories of ignorance and enlightenment. The tragic hero knows not his own frustration, he knows not the extent of his own *wait*; he is on the horizon, waiting to be in-formed of the appearance of the not-yet there essence of tragedy, in the endlessness of the tragic vision.

The Tragic Wait

Et lavit nos a peccatis nostris in Sanguine.

Something is there in this elusive tragic ground. We are ontologically familiar with it but *noetically* stranded like Philoctetes. If the eternal is not present in a form commensurate with man's being, it is as if it is not there at all. Yet at the same time, it is always there: the possibility of man's *noetic distance*, the need for language and thought to play *catch-up* to Being is prefigured on our irreducible involvement in eternity. In tragedy we are at the origin of our ontological familiarity, at the ground of the possibility of knowledge, but a groundless ground, a homeless home because since Being has not-yet-appeared in a form commensurate with man's embodied act of knowledge.

Tragedy is given its essence in the dying God-Man: in Christ. Tragedy is fulfilled, when He puts on the greatest tragic burden, the sins of mankind. Christ gives *Himself* to tragedy as *its telos*.

Christ does not rid the world of its encounter with nothingness, of the place of the furies, and of the tragic; this would be to turn faith into magic, to circumvent the *longior viae* and to deny how man knows only in the face of the particular, the individual, the finite and the temporal, where all things are shot through with the irretrievable, the irreducible, the tragic.

Christ is the one Being-in-act who overcomes tragedy by *fulfilling* the terms through which we can answer "yes and no" to the question, "isn't this, this world of being, enough?" What has Christ taken *on* when he has taken *away* our sins? To understand this is to uncover what makes tragedy tragic. Christ has, by taking away our sins, *become* and thus fulfilled the essence of tragedy, or rather gave tragedy its essence. By giving tragedy essence, Christ overcame what makes tragedy the tragic: its non-essence. Christ is the very essence of tragedy. Yet when we ask if tragedy, this *not-yet-there* essence, has been eradicated from man's engagement with Being, the answer must be as all answers must be for those accepting the risk of the horizon: "yes and no."

Christian tragedy is rejected only on the basis of a vulgar historicism. The presence of Christ is there sorted out in a linearized existence that all too easily forgets that Christ is not a figure in history but figure *of* history. Historicism, in its chronological reductionist order proclaims the incompatibility of tragedy with Christianity. In their compact and abstracted view: tragedy existed, Christ came, and tragedy was overcome. What a neat and empty idealism, a story told against the mythic patterns and formed out of clear woven ideas. But if each man acts out the universal in his particularity, then Christ's death and the tragic vision must be acted out again and again through each man.

Christianity recognizes the paradoxical nature of temporality: the drama of man's existence *is both* unrepeatable and yet an eternal return or repetition. Christ is not some universal static template by and through which all men are automatically saved and saved the same way. Why *did* God become Man? God became man to unveil the eternal in a form that befits man. This form thus extends to the particularity of each man and every man to come. Every man must make the choice to enter the tragic, become more than himself and then, unable to come home again, he surrenders to the *tragic distance* where he is even unaware that he is *waiting* for Christ.

Christ is the essence of tragedy. When He entered the world He took on the sins and became the sinful. He became the essence of tragedy, and gave it a ground by and through which man can take it in. Christ overcomes tragedy only by overcoming what makes it tragic, its not-yet-there essence; but in another way, He fulfills the existential terms of tragedy. Tragedy is not eradicated: if man knows only through the particular, then the tragic act must be reenacted within each man in every epoch. This is the meaning of history, that other not-yet-there-essence fulfilled only in the idea of Christ.

Christianity and the Tragic Choice

The tragic act begins cloaked and hidden in the resplendent possibilities of the *telos*, in the sense that man is more than himself. Man can in time *leap ahead* to the end of time. We see this in the aphoristic enunciations of myth, in speaking of the beginning and the beyond. The hero's descent into the *tragic distance* begins in a sensuous *elan vital*; it appears to be an ascent, a desire to complete in action the teleological inclination of man. Yet somewhere, in some place between time and eternity, the ascent becomes the descent, the up becomes the way down, the hero cannot go home. His *noetic* loss awakens those tragic descriptions of dread, terror, agony and suffering without purpose. The tragic hero is unaware of the magnitude of his leap and what will become of him; his final resignation is an acceptance of the endlessness of tragic knowledge.

What is more tragic, pre-Christian tragedy where the hero does not know that he has thrown himself to the pits of endlessness, or Christian tragedy where Christian man knows the terms of tragedy and makes the choice, to throw himself outside himself unable to return home without Christ? Isn't this the wager of all time?

In Christianity, the framework of the "yes and no" only makes the tragic choice all the more real, as real as the risk in the leap of faith. I can do nothing for Christ or for myself but this tragic act, a choice that is more than all or nothing, the act of total surrender, of throwing all that I know of all that I am into nothingness; into the dark night of passive purification, first of the senses, then of the soul.

Christian man, unlike the tragic hero, knows the stakes of choosing the *tragic distance*. He knows that his own *noetic* privilege is surrendered when he *throws* himself to the brink of time. To know this before leaping ahead makes the act all the more tragic because it begins in the recognition of the *tragic distance*, not in the safety of transcendent ends. Christian man knows that the not-yet-there-essence carries no reflexive ground. Once he makes the wager of faith, he may lose himself and all awareness that he is a lost lamb. Christian man is the farthest along the *tragic distance*. He is blood brother to the Greek tragic hero, as Christ is blood brother to both.

When Christian man chooses *waiting* for Christ he must surrender his *noetic* distance and reside beyond the categories of good and evil, beyond the realm of essences. He surrenders himself to the groundlessness where there is nothing he can do. He knows prior to *leaping* that he will lose himself, that once he throws himself *ahead*, he would be outside the possibility of wanting or knowing how to stay or to return. He would be *noetically* lost unto himself, not knowing where he is or how to come home.

What does this dark night have in store for man? Man cannot know. Its darkness beckons man to come to Christ, but it resides beyond the realm of light and dark and to take it in requires total surrender of the sight. This is no simple choice.

Most choices are made within the comforts and confines of *noetic* distance, where man thinks he is merely reading off the appearances of Being, that he has the primacy in choice and can come back and revisit or undue his action. The irreducibility and repeatable unrepeatability of tragic choice is the one true reality behind genuine faith and free will. The tragic choice is made with the recognition that each act has primacy and constitutes our relationships and our being-in the-world. The ultimate and the freest act is the tragic choice, because it is the final release of man's errant and self-imposed primacy over and against the existential possibilities of the world that give him the possibility of participation in the first place.

The act of Christian tragedy is thus the most rigorous of tragic acts. Christ does not wash away the tragic tension essential to salvation. Instead, Christ fulfills the terms, heightens the stakes that make man's choice to leap into the tragic not-yet-there-essence choice an in-formed choice, a choice that moves man far deeper into the tragic vision than the tragic hero. Why? Because the tragic hero, unlike Christian man, did not know the wager or the dark night behind his choice when he was *compelled* to *leap ahead*. But Christian man does.

Christian man answers "yes and no" because he understands the lengths of tragedy and the meaning of its essence in Christ. This "yes and no," this seamless unity whose unity is *impossible* except for Christ, signals something essential: on man's side, we make the Christian wager in the face of the irretrieved or uncanny, in the face of the essence of Christ's wager. We make our surrender toward or patterned after Christ's surrender. We leap, unsure whether we will make it over the *confinium* upon which we reside to meet Him on the terms He made for us *out of nothing*, out of utter finality. The tragic move is intact; we must always *wait* for Christ.

Hope: The Horizon of the Transcendent and the Tragic

Man's ultimate transcendence would be to enter that reflexive ground where man is not only more than himself in knowledge, but has reached the terminus of more-than-man. All knowledge is an exteriorization of the soul in the world. When Christian man makes the tragic choice, he knows he wants to see himself in God and thus become irreducibly more than himself. But God is the one knowledge man cannot take in on his own.

God is not knowledge but the irreducible ground or Being of knowledge. While God has created the realm of our reflexive possibilities, those things we can take in, He is, in himself distinct, He is the Act of Being, the ground of the possibility of reflexivity and thus is not like everything else we can know or take in. What we may know exists from and reflects the Being of God, but God is the groundless ground of that reflexivity. Thus, how can we know Him?

Here is the startling paradox: God is the one Being that could make each man the most of himself in knowledge, yet God is not an object of knowledge, He is the irreducible ground of the possibility of knowledge and thus cannot be *taken in* by man in normal reflexive knowledge. In terms of the tragic ground, the not-yet-there essence is a genuine recognition of God's profound involvement in and radical distinction from reflexive objects of knowledge.

When God became man, God gave man the ultimate gift, He brought into the horizon the appearance of the eternally non-apparent. In Christ, God made himself an act of knowledge man could *finally* take in and become.

Desirous of union with Christ, man leaps ahead past the temporal crea-tions that are, on man's side, the starting point of transcendence. Man has thrown himself to the ground of the possibility of transcendence. And as source or ground, it cannot be broken down or reflected upon, it is irreduc-ible and as such leaves man in the irretrieved. This is the *tragic distance* where the horizon of transcendence is at the same time the tragic endless-ness. At this point man can do nothing, he is at the well-spring of *ex nihilo*, and if this tragic ground is to take on the appearance of the transcendent it is only because God, the ground of the possibility of transcendence, decides to appear, to participate in form and being so that man can take in this ulti-mate transcendence. Isn't this the meaning of the sacrament of the body and blood of Christ?

Beauty, as Heidegger once noted, is the appearance of the eternally non-apparent, and so, in the most Beautiful of acts, God became man and unveiled the *tragic distance* for what it always was—the transcendent horizon.

Christ-as-God is the ground of the possibility of knowledge and cannot be taken in by man. Man's participation with God is in the *tragic distance*. Christ-as-man is the greatest gift, the impossible *non sequitur*: the appearance of that ground for knowledge through faith. As it appeared through and in Christ, in the form that befits man's nature, it is the realm of transcendence. Perhaps, in this inseparable horizon of the tragic and the transcendent held within the being of Christ lies the real possibility of Faith, Hope and Love. Since Hope lies in-between its sister virtues like man lies in-between time and eternity, what does Hope say about man?

The tragic vision is often described by those marks that seem contrary to or undo hope. Tragedy confounds us and our descriptions overflow in attempts to measure the loss within these dark nights. Tragedy is described as dread, terror, pessimism, as an overwhelming grief with no object but the fact of its own grief.

But faith is not a fairy tale dissolving under the historicist touch and hope is not its empty handmaiden. Hope, instead, hopes for the unseen things and this activity resides at the core of the tragic vision. Rather than the pseudo-certitudes of cheap grace and easy wish-fulfilling hope, transcending the presumptuousness of postmodernist humanism as well as the despair of everyday emptiness lies the unique and irreducible reality of the theological virtue of hope in which faith carries the greatest risk and love the most ardent fear.

As so often in St. Thomas an explosive doctrine is hidden within and by his seemingly dry scholastic presentation. For St. Thomas, Hope denotes movement or a stretching forth of the appetite toward an arduous Good. What a strange and magnificent description! Hope is active and its *stretching* forth carries the primal truth of man's *aeviternal* status.

In-formed hope—how hope unfolds through man's participation—originates in the genuine certitude of faith. Its end, desirous of the arduous Good, is transformed into the lover-and-beloved union of caritas, which, irreducibly united to filial fear, enters the mutually intensified union with God. It is thus a kind of *onto-logical in-between*. In-between what?—In-between Faith and Love.

The theological virtues are each distinct, and at the same time they signal a fundamental union, so much so that the certitude of faith and the filial fear united to caritas can be understood or appreciated only through hope, and its transformational involvement with its sister virtues.

"Hope is the certain expectation of future happiness." Genuine certitude goes so far in its neediness that without the groundless Fact of God's divine love man would enter annihilation. The certain expectation of future happiness is the same certitude by which man must accept his own nothingness, the fact of his grounded existence. Man can be certain of the manifold implications of the twofold meaning of *ex nihilo*: (1) there is an infinite distance from man to nothingness and (2) there is a parallel infinite distance from man to God.

The ontological structure of creative causality *ex nihilo* secures the necessity for and thus the certitude of faith, as well explains why filial fear grows with greater union with God! The act of creative causality *ex nihilo* requires God's existential nearness within the infinite distance between nothingness and man. Man is thus a created perfection, a complete ontological unity forever dependent on God. But, through that same certitude, man begins to fear separation from God which, paradoxically, faith holds to be impossible. Man's infinite distance to nothingness requires his infinite distance to God, the irreducible difference between created and uncreated. Because man can never overcome that divide, the more he desires to cross what is infinite and un-crossable, the more he fears his creaturely separation from Him. When caritas attempts to bridge the divide, the infinite distance from creature to Creator only strengthens man's filial fear.

The theological virtue of hope stretching forth from faith to love encompasses this paradox. Hope is thus certain of God's love and certain of all the risks of loving Him.

Hope's perdurance lies between the two Sundays, after the palms fall and before Christ rises from the grave. This is where each man takes up the Cross on Good Friday. It is hope's ontological in-between that announces man's privileged status. Man is a composite unity, where the addition does not add up: where one soul united to one body equals one embodied soul, one man where his *aeviternal* status cannot be neatly added to express his being, because man must be more than himself to be a man. This is the risk of the longer way and of reflexive knowledge: when man hunts for the origin, he adds to himself only the act of surrender, where the tragic is the transcendent and the transcendent is the tragic. Existence does not add up: this is the logic of perfection: this is Christ.

As Christian tragedy is not only possible but the actual fulfillment of tragedy itself, so Christian Philosophy is not only merely possible but the actual fulfillment of the essence of philosophy itself, because it has more than anticipated Heidegger's claim that such a philosophy bathed in the eternal can no longer think Being Is-Not. Only in Christian Philosophy can the possibility of nonbeing be genuinely given its due, its length and limit. The stop in the order of Christian philosophical explanation as the perfection of the stop in the order of all philosophical inquiry points toward a unique kind of reciprocal groundlessness wherein nonbeing finally has its place in existence. The act of creating *ex nihilo* is not an act that is left behind in its creatures, it is the very formative act of existence itself. As such, man cannot possibly exist without his formation from nonbeing, nor can he think meaningfully about Being-Is without the possibility of nonbeing as fundamental guide. Christian man understands nonbeing when he contemplates his formational relationship with God. He cannot think about God and not recognize in his being-in the possibility of nonbeing. The possibility of nonbeing, the reality of his formation, is with him at every moment of his existence, and this possibility has both an uncanny proximity to and an essential distance from man. Because it is there in this strange way, as both near and far, he asks himself "isn't this enough?" The proximity to nonbeing is there in the onto-theo-logical fact that he was created out of nothing, and the infinite distance is there because his act of to-be has an infinite distance to nullity. In this distance that is a nearness made manifest by his answer "yes and no," Christian man doesn't just entertain the possibility of nonbeing but is its existential gauge in the world. Man's intensified privileged access in-and-to-the-world is to know the origins of being-in, to enter the plenitude at the ground of Being-Is and to fathom the act of creation *ex nihilo* because he knows what can possibly spring from and be formed out of nothing.

In Christian Philosophy, nonbeing doesn't take over and annihilate the path to Being-Is. As an essential tension that announces the inseparability factor, the possibility of nonbeing situates man fully in the world but in a world open, from its very origins to the infinite. As radical possibility, nonbeing is the unitary force beneath the entire fourfold and the essence of Christian Philosophy as the inseparable existential signature of creative formation *ex nihilo*. It is this possibility of nonbeing that enables man to see the No-thing. And because the possibility of nonbeing is no longer a metaphysical embarrassment lurking around the body of Being which needs to be explained away, Being can truly be seen as both self-identical and causally creative, thus resolving Plato's problem of how Being could endure otherness. Not only can it endure otherness but it can and does rejoice in it. Why? Because I know all things, especially and including myself, only from the fact that I am the other as other first. I have always been the other first ontologically, most especially in the fact of my existence *ex nihilo* where I first was formed to be the other in the relationship that constitutes my privileged access into the meaning of Being.

My being-in Being-Is has always required a relationship, a unity, an exteriorized existence. I come to know that Being is self-identical only from the onto-theo-logical fact of my existence in which, as the formation of the creative act *ex nihilo*, I am the other as other. I do not calculate that Being is self-identical and then strain to make some facile connections to prove that Being endures otherness. As a primordially relational being I am always an exteriorized existence. I know that Being is self-identical only from the difference as difference between myself and Being-Is that is prefigured on our unity *ex nihilo.* I can never be a sole cogito. I have always been the other that Being enjoys, that Being has brought into existence out of nothing. I know this because I am originally and *aeviternally* formed in this relationship and have always been for all time. There are things and there is a way for things to be, and that way is understood in my relational being-in-and-to-the-world as in-and-to-God. I am the privileged formation of that relationship, announcing the meaning of original Being.

Has arguing the validity of the Christian philosophical enterprise been merely a means to justify the perfectly aligned a-historicality of the Christian, to validate his specific kind of spectatorial stance in or, rather, out-of-the-world? Or more covertly, to redirect his palliative mumblings about the Absolute back into the world? Have we as Christians accepted the Wager without any sense of its breadth and *nihil*; in a word, without any burden of its un-becomingness. Have we accepted it in name only? The fundamental cohesion between the Philosophical and the Christian as a being-in-kind-being-in-the-world isn't based on the birth of an intellectual attitude or posture by and through which we come to observe or encounter the ready-made theoretical pseudo-certitudes. It can not be a short cut, but must be the longer way. The Christian who thinks he knows all the answers before the questions are even asked is at a human disadvantage and, worse, does no service to the faith. It is, and must be, so much more, it is the wager of a lifetime of all lifetimes. The question or possibility of Christian Philosophy penetrates in its radicality into the meaning of tragedy and the tragic in its fully articulated essence, it is a question of the existential activity of the Christian incarnational-intentional presence, prefigured in the encounter with Nothingness and thus acknowledging the place of the Furies.

Now when we ask, "what does Athens have to do with Jerusalem?" "nothing" is the answer. The entire wait structure of the fourfold is encountered on the path from Athens to Jerusalem, as Christ was encountered on the road to Emmaus. The only thing we own is our nothingness, says St. Anselm. As travelers on the road from Athens to Jerusalem, this possibility of nonbeing is all we can take; but look, so far, where it has taken us.

Notes

Preface

[1] See G. K. Chesterton, *William Blake* (London, UK: Duckworth, 1910), 106–7.

[2] Martin Heidegger, *Nietzsche*, trans. J. Stambaugh, D. Krell, and F. Capuzzi (San Francisco: Harper, 1991), 4–5.

Chapter 1

[1] Eric Voegelin, *The World of the Polis* (Baton Rouge, LA: Louisiana State Univ. Press, 1957), 208. Future citations will be as follows: Voeg., *WP*.

[2] Aristotle, *Metaphysics*, trans. H. G. Apostle (Bloomington, IN: Indiana Univ. Press, 1966) (980a, 21). Future citations will be as follows: Arist., *M*.

[3] See M. J. Henn, *Parmenides of Elea* (Santa Barbara, CA: Praeger, 2003), 134. Future citations will be as follows: Henn, *PE*.

[4] M. Heidegger, *Parmenides*, trans. A. Schuwer & R. Rojcewicz (Bloomington, IN: Indiana Univ. Press, 1992), 5. Future citations will be as follows: Heid., *P*.

[5] See Ibid.

[6] See Henn, *PE*, 81.

[7] See Heid., *P*, 5–6.

[8] See Henn, *PE*, 85–6.

[9] J. D. Caputo, *Heidegger and Aquinas* (Bronx, NY: Fordham Univ. Press, 1982), 108.

[10] This is not the so-called essence (what) existence (that) distinction which comes to dominate much later. See C. Kahn, "The Greek Word 'to-Be' and the Concept of Being," *Foundations of Language* 2 (1966): 245–65. Also his "Thesis of Parmenides," *Review of Metaphysics* 23 (1969–1970): 700–24.

[11] Voeg., *WP*, 207.

[12] H. G. Gadamer, *The Beginning of Philosophy*, trans. R. Coltman. (New York: Continuum, 1998), 97. Future citations will be as follows: Gad., *BP*.

[13] Heid., *P*, 16.

[14] Henn, *PE*, 9.

[15] W. Jaeger, *Theology of the Early Greek Philosophers* (New York: Oxford Univ. Press, 1947), 98. Future citations will be as follows: Jaeg., *TEGP*.

[16] Heid., *P*, 26.

[17] Ibid., 48.

18 See Heidegger's "Letter on Humanism," *Basic Writings*, ed. D. F. Krell (San Francisco: Harper, 1993), 213–66. He notes that by the time of Plato and Aristotle the logos has long since been dead and buried.

19 Heid., *P*, 36.

20 Correspondingly, of course, to this collapse of aletheia/pseudos into the mere "true" and "false" is the ultimate collapse of Being and Nothing into the real and the unreal. We shall be discussing this more fully in Chapter 3. But see Heidegger's *The Essence of Truth*, trans. T. Sadler (New York: Continuum, 2002); and "What is Metaphysics?" *Existence and Being*, ed. W. Brock (Chicago: Henry Regnery Co., 1949). See also Heid., *P*, 13.

21 See Voeg., *WP*, 210.

22 See M. Heidegger, *Being and Time*, trans. J. Macquarrie and E. Robinson (New York: Harper & Row, 1962), 272, para. 230. Future citations will be as follows: Heid., *B&T*.

23 See Gad., *BP*, 123.

24 See G. E. L. Owen, "Eleatic Questions," in *Logic, Science, and Dialectic*, ed. M. Nussbaum (Ithaca, NY: Cornell Univ. Press, 1986), 3–26.

25 See D. Gallop, *Parmenides of Elea: A Text and Translation* (Toronto: Univ. of Toronto Press, 1984), 27.

26 See Jaeg., *TEGP*, 106.

27 See M. Heidegger, "Letter on Humanism" in *Basic Writings*, ed. D. F. Krell (San Francisco: Harper, 1993), 213–66. Future citations will be as follows: Heid., *LH*, 213.

28 See St. Thomas Aquinas, *De Veritate*, trans. R. W. Mulligan (Chicago: Henry Regnery Co., 1952), I.I. Future citations will be as follows, ST., *DV*.

29 Voeg., *WP*, 212.

30 Voeg., *WP*, 217–18.

31 Voeg., *WP*, 213.

32 Gad., *BP*, 97.

33 Henn, *PE*, 139.

34 Voeg., *WP*, 210.

35 Jaeg., *TEGP*, 92.

36 Jaeg., *TEGP*, 92.

37 Heidegger, *Identity and Difference*, trans. J. Stambaugh (New York: Harper & Row, 1969), 59. Future citations will be as follows: Heid., *I&D*.

38 Heid., *B&T*, 272, para. 229.

39 Jaeg., *TEGP*, 92.

40 Voeg., *WP*, 218. One might note that for St. Thomas, once Christ has entered existence not as an addition to or defect of, but as the radical intelligible fulfillment of existence as existence itself, to think about Being is to think about Christ, that is, the structure of being-in-the-world is onto-theologic. Does this Christian notion of Being lessen the integrity of something like the poem of Parmenides or actually reflect its goal or telos? See also D. G. Leahy's, *Novitas Mundi* (New York: New York Univ. Press, 1980); and *Faith and Philosophy* (New York: Ashgate Pub., 2003).

41 Voeg., *WP*, 219.

42 Henn, *PE*, 33.

[43] Caputo, J. D., *Heidegger and Aquinas*, 168–9.

[44] See Gad., *BP*, 98.

[45] Henn., *PE*, 36.

[46] Gad., *BP*, 111.

[47] M. Dufrenne, *The Notion of the A Priori*, trans. E. S. Casey (Evanston, IL: Northwestern Univ. Press, 1966), 230.

[48] Jaeg., *TEGP*, 102.

[49] Gad., *BP*, 105.

[50] Structurally important, the dialogue *Parmenides* is divided into eight arguments, the first four beginning with the assertion "One is" while the latter claim "One is not." The arguments defend either on behalf of the One or in support of everything else that isn't One, i.e., the different things. The pattern of the arguments is to assert and then to contradict: The subsequent argument always negates the preceding one. The unifying theme within every argument whether it claims the One is or is not, is resoundingly that "One is not."

[51] See A. E. Taylor, *Plato: The Man and His Works* (London: Methuen Pub., 1927), 351.

[52] See Ibid., 370.

[53] See S. Rosen, *Plato's Symposium* (New Haven, CT: Yale Univ. Press, 1997), xxviii.

[54] Plato, *Parmenides*, trans. A. K. Whitaker (Newburyport, MA: Focus Pub., 1996), 137b.

[55] "We should keep our seriousness for serious things, and not waste it on trifles, and that, while God is the real goal of all beneficent serious endeavor, man as we said before, has been constructed as a toy for God, and this is, in fact, the finest thing about him. All of us, then, men and women alike, must fall in with our role and spend life in making our play as perfect as possible—to the complete inversion of current theory." (Plato, *Laws*, trans. B. Jowett [New York: Random House, 1937], Bk. VII, 803b1–c8.)

[56] It should be noted that we are not engaging the question of the specific problems engendered by Platonic, let alone Neo-Platonic, metaphysics any more than we did so in the discussion of *Parmenides*. Our sole concern is to demonstrate that any genuine metaphysics requires the fourfold intentional presupposition. In this sense, and perhaps only in this sense can it be said that St. Thomas, as we shall see, is the supreme representative of even the Platonic tradition.

[57] See R. E. Allen, *Plato's Parmenides* (New Haven, CT: Yale Univ. Press, 1997), xiii.

[58] See Plato, *Phaedo* trans. B. Jowett (New York: Random House, 1937), 101d–e.

[59] Although the arguments lack the proper ontology to support the "no-thingness" or the ananke stenai of the One, nevertheless, they are directed towards the same goal found in Thomistic analogy, i.e., grounding knowledge in Being's radical Otherness which is essentially needed in order to fully support or explain the existence of the different things.

[60] S. Scolnicov, *Plato's Parmenides* (Berkeley, CA: California Univ. Press, 2003), 5.

[61] Plato, *Sophist*, trans. N. P. White (Indianapolis, IN: Hackett, 1993), 238d.

[62] M. Dufrenne, *The Notion of the A Priori*, 228.

[63] S. Scolnicov, *Plato's Parmenides*, 138.

[64] K. M. Sayre, *Parmenides' Lesson* (Notre Dame, IN: Notre Dame Univ. Press, 1996), 347–8.

[65] Argument III returns to the problem of predication, supporting the same conclusion as argument I. It shows that if the One is, it is nothing: for the different things

to experience everything, mustn't the One, in order to be different than them, experience nothing?

66 Parmenides, *Poem of Parmenides*, trans. M. Miller (n.p., n.d.), fr. 5: "And it is all one to me where I am to begin; for I shall return there again."

67 The text and structure of the *De Anima* have been the subject of considerable historical discussion. If we follow the historical consensus, the text seems to be the manuscript of lecture notes, perhaps recorded by students, and thus "private" or "esoteric" at least in that sense. In terms of Aristotle's own development the scholarly consensus places *De Anima* in the final phase of Aristotle's tripartite development. In the first phase, Aristotle adheres closely to Plato's doctrine set forth in the *Phaedo* in which the soul appears imprisoned in the body, but in command. This dualism succeeded in the second phase by Aristotle's biological investigations which lead to a wider conception of the soul, while in the third phase Aristotle achieves some form of unity of body and soul, thus bringing his psychology into line with the universal principles of his philosophy. In this regard see W. K. C. Guthrie, *A History of Greek Philosophy*, vol. 6 (New York: Cambridge Univ. Press, 1993); also the *Cambridge Companion to Aristotle*, ed. J. Barnes (New York: Cambridge Univ. Press, 1996). See also the notable essay by M. Nussbaum, "The Text of Aristotle's *De Anima*" in *Essays on Aristotle's* De Anima, ed. M. Nussbaum and R. Rorty (Oxford: Clarendon Press, 1992).

68 Aristotle, *De Anima*, trans. G. P. Goold (Cambridge, MA: Harvard Univ. Press, 1975), 415a, 18–20. Future citations will be as follows, Arist., *DA*.

69 *Parmenides*, 134e.

70 Arist., *M*, 994a1–6.

71 Ibid., 994b10–16.

72 Arist., *DA*, 406a2–4.

73 Arist., *DA*, 411a24–26.

74 Ibid., 425a32–33.

75 See J. Owens, *The Doctrine of Being in the Aristotelian Metaphysics* (Toronto: PIMS, 1951), 223.

76 Ibid., 413b26–29.

77 Ibid., 430a22–25.

78 In this regard, one can only benefit by referring to the astonishing conclusion of the *Nichomachean Ethics* where Aristotle concludes that the philosophic life is the happy life: "But such a life will be higher than the human plane; for it is not insofar as he is human that he will live like this, but insofar as there is something divine in him . . . If then intelligence is something divine as compared to a human being, so too a life lived in accordance with this will be divine as compared to a human life. One should not follow the advice of those who say 'human, you are to think human thoughts,' and 'mortal you are, think mortal ones,' but instead, so far as is possible immortalize yourselves and do everything with the aim of living in accordance with what is highest in us" (Trans. D. Ross [New York: Oxford Univ. Press, 1998], 1177b25–1178a8.

79 Ibid., 402a7–402a8.

80 Ibid., 402a16–18.

81 Ibid., 424b16–17.

82 Ibid., 430a15–21.

83 Ibid., 430a7–9.

84 Ibid., 417a19–21.

85 Ibid., 425b27–426a1.

86 Ibid., 418a3–5.

87 Ibid., 431a1–2, 431b17–22.

88 Parmenides, *Poem of Parmenides*, fr. 5.

89 The emphasis on touch here tends to belie the traditional understanding of ancient and medieval thought wherein the priority of the sight as the analogy of the intellectual soul characterizes a kind of Platonic hyper-intellectuality. Here we see on the other hand that whatever priority sight may have, it is equally rooted in the priority of touch; these are mutual priorities as representative or characteristic of man's sensible being-in-the-world. And it is this that fundamentally, contra Heidegger, distinguishes the classic vision from any Idealistic vision. This is a non-participating spectator fully participant at the epistemological ontological level in the world unlike the Idealistic all-seeing I. In this sense one might even redeem Plato from the idea of the correct vision for he too, as indicated in this chapter, stresses the analogy of touch as the connective or causal signate between man and world. St. Thomas' remark in *De Spiritualibus Creaturis* that "ad primum ergo dicendum quod substantia spiritualis, licet non comprehendatur a corpore, attingitur tamen aliqualiter ab eo, ut dictum est" is of more than passing interest, as well as Heidegger's remarks on touch in Being and Time, 55–6, para. 32–3.

90 If then, finitude is the enclosure (veritas) of the knower around the object it apprehends, and this enclosure is realized within the framework of an end qua origin, can the endlessness of the phenomenological phenomenon really reclaim a positive finitude? And without finitude, can it really claim to "touch" upon being-in-the-world or is it merely marking off semblances or appearances of things that cannot be themselves?

91 See Arist., *DA*, 422b34–35, 423a7–12.

92 Ibid., 435a18–435b5.

93 Ibid., 413b5–6.

94 Ibid., 414a3–4.

95 Ibid., 421a22–24.

96 Ibid., 414a5–15.

97 Ibid., 407a18–26.

98 Ibid., 416b19–20.

Chapter 2

1 See Arist., *M.*, 1048b28–1050a.

2 See ST., *DV*, Q10, a8.

3 St. Thomas' first three demonstrations of the existence of God especially, but all five, have as their linchpin the necessity of the ananke stenai; the primordial appropriation of man's being-in-the-world as inherently onto-theologic. Without it wouldn't the proofs inevitably collapse, succumbing to the criticisms that they are but products of a naive realism? We shall address this separately below.

⁴ St. Thomas Aquinas, *Summa Theologiae* I, ed. T.Gilby (New York: Cambridge Univ. Press, 1967), Q84, a2, R. Future citations will be as follows: ST., I. See also St. Thomas Aquinas, *Commentary on the* De Anima, trans. K. Foster and S. Humphries (New Haven, CT: Yale Univ. Press, 1951), 13, lect. III.

⁵ Arist., *DA*, 431b24–432a2.

⁶ See Arist., *M*, 1050a.

⁷ Our discussion of Parmenides and Plato, as noted earlier, prescinded from any emphasis on any internal problems arising from their conceptions of Being; our interest was in the fourfold intentional presupposition of all classical metaphysics. Now, however, in order to do justice to St. Thomas, such discussion is inevitable.

⁸ See ST., I, Q84, a2, R. See also St. Thomas Aquinas, *Commentary on the* De Anima, lect III, a13 n.4.

⁹ St. Thomas Aquinas, *Commentary on the* De Anima, lect III, a13 n.4.

¹⁰ J. Maritain, *Degrees of Knowledge*, trans. G. Phelan (New York: Charles Scribner's Sons, 1959), 114. Future citations will be as follows: Maritain, *DK*, 114.

¹¹ This confusion about intentionality in St. Thomas continues; one need only read A. Kenny's dispute with P. Geach and B. Lonergan in his essay "Intentionality: Aquinas and Wittgenstein" in *Thomas Aquinas: Contemporary Philosophical Perspectives*, ed. B. Davies (New York: Oxford Univ. Press, 2002) to get the full sense of the problem of a genuine understanding of intentionality.

¹² See ST., I, Q78, a3, R. See also ST., *DV*, Q2, a2.

¹³ See ST., I, Q55, a2, R; see also ST., I, Q85, a1, R.

¹⁴ Ibid.

¹⁵ Ibid.

¹⁶ Ibid.

¹⁷ ST., I, Q85, a2, ad 1.

¹⁸ Ibid.

¹⁹ Ibid.

²⁰ Ibid.

²¹ ST., I, Q85, a1, arg. 2.

²² See St. Thomas Aquinas, *On Being and Essence*, trans. A. Maurer (Toronto: PIMS, 1949), 40.

²³ Maritain, *DK*, 35.

²⁴ ST., I, Q85, a1, ad 2.

²⁵ Insofar as they do not affect the object of our immediate inquiry, we shall leave out of consideration both mathematical and metaphysical abstraction.

²⁶ ST., I, Q85, a1, ad 3.

²⁷ ST., I, Q79, a2, R.

²⁸ ST., I, Q79, a2, R.

²⁹ ST., I, Q79, a2, R.

³⁰ ST., I, Q79, a3, R.

³¹ E. Gilson, *The Christian Philosophy of St. Thomas* (New York: Random House, 1956), 220. Future citations will be as follows: Gilson, *CPST.*, 220.

³² ST., I, Q85, a1, ad 4.

³³ By "intelligible intentions" here St. Thomas means intelligible species that possess the intentional presence, and not ratio or conceptio.

³⁴ Maritain, *DK*, 116.

35 ST., I, Q85, a1, ad 4.

36 ST., I, Q85, a1, ad 5.

37 ST., I, Q85, a2.

38 ST., I, Q85, a2, R.

39 ST., I, Q85, a2, R.

40 Gilson, *CPST*, 227.

41 ST., I, Q85, a2, R.

42 ST., I, Q85, a2, ad 1.

43 ST., I, Q85, a2, ad 2.

44 Gilson, *CPST*, 228.

45 ST., I, Q85, a2, ad 3.

46 ST., I, Q87, a1, R.

47 Jean-Paul Sartre, *Transcendence of the Ego*, trans. F. Williams and R. Kirkpatrick (New York: Noonday Press, 1962), 40.

48 ST., *DV*, Q10, a8.

49 ST., *DV*, Q10, a8.

50 ST., *DV*, Q10, a8.

51 See ST., *DV*, Q10, a8.

52 ST., *DV*, Q10, a8.

53 ST., *DV*, Q10, a8.

54 ST., I, Q87, a1, R.

55 See ST., I., Q87, a1, R.

56 ST., *DV*, Q10, a8.

57 ST., I, Q87, a1, R.

58 Gilson, *CPST*, 227.

59 See ST., I, Q62, a5, ad 1.

60 ST., I, Q87, a1, R; ST., I, Q84, a7.

61 "Hence, our mind cannot so understand itself that it immediately apprehends itself. Rather, it comes to a knowledge of itself through apprehension of other things, just as the nature of first matter is known from its receptivity for forms of a certain kind" (*De Veritate*, Q10, a8).

62 See ST., I, Q76, a2, ad 4.

63 Heid., *B&T*, para., 55, 81.

64 See St. Thomas Aquinas, *Commentary on the* De Anima, lect III, 23.

65 See ST., I, Q76, a1, ad 5; see also St. Thomas Aquinas, *De Spiritualibus Creaturis*, ed. L. W. Keeler (Rome, Italy: Gregoriana Univ. Press, 1938), a2 responsio.

66 ST., I, Q77, a3, R.

67 ST., I, Q76, a5, ad 4.

68 See ST., I, Q14, a1, R.

69 ST., II-II, Q8, a1, R.

70 ST., I, Q79, a1, ad 4; ST., *DV*, Q23, a1. R.

Chapter 3

1 E. Gilson, *Reason and Revelation in the Middle Ages* (New York: Charles Scribner's Sons, 1966), 70–1.

[2] See Heid., *I&D* for the development of this train of thought in Heidegger.

[3] Martin Heidegger, *Kant and the Problem of Metaphysics*, trans. J. S. Churchill (Bloomington, IN: Indiana Univ. Press, 1963). Future citations will be as follows: Heid., *KPM.*

[4] See Heid., *I&D*, 31.

[5] See Husserl, *Experience and Judgment*, trans. J. S. Churchill and K. Ameriks (Evanston, IL: Northwestern Univ. Press, 1973), 48–50.

[6] Husserl, *Cartesian Meditations*, trans. D. Cairns (The Hague: Nijhoff, 1960), 57.

[7] See Husserl, *The Crisis of European Sciences and Transcendental Phenomenology*, trans. D. Carr (Evanston, IL: Northwestern Univ. Press, 1970), 198–201. Future citations will be as follows: Husserl, *CESTP.*

[8] Husserl, *CESTP*, 198–201.

[9] Ibid.

[10] Ibid.

[11] Ibid.

[12] Ibid.

[13] Husserl, *Paris Lectures*, trans. P. Koestenbaum (The Hague: Nijhoff, 1970), 8–9. Future citations will be as follows: Husserl, *PL*, 8–9.

[14] Husserl, *PL*, 8–9.

[15] Husserl, *Ideas I*, trans. W. R. B. Gibson (New York: Collier Books, 1967), 39. Future citations will be as follows: Husserl, *I I*, 39.

[16] Ibid., 78.

[17] Ibid., 72.

[18] Paul Ricoeur, *Husserl: An Analysis of His Phenomenology*, trans. E. G. Ballard and L. E. Embree (Evanston, IL: Northwestern Univ. Press, 1967), 9.

[19] See Husserl, *Husserliana II* (The Hague: Nijhoff, 1950), 23.

[20] Husserl, *The Idea of Phenomenology*, trans. W. P. Alston and G. Nakhnikian (The Hague: Nijhoff, 1974), 174. Future citations will be as follows: Husserl, *IP*, 174.

[21] Husserl, *I I*, 102–3.

[22] Ibid., 67; also see R. Boehm, "Husserl's Concept of the Absolute," in *The Phenomenology of Husserl*, ed. R. O. Elveton (Chicago: Quandrangle Books, 1970), 181–2.

[23] Husserl, *I I*, 194.

[24] Ibid., 67.

[25] Husserl, *IP*, 17–18.

[26] Ibid.

[27] Ibid.

[28] Ibid.

[29] Ibid.

[30] Ibid.

[31] Husserl, *PL*, 6–8.

[32] See Quentin Lauer, "On Evidence," in *Phenomenology: The Philosophy of Edmund Husserl and Its Interpretation*, ed. J. Kockelmans (New York: Doubleday, 1967), 154.

[33] Mikel Dufrenne, *The Notion of the A Priori*, 88–93.

[34] Husserl, *PL*, 27–9.

[35] Husserl, *PL*, 8–9.

[36] Mikel Dufrenne, *The Notion of the A Priori*, 77.

[37] See my article, "Edmund Husserl and the Crisis of Europe," *Modern Age* 48, (Winter 2006): 28–36.

[38] See Gaston Berger, *The Cogito in Husserl's Phenomenology*, (Evanston, IL: Northwestern Univ. Press, 1972), 57.

[39] See David Leahy, *Novitas Mundi*, 269.

[40] See Rudolf Boehm, "Husserl's Concept of the Absolute," in *The Phenomenology of Husserl*, 175.

[41] Ibid., 3–5.

[42] See Heid., *KPM*, 167–170, 221–2.

[43] See M. Merleau-Ponty, *Humanism and Terror* (Boston, MA: Beacon Press, 1971), 15.

[44] While it is not as such our issue, does this not shed some light on the absence of an ethics in Heidegger and his own disastrous political allegiances about which there is such a constant controversy? Does this signal the triumph of Will over Intellect?

[45] This notion of the causal reversal which places the primacy in thought is best spoken by Etienne Gilson in *Methodical Realism*: "A thought which starts from a mental representation will never get beyond it: from the duplicate or image there is no way of reaching the thing itself. Once trapped in immanence, the duplicate is only a mental symbol and will remain such. The principle of causality does not in the least change the situation. . . . In other words, he who begins an Idealist ends as Idealist. . . . Nobody has tried as hard as Descartes to build a bridge from thought to things, by relying on the principle of causality. He was also the first to make the attempt, and did so because he was forced to by having set the starting point for knowledge in the intuition of thought. . . . St. Augustine, logically or not, never required of thought that it should guarantee the existence of matter, and if one . . . expected thought to perform such a task . . . the being I grasp is only through and in my thought, how by this means shall I ever succeed in grasping a being which is anything other than that of thought." (trans. P. Trower [Poulsbo, WA: Christendom Univ. Press, 1990], 21–4). Gilson's remark that Descartes was forced to start with thought rather than Being because he had set the starting point for knowledge in the intuition of thought is critical to our analysis of Heidegger's implementation of Kantian finitude.

[46] Heid., *KPM*, 213.

[47] Ibid., 221–2.

[48] Ibid., *KPM*, 200.

[49] Etienne Gilson, *Being and Some Philosophers* (Toronto: PIMS, 1952), 172.

[50] See Joseph Owens, "Aquinas on Infinite Regress," *Mind* 71 (1962): 244–6.

[51] Anton C. Pegis, "Man as Nature and Spirit," in *Doctor Communis* 4 (1951): 52–63. See also Pegis, *At the Origins of the Thomistic Notion of Man* (New York: Macmillan, 1963).

[52] Heid., *KPM*, 225.

[53] Ibid., 96.

[54] Heid., *B&T*, 74–5, para. 48–50.

[55] ST., I-II, Q2, a8, ad 3.

[56] Heid., *B&T*, 378–9, para. 329–30.

[57] Ibid., 402, para. 351.

[58] Ibid., 378–9, para. 329–30.

59 Ibid., 240–1, para. 196.
60 Heid., *KPM*, 153.
61 Ibid., 3–5.
62 Heid., *B&T*, 333, para. 287.
63 Ibid., 308–9, para. 264.
64 Ibid., 321, para. 276–7.
65 See Martin Heidegger's, "Letter on Humanism," 270–302 and *Plato's Doctrine of Truth in Philosophy in the Twentieth Century*, eds H. D. Aiken and W. Barrett (New York: Random House, 1962), 251–70.
66 Heid., *B&T*, 133, para. 100.
67 Ibid., 246–7, para. 202–3.
68 Ibid., 133, para. 100.
69 Ibid., 313–15, para. 268–70.
70 Heid., *KPM*, 221–2.
71 Ibid., 44.
72 Ibid., 42–3.
73 See Etienne Gilson, *The Elements of Christian Philosophy* (New York: Mentor Omega, 1963), 253.
74 Heid., *B&T*, 119–21, para. 86–7.
75 Heid., *KPM*, 233.
76 Ibid., 122.
77 Heid., *B&T*, 359, para. 311.
78 Ibid., 143–4.
79 Ibid., 82, para. 56.
80 Ibid., 184, para. 144.
81 Ibid., 118, para. 85–6.
82 Heid., *KPM*, 236.
83 Voegelin sees in Heidegger's notion of Geworfenheit a clear gnostic symbol and does not hesitate to see in Heidegger himself "that ingenious gnostic of our own time." Regrettably, this goes far beyond the scope of this work. (See Eric Voegelin, *Science, Politics, Gnosticism* (Chicago: Henry Regnery Co., 1968), 10, 48.
84 Heid., *KPM*, 231.
85 Ibid., 213.
86 Heid., *B&T*, 226, para. 181–2.
87 Heid., *B&T*, 111, para. 80.
88 Heid., *KPM*, 75.
89 Heid., *B&T*, 360–1, para. 312–13.
90 Heid., *B&T*, 372–3, para. 325–6.
91 Ibid., 236, para. 191–2.
92 Ibid., 162–3, para. 125.
93 Ibid., 174–5, para. 135–6.
94 "The problem of the laying of the foundation of metaphysics is rooted in the question of the Dasein in man, i.e., in the question of his ultimate ground, which is the comprehension of Being as essentially existent fintude . . . the laying of the foundation of metaphysics is based upon a metaphysics of Dasein" (Heid., *KPM*, 238).

95 Heid., *B&T*, 374–5, para. 326–7.

96 "In realism there is a lack of ontological understanding. Indeed realism tries to explain Reality ontically by Real connections of interaction between things that are Real. As compared with realism, idealism, no matter how contrary and untenable it may be in results, has an advantage in principle, provided that it does not misunderstand itself as 'psychological' idealism. If idealism emphasizes that Being and Reality are only 'in the consciousness', that expresses an understanding of the fact that Being cannot be explained through entities. But as long as idealism fails to clarify what this very understanding of Being means ontologically, or how this understanding is possible, or that it belongs to Dasein's state of Being, the interpretation of Reality that idealism constructs is an empty one" (Heid., *B&T*, 251, para. 207).

97 Heid., *B&T*, 205, para. 162. Is it any wonder that Santayana is reported to have said upon reading Sein und Zeit: "This man understands essence" (John McCormick, *George Santayana: A Biography* [Edison, NJ: Transaction Publishers, 2003]).

98 Heid., *B&T*, 65, para. 41.

99 Ibid., para. 76.

100 Ibid., 236, para. 191–2.

101 ST., I, Q10, a4–5.

102 Ibid., a4, R.

103 ST., I, Q2, a3, resp.; For a penetrating account of St. Thomas' five ways, see L. Clavell and M. Perez De Laborda, *Metafisicia* (Rome: Armando Editore, 2006).

104 See Martin Heidegger, *The End of Philosophy*, trans. J. Stambaugh (New York: Harper & Row, 1973).

105 Heid., *I&D*, 59.

106 Ibid., 60.

107 Heid., *B&T*, 213, para. 169.

108 Ibid., 313, para. 267.

109 Heid., *KPM*, 167–70.

110 Heid., *B&T*, 35, para. 303–4.

111 Heid., *KPM*, 198–9.

112 Heid., *B&T*, 116–17, para. 84.

113 Ibid., 119–21, para. 86–7.

114 Ibid., para. 274.

115 Ibid., 149, para. 114.

116 Ibid., 142–3, para. 108.

117 "Resoluteness, as authentic Being-one's-Self, does not detach Dasein from its world, nor does it isolate it so that it becomes a free-floating 'I'. And how should it, when resoluteness as authentic disclosedness is authentically nothing else than Being-in-the-world? Resoluteness brings the Self right into its current concernful Being-alongside what is ready-to-hand, and pushes it into solicitous Being with Others" (Heid., *B&T*, 344, para. 298).

118 Heid., *B&T*, 330–1, para. 284–5.

119 "Phenomenological Interpretation must make it possible for Dasein itself to disclose things primordially; it must, as it were, let Dasein interpret itself" (Heid., *B&T*, 179, para. 140).

Chapter 4

1 To understand Heidegger's question "why being instead of nothing?" see Heidegger's commentary in *Plato's Sophist*, trans. A. Schuwer and R. Rojcewicz (Bloomington, IN: Indiana Univ. Press, 1997); and "The Fundamental Question of Metaphysics," in *Philosophy in the Twentieth Century*, ed. W. Barrett and H. D. Aiken (New York: Random House, 1962). Future citations will be as follows, Heid., *FQM*.

2 "Dionysus versus the Crucified: there you have the antithesis. It is not a difference in regard to their martyrdom: it is a difference in the meaning of it. Life itself, its eternal fruitfulness and recurrence, creates torment, destruction, the will to annihilation. In the other case, suffering—'the crucified as the innocent one'—counts as an objection to this life, as a formula for its condemnation. One will see the problem is that of the meaning of suffering: whether a Christian meaning or a tragic meaning. . . . The tragic man affirms even the harshest suffering: he is sufficiently strong, rich and capable of deifying to do so. . . . The god on the cross is a curse on life, a signpost to seek redemption from life" (Nietzsche, *The Will to Power*, trans. W. Kaufmann and R. J. Hollingdale [New York: Random House, 1967], 542, section 1052).

3 Augustine, *The Confessions*, trans H. Chadwick (New York: Oxford Univ. Press, 1998), Bk. X, Ch. 6.

4 ST., I-II, Q2, a5, ad2; ST., I, 43; and *Summa Contra Gentiles*, trans. J. E. Anderson (Notre Dame, IN: Univ. of Notre Dame Press, 1992), II, 30. Future citations will be as follows: ST., SCG.

5 G. M. Hopkins, Pied Beauty; Hopkins' poem Wreck of Deutschland speaks the terror of existence (*Selected Poems of G. M. Hopkins* [Portsmouth, NH: Heinemann, 1975]).

6 See A. C. Pegis, "St. Thomas and The Meaning of Human Existence," in *Calgary Aquinas Studies* (Toronto: PIMS, 1978), 23–37.

7 See Heidegger's "What is Metaphysics."

8 M. Heidegger, *Schelling's Treatise on the Essence of Human Freedom*, trans. J. Stambaugh (Athens, OH: Ohio Univ. Press, 1985), 186.

9 See Spinoza's *Ethics*, D7: "That thing is called free which exists from the necessity of its nature alone, and it is determined to act by itself alone. But a thing is called necessary, or rather compelled, which is determined by another to exist and to produce and effect in a certain and determinate manner" (trans. E. Curley [New York: Penguin Classics, 2005]).

10 When Pascal dismisses the "god of the philosophers" isn't this precisely and correctly what he dismisses? In Fr 77, he finds Descartes unforgivable because "in all his philosophy he would have been quite willing to dispense with God but had to make him give a fillip to set the world in motion; beyond this, he has no further need of God" (Pascal, *Pensees*, trans. W. F. Trotter [New York: EP Dutton, 1958]).

11 Heid., *FQM*, 233–4.

12 Even so renowned a historian of philosophy, and a Thomist himself, as Father Frederick Copleston in his famous debate with Bertrand Russell generally interprets St. Thomas' third way in terms of the principle of sufficient reason: "I have made use of this argument from contingent to necessary Being, basing the argument on the principle of sufficient reason, simply because it seems to me a brief

and clear formulation of what is, in my opinion, the fundamental metaphysical argument for God's existence" ("The Existence of God: A Debate," in *A Modern Introduction to Philosophy*, ed. P. Edwards, with intro. by A. Pap [New York: Free Press, 1965], 473–90).

[13] See Eric Voegelin, *Order and History*, vol. II (Baton Rouge, LA: Louisiana State Univ. Press, 1957) and Eric Voegelin, *The World of the Polis*.

[14] A being-meaningfully-in-and-to-the-world which, as Heidegger describes, includes the essential possibility of forgetfulness of our being-in-the-world and the oblivion of Being itself: fallenness. Perhaps this is what Plato was trying to articulate in the so-called theory of anamnesis.

[15] Leibniz, *Monadology*, trans. G. R. Montgomery (New York: Dover, 2005), 36.

[16] Ibid.

[17] Heid., *FQM*, 224–5.

[18] Heidegger, *The Principle of Reason*, trans. R. Lilly (Bloomington, IN: Indiana Univ. Press, 1996), 105. Future citations will be as follows: Heid., *PR*, 105.

[19] See ST., I, Q 82, a5, R.

[20] Spinoza, *Ethics*, proposition II.

[21] Heid., *PR*, 26–8.

[22] Ibid.

[23] Heid., *PR*, 30.

[24] Heid., *FQM*, 231.

[25] Heid., *PR*, 6–7.

[26] Heidegger, *Nietzsche*, vol. I, 5.

[27] Heid., *FQM*, 223.

[28] Ibid., 235–7.

[29] See Arist., *M*, 980a–983b, 1002b20–1004a9.

[30] Heid., *FQM*, 244–5.

[31] Ibid., 246. Also see *What is Called Thinking*, trans. F. D. Wieck and J. G. Gray (New York: Harper & Row, 1968), 43.

[32] Heid., *PR*, 44–5.

[33] Aristotle, *Nichomachean Ethics*, trans. D. Ross (New York: Oxford Univ. Press, 1998), Bk. X, 1177.

[34] Descartes, *Meditation VI*, In *The Philosophical Works of Descartes*, vol. 1, trans. E. S. Haldane and G. R. T. Ross (London: Cambridge Univ. Press, 1975), 199.

[35] See E. Gilson, *Being and Some Philosophers*, 207.

[36] "As eternity is the proper measure of being, so time is the proper measure of movement" (ST., I, Q10, a3, ad 3).

[37] Heid., *PR*, 46.

[38] ST., *DV*, I.I.

[39] ST., I, Q2, a2, obj3–ad 3.

[40] Ibid.

[41] M. Heidegger, *Schelling's Treatise on the Essence of Human Freedom*, 182.

[42] Heid., *FQM*, 219–22.

[43] See Heidegger's *Discourse on Thinking*, trans. J. M. Anderson and E. H. Freund (New York: Harper & Row, 1966), 62.

[44] Heid., *FQM*, 249.

[45] Heid., *PR*, 94.

46 Heid., *FQM*, 226.

47 Ibid., 223.

48 "What is Being? It is Itself" (Martin Heidegger, "Letter on Humanism," 281).

49 Heid., *PR*, 93.

50 E. Gilson, *Being and Some Philosophers*, 91.

51 Heid., *PR*, 47–8.

52 E. Gilson, *Being and Some Philosophers*, 93.

53 ST., *SCG* II, 68; ST., *SCG* III, 66.

54 Ibid., 68.

55 See ST., I, 75–89.

56 See A. C. Pegis, *At the Origin of the Thomistic Notion of Man* (New York: Macmillan Press, 1963).

57 ST., I, Q85, a4, 1.

58 Ibid., ad 1.

59 Not only Plato's problem in the *Phaedo* but Descartes' in the *Meditations*.

60 ST., I, Q10, a5, R.

61 Ibid.

62 Heid., *B&T*, 73–5, para. 48–9, as well as the entire thrust of the "Letter on Humanism."

63 Heid., *LH,*. 278–9.

64 E. Gilson, *The Spirit of Thomism* (New York: Harper and Row, 1964), 34.

65 See ST., I, Q10 a6 obj1-resp.

66 Ibid., a2, ad 1.

67 Heid., *FQM*, 243.

68 Ibid., 228.

69 Ibid., 241.

70 Ibid., 234–5. Carnap's ridicule of Heidegger's meditation on Nothing in "What is Metaphysics?" perhaps triggered Heidegger's remarks on the "cheap acid of a merely logical science." See Rudolf Carnap, "The Elimination of Metaphysics through Logical Analysis of Language" in *Logical Positivism*, ed. A. J. Ayer (Westport, CT: Greenwood Press, 1978), 60–81.

71 Aristotle, *Posterior Analytics*, trans. R. McKeon (New York: Random House, 1941), Bk. I, Ch. 3, 72b, 18–23; also see ST., I, Q2, a1, ad 3.

72 St. Anselm, "In Reply to Gaunilo's Answer on Behalf of the Fool," *Basic Writings*, trans. S. N. Deane (Chicago: Open Court, 1962), Ch I.

Bibliography

Primary Sources

Anselm, S. *Basic Writings*. Translated by S. N. Deane. Lasalle, IL: Open Court Publishing, 1962.

Aristotle. *De Anima*. Translated by G. P. Goold. Cambridge: Harvard Univ. Press, 1975.

—. *Metaphysics*. Translated by H. G. Apostle. Bloomington, IN: Indiana Univ. Press, 1966.

—. *Nichomachean Ethics*. Translated by D. Ross. New York: Oxford Univ. Press, 1998.

—. *Posterior Analytics*. Translated by R. McKeon. New York: Random House, 1941.

Augustine. *The Confessions*. Translated by H. Chadwick. New York: Oxford Univ. Press, 1998.

—. *On Free Choice of the Will*. Translated by T. Williams. Indianapolis, IN: Hackett, 1993.

Descartes. *The Philosophical Works of Descartes*. Translated by E. S. Haldan and G. R. T. Ross. New York: Cambridge Univ. Press, 1955.

Heidegger, M. "Art and Space." Translated by C. H. Seibert. *Man and World* 6, no.1 (1973): 3–8.

—. *Basic Problems of Phenomenology*. Translated by A. Hofstadter. Bloomington, IN: Indiana Univ. Press, 1982.

—. *Being and Time*. Translated by J. Macquarrie and E. Robinson. New York: Harper & Row, 1962.

—. *Discourse on Thinking*. Translated by J. M. Anderson and E. H. Freund. New York: Harper & Row, 1966.

—. *Early Greek Thinking*. Translated by D. F. Krell and F. A. Capuzzi. New York: Harper & Row, 1975.

—. *The End of Philosophy*. Translated by J. Stambaugh. New York: Harper & Row, 1973.

—. *The Essence of Reasons*. Translated by T. Malick. Evanston, IL: Northwestern Univ. Press, 1969.

—. *The Essence of Truth*. Translated by T. Sadler. New York: Continuum, 2002.

—. "The Fundamental Question of Metaphysics." *Philosophy in the Twentieth Century*, vol. 3. Edited by W. Barrett and H. D. Aiken. New York: Random House, 1962: 219–50.

—. *Hegel's Concept of Experience*. Translated by J. G. Gray and F. D. Wieck. New York: Harper & Row, 1970.

—. *Hegel's Phenomenology of Spirit*. Translated by P. Emad and K. Maly. Bloomington, IN: Indiana Univ. Press, 1988.

—. *Heraclitus Seminar, 1966–1967*. With E. Fink. Translated by C. H. Seibert. Tuscaloosa, AL: Univ. of Alabama Press, 1979.

—. *History of the Concept of Time: Prolegomena*. Translated by T. Kisiel. Bloomington, IN: Indiana Univ. Press, 1985.

—. *Identity and Difference*. Translated by J. Stambaugh. New York: Harper & Row, 1969.

—. *An Introduction to Metaphysics*. Translated by R. Manheim. New York: Doubleday-Anchor Books, 1961.

—. *Kant and the Problem of Metaphysics*. Translated by J. S. Churchill. Bloomington, IN: Indiana Univ. Press, 1963.

—. "Letter on Humanism." *Basic Writings*. Edited by D. F. Krell. San Francisco: Harper, 1993: 213–66.

—. *The Metaphysical Foundations of Logic*. Translated by M. Heim. Bloomington, IN: Indiana Univ. Press, 1984.

—. *Nietzsche*. Translated by J. Stambaugh, D. Krell, and F. Capuzzi. San Francisco: Harper, 1991.

—. *On the Way to Language*. Translated by P. D. Hertz and J. Stambaugh. New York: Harper & Row, 1971

—. *On Time and Being*. Translated by J. Stambaugh. New York: Harper & Row, 1972.

—. "Only a God can Save us Now": An interview with Martin Heidegger." Translated by D. Schlender. *Graduate Faculty Philosophy Journal* 6, no. 1 (1977): 5–27.

—. *Parmenides*. Translated by A. Schuwer and R. Rojcewicz. Bloomington, IN: Indiana Univ. Press, 1992.

—. *Phenomenological Interpretations of Aristotle*. Translated by R. Rojcewicz. Bloomington, IN: Indiana Univ. Press, 2001.

—. *The Piety of Thinking*. Translated by J. G. Hart and J. C. Maraldo. Bloomington, IN: Indiana Univ. Press, 1976. (Contains Heidegger's review of Ernst Cassirer's "Mythical Thought," 1928.)

—. *Plato's Doctrine of Truth in Philosophy in the Twentieth Century*. Edited by H. D. Aiken and W. Barrett. New York: Random House, 1962.

—. *Plato's Sophist*. Translated by A. Schuwer and R. Rojcewicz. Bloomington, IN: Indiana Univ. Press, 1997.

—. *Poetry, Language, Thought*. Translated by A. Hofstadter. New York: Harper & Row, 1971.

—. *The Principle of Reason*. Translated by R. Lilly. Bloomington, IN: Indiana Univ. Press, 1996.

—. *The Question Concerning Technology and Other Essays*. Translated by W. Lovitt. New York: Harper & Row, 1977.

—. *The Question of Being*. Translated by W. Kluback and J. T. Wilde. New Haven, CT: Yale Univ. Press, 1958.

—. *Schelling's Treatise on the Essence of Human Freedom*. Translated by J. Stambaugh. Athens, OH: Ohio Univ. Press, 1985.

—. "The Self-Assertion of the German University." Translated by K. Harries. *Review of Metaphysics* 38 (1985): 467–80. (With "The Rectorate 1933-34: Facts and Thoughts.")

—. *What is a Thing?* Translated by W. B. Barton, Jr. and V. Deutsch. Chicago: Henry Regnery Co., 1967.

—. *What is Called Thinking?* Translated by F. D. Wieck and J. G. Gray. New York: Harper & Row, 1968.

—. "What is Metaphysics?" *Existence and Being*. Edited by W. Brock. Chicago: Henry Regnery Co., 1949.

—. *What Is Philosophy?* Translated by W. Kluback and J. T. Wilde. New Haven, CT: Yale Univ. Press, 1958.

Husserl, E. *Cartesian Meditations*. Translated by D. Cairns. The Hague: Nijhoff, 1960.

—. *The Crisis of European Sciences and Transcendental Phenomenology*. Translated by D. Carr. Evanston, IL: Northwestern Univ. Press, 1970.

—. *Experience and Judgment*. Translated by J. S. Churchill and K. Ameriks. Evanston, IL: Northwestern Univ. Press, 1973.

—. *Husserl, Paris Lectures*. Translated by P. Koestenbaum. The Hague: Nijhoff, 1970.

—. *Husserliana II*. The Hague: Nijhoff, 1950.

—. *The Idea of Phenomenology*. Translated by W. P. Alston and G. Nakhnikian. The Hague: Nijhoff, 1974.

—. *Ideas I*. Translated by W. R. B. Gibson. New York: Collier Books, 1967.

—. *Logical Investigations*. Translated by J. N. Findlay. New York: Humanities, 1970.

Kant, I. *Critique of Pure Reason*. New York: Hackett, 1996.

Leibniz, G. W. *Monadology*. Translated by G. R. Montgomery. New York: Dover, 2005.

Parmenides. *Poem of Parmenides*. Translated by M. Miller. N.p., n.d.

Plato. *Laws*. Translated by B. Jowett. New York: Random House, 1937.

—. *Parmenides*. Translated by A. K. Whitaker. Newburyport, MA: Focus Pub., 1996.

—. *Phaedo*. Translated by B. Jowett. New York: Random House, 1937.

—. *Sophist*. Translated by N. P. White. Indianapolis, IN: Hackett, 1993.

—. *Theaetetus*. Translated by B. Jowett. New York: Random House, 1937.

Spinoza. *The Collected Works of Spinoza*. Edited and translated by E. Curley. Princeton, NJ: Princeton Univ. Press, 1985.

—. *Ethics*. Translated by E. Curley. New York: Penguin Classics, 2005.

St. Thomas Aquinas. *On Being and Essence*. Translated by A. Maurer. Toronto: PIMS, 1949.

—. *Commentary on the* De Anima. Translated by K. Foster and S. Humphries. New Haven, CT: Yale Univ. Press, 1951.

—. *Commentary on the Metaphysics*. Translated by J. P. Rowen. South Bend, IN: Dumb Ox Books, 1995.

—. *De Spiritualibus Creaturis*. Edited by L. W. Keeler. Rome, Italy: Gregoriana Univ. Press, 1938.

—. *De Veritate*. Translated by R. W. Mulligan. Chicago: Henry Regnery Co., 1952.

—. *Summa Contra Gentiles*. Translated by J. E. Anderson. Notre Dame, IN: Univ. of Notre Dame Press, 1992.

—. *Summa Theologiae*. Edited by T. Gilby. New York: Cambridge Univ. Press, 1967.

Secondary Sources

Allen, R. E. *Plato's Parmenides*. New Haven, CT: Yale Univ. Press, 1997.

—. *Studies in Presocratic Philosophy*. Edited by R. E. Allen and D. Furley. London: Routledge, 1975.

—. "Unity and Infinity: Parmenides 142b–145a." *Review of Metaphysics* 27 (1974): 697–725.

Arendt , H. "Martin Heidegger at Eighty." *The New York Review of Books* 17, no. 6 (1971): 41–55.

Barnes, J., ed. *Cambridge Companion to Aristotle.* New York: Cambridge Univ. Press, 1996.

Barrett, W. and H. Aiken, eds *Philosophy in the Twentieth Century.* New York: Random House, 1962.

Beaufret, J. *Dialogue avec Heidegger.* Vol. 3, *Approche de Heidegger.* Paris: Minuit, 1974.

Berger, G. *The Cogito in Husserl's Phenomenology.* Evanston, IL: Northwestern Univ. Press, 1972.

Bernet, R. "Husserl and Heidegger on Intentionality and Being." *Journal of the British Society of Phenomenology* 21 (1990) 136–52.

Boehm, R. "Husserl's Concept of the Absolute." In *The Phenomenology of Husserl.* Edited by R. O. Elveton. Chicago: Quandrangle Books, 1970.

Caputo, J. D. *Heidegger and Aquinas.* Bronx, NY: Fordham Univ. Press, 1982.

Carnap, R. "The Elimination of Metaphysics Through Logical Analysis of Language." In *Logical Positivism.* Edited by A. J. Ayer. Westport, CT: Greenwood Press, 1978.

Charlesworth, M. J. *Philosophy and Linguistic Analysis.* Pittsburgh, PA: Duquesne Univ. Press, 1961.

Cherniss, H. F. "Parmenides and the 'Parmenides' of Plato." *American Journal of Philology* 53 (1932): 122–38.

Chesterton, G. K. *William Blake.* London, UK: Duckworth, 1910.

Clarke, W. N. "The Limitation of Act by Potency: Aristotelianism or Neoplatonism." *The New Scholasticism* 26 (1952): 167–94.

Clavell, L. and M. Perez De Laborda. *Metafisicia.* Rome: Armando Editore, 2006.

Copleston, F. and B. Russell. "The Existence of God: A Debate." In *A Modern Introduction to Philosophy.* Edited by P. Edwards, with introduction by A. Pap. New York: Free Press, 1965.

Cornford, F. M. *Plato and Parmenides.* London: Routledge and Paul Kegan Ltd., 1939.

Davies, B., ed. "Intentionality: Aquinas and Wittgenstein." In *Thomas Aquinas: Contemporary Philosophical Perspectives.* Edited by B. Davies. New York: Oxford Univ. Press, 2002.

Dilthey, W. *Introduction to the Human Sciences.* Translated by R. J. Betanzos. Detroit, MI: Wayne State Univ. Press, 1988.

Dufrenne, M. *The Notion of the A Priori.* Translated by E. S. Casey. Evanston, IL: Northwestern Univ. Press, 1966.

Fabro, C. *God in Exile.* Translated by A. Gibson. New York: Newman Press, 1964.

—. *Participation et Causalite selon Saint Thomas d'Aquin.* Belgium: Louvain Univ. Press, 1961.

Francis M. C. *Plato's Theory of Knowledge: The "Theaetetus" and the "Sophist."* London: Routledge, 1935.

Furth, M. "Elements of Eleatic Ontology." *Journal of the History of Philosophy* 7 (1969): 111–32.

Gadamer, Hans-Georg. *The Beginning of Philosophy.* Translated by R. Coltman. New York: Continuum, 1998.

—. "Plato's Parmenides and Its Influence." *Dionysius* 7 (1983): 3–16.

—. *Truth and Method.* Translated by W. Glen-Doepel. London: Sheed & Ward, 1979.

Gallop, D. *Parmenides of Elea: A Text and Translation.* Ontario: Univ. of Toronto Press, 1984.

Geach, P. T. "The Third Man Again." *Philosophical Review* 55 (1956): 72–82.

Gilson, E. "Autour de Pompanazzi." In *Archives d'Histoire Doctrinale et Litteraire du Moyen Age* xxviii (1961): 163–278.

—. *Being and Some Philosophers.* Toronto: PIMS, 1952.

—. *The Christian Philosophy of St. Thomas.* New York: Random House, 1956.

—. *The Elements of Christian Philosophy.* New York: Mentor Omega, 1963.

—. *God and Philosophy.* New Haven, CT: Yale Univ. Press, 1941.

—. *Jean Dun Scot: Introduction a ses positions fondamentales. Librairie Philosophique J. Vrin.* Paris: Vrin, 1952.

—. *Linguistics and Philosophy.* Notre Dame, IN: Univ. of Notre Dame Press, 1988.

—. *Methodical Realism.* Translated by P. Trower. Poulsbo, WA: Christendom Univ. Press, 1990.

—. *The Philosopher and Theology.* Translated by C. Gilson. New York: Random House, 1962.

—. *Reason and Revelation in the Middle Ages.* New York: Charles Scribner's Sons, 1966.

—. *The Spirit of Mediaeval Philosophy.* Translated by A. C. H. Downes. New York: Charles Scribner's Sons, 1940.

—. *The Spirit of Thomism.* New York: Harper, 1964.

—. *The Unity of Philosophical Experience.* San Francisco: Ignatius Press, 1999.

Guthrie, W. K. C. *A History of Greek Philosophy,* vol. 6. New York: Cambridge Univ. Press, 1993.

Henn, M. J. *Parmenides of Elea.* Santa Barbara, CA: Praeger, 2003.

Hopkins, G. M. "Pied Beauty" and "Wreck of Deutschland." In *Selected Poems of G. M. Hopkins.* Portsmouth, NH: Heinemann, 1975.

Inciarte, F. *First Principles, Substance and Action. Studies in Aristotle and Aristotelianism.* Zurich: Olms, 2005.

Jaeger, W. *Theology of the Early Greek Philosophers.* New York: Oxford Univ. Press; 1947.

Jaffa, H. V. *Thomism and Aristotelianism.* Chicago: Univ. of Chicago Press, 1952.

Kahn, C. *Aquinas.* Edited by A. Kenny. New York: Doubleday, 1969.

—. *The Five Ways. St. Thomas Aquinas' Proofs of God's Existence.* Notre Dame, IN: Univ. of Notre Dame Press, 1980.

—. "The Greek Word 'to-Be' and the Concept of Being." *Foundations of Language* 2 (1966): 245–65.

—. "Thesis of Parmenides." *Review of Metaphysics* 23 (1969–1970): 700–24.

—. *The Verb 'Be' in Ancient Greek.* Indianapolis, IN: Hackett, 2003.

Kirk, G. S., J. E. Raven, and M. Schofield. *The Presocratic Philosophers.* New York: Cambridge Univ. Press, 1983.

Kisiel, T. *The Genesis of Heidegger's Being & Time.* Berkeley, CA: Univ. of California Press, 1993.

Kretzmann, N. and E. Stump, eds *The Cambridge Companion to Aquinas.* New York: Cambridge Univ. Press, 1993.

Lauer, Q. "On Evidence." In *Phenomenology: The Philosophy of Edmund Husserl and Its Interpretation.* Edited by J. Kockelmans. New York: Doubleday, 1967.

Leahy, D. G. *Faith and Philosophy.* New York: Ashgate Pub., 2003.

—. *Novitas Mundi*. New York: New York Univ. Press, 1980.

Lonergan, B. *Verbum: Word and Idea in Aquinas*. Notre Dame, IN: Univ. of Notre Dame Press, 1967.

Maritain, J. *Degrees of Knowledge*. Translated by G. Phelan. New York: Charles Scribner's Sons, 1959.

—. *Existence and the Existent*. Translated by G. Phelan. New York: Vintage Books, 1996.

McCormick, J. *George Santayana: A Biography*. Edison, NJ: Transaction Publishers, 2003.

McInerny, R. M. *Aquinas and Analogy*. Washington, DC: Catholic Univ. Press, 1996.

—. *Aquinas against the Averroists: On There Being Only One Intellect*. West Lafayette, IN: Purdue Univ. Press, 1993.

—. *The Logic of Analogy: An Interpretation of St. Thomas*. The Hague: Nijhoff, 1961.

Merleau-Ponty, M. *Humanism and Terror*. Boston: Beacon Press, 1971.

Miller, M. H. Plato's *"Parmenides": The Conversion of the Soul*. Princeton, NJ: Princeton Univ. Press, 1986.

Nietzsche, F. *The Will to Power*. Translated by W. Kaufmann and R. J. Hollingdale. New York: Random House, 1967.

Nussbaum, M. "The Text of Aristotle's *De Anima*." In *Essays on Aristotle's De Anima*. Edited by M. Nussbaum and R. Rorty. Oxford: Clarendon Press, 1992.

Owen, G. E. L. "Eleatic Questions." In *Logic, Science, and Dialectic*. Edited by M. Nussbaum. Ithaca, NY: Cornell Univ. Press, 1986.

Owens, J. "Aquinas on Infinite Regress." *Mind* 71 (1962): 244–6.

—. *The Doctrine of Being in the Aristotelian Metaphysics*. Toronto: PIMS: 1951.

—. *St. Thomas Aquinas on the Existence of God*. Albany, NY: SUNY, 1980.

—. *St. Thomas and the Future of Metaphysics*. Milwaukee, WI: Marquette Univ. Press, 1957.

Pascal, B. *Pensees*. Translated by W. F. Trotter. New York: EP Dutton, 1958.

Pegis, A. C. *Introduction to St. Thomas Aquinas*. New York: Modern Library, 1948.

—. "Man as Nature and Spirit." *Doctor Communis* 4 (1951): 52–63.

—. *At the Origins of the Thomistic Notion of Man*. New York: Macmillan, 1963.

—. *The Problem of the Soul in the 13th Century*. Toronto: PIMS: 1934.

—. "Some Reflections on Summa Contra Gentiles II, 56." In *An Etienne Gilson Tribute*. Edited by C. O'Neil. Milwaukee, WI: Marquette Univ. Press, 1959.

—. *St. Thomas and the Greeks*. Milwaukee, WI: Marquette Univ. Press, 1939.

—. "St. Thomas and the Meaning of Human Existence." In *Calgary Aquinas Studies*. Toronto: PIMS, 1978: 49–64.

—. "St. Thomas and the Unity of Man." In *Progress in Philosophy*. Edited by J. McWilliams. Milwauke, WI: Marquette Univ. Press, 1955.

Poggeler, O. *Martin Heidegger's Path of Thinking*. Translated by D. Magurshak and S. Barber. Atlantic Highands, NJ: Humanities Press, 1987.

Richardson, W. J. *Heidegger: Through Phenomenology to Thought*. Bronx, NY: Fordham Univ. Press, 2003.

Ricoeur, P. *Husserl: An Analysis of His Phenomenology*. Translated by E. G. Ballard and L. E. Embree. Evanston, IL: Northwestern Univ. Press, 1967.

Rosenp, S. *Plato's Symposium*. New Haven, CT: Yale Univ. Press, 1997.

Rousselot, P. *The Intellectualism of St. Thomas*. New York: Sheed & Ward, 1935.

Ryle, G. "Plato's Parmenides." In *Studies in Plato's Metaphysics*. Edited by R. E. Allen. London: Routledge, 1939.

Sanguineti, J. J. *Introduzione Alla Gnoseologia*. Florence, Italy: Le Monnier, 2003.

Sartre, Jean-Paul. *Being and Nothingness*. Translated by H. E. Barnes. New York: Washington Square Press, 1993.

—. *Transcendence of the Ego*. Translated by F. Williams and R. Kirkpatrick. New York: Noonday Press, 1962.

Sayre, K. M. *Parmenides' Lesson*. Notre Dame, IN: Univ. of Notre Dame Press, 1996.

—. "Plato's Parmenides: Why the Eight Hypotheses are not Contradictory." *Phronesis* 23, no. 2 (1978): 133–50.

Schelling, F. W. J. *Philosophical Inquiries into the Nature of Human Freedom*. Translated by R. Gutman. LaSalle, IL: Open Court, 1989.

Scolnicov, S. *Plato's Parmenides*. Berkeley, CA: California Univ. Press, 2003.

Smith, C. "Edmund Husserl and the Crisis of Europe." *Modern Age* 48, no. 1 (2006): 28–36.

Strauss, L. "An Introduction to Heideggerian Existentialism." In *The Rebirth of Classical Political Rationalism*. Chicago: Univ. of Chicago Press, 1989.

Taylor, A. E. *The "Parmenides" of Plato*. New York: Oxford Univ. Press, 1934.

—. *Plato*. New York: New York Univ. Press, 1926.

—. *Plato: The Man and His Works*. London: Methuen Publishers, 1927.

Veatch, H. "Why Be Uncritical about the Life-World." In *Patterns of the Life-World*. Edited by J. Edie, F. Parker, and C. Schrag. Evanston, IL: Northwestern Univ. Press, 1970.

Vlastos, G. "The Third Man Argument in the Parmenides." *Philosophical Review* 63 (1954): 319–39.

Voeglin, E. *Order and History*, vol. II. Baton Rouge, LA: Louisiana State Univ. Press, 1957.

—. *Plato and Aristotle*. Vol. 3, *Order and History*. Baton Rouge, LA: Louisiana State Univ. Press, 1957.

—. *Science, Politics, Gnosticism*. Chicago: Henry Regnery Co., 1968.

—. *The World of the Polis*. Baton Rouge, LA: Louisiana State Univ. Press, 1957.

Wippel, J. F. "Truth in Thomas Aquinas (Part I–II)" *Review of Metaphysics* 43 (1989–1990): 295–326.

Zubiri, X. *On Essence*. Translated by R. Caponigri. Washington, DC: Catholic Univ. Press, 1980.

Index